Triangle Mesh Watermarking and Steganography

Hang Zhou • Kejiang Chen • Zehua Ma •
Feng Wang • Weiming Zhang

Triangle Mesh Watermarking and Steganography

Hang Zhou
Computer Science Department
Simon Fraser University
Burnaby, BC, Canada

Kejiang Chen
School of Cyberspace Science
and Technology
University of Science and Technology
of China
Hefei, China

Zehua Ma
School of Information Science
and Technology
University of Science and Technology
of China
Hefei, China

Feng Wang
University of Science and Technology
of China
Hefei, China

Weiming Zhang
School of Information Science
and Technology
University of Science and Technology
of China
Hefei, China

ISBN 978-981-19-7722-0   ISBN 978-981-19-7720-6   (eBook)
https://doi.org/10.1007/978-981-19-7720-6

This Springer imprint is published by the registered company Springer Nature Singapore Pte Ltd.
The registered company address is: 152 Beach Road, #21-01/04 Gateway East, Singapore 189721, Singapore

To our families and friends.

Foreword by Nenghai Yu

Information hiding is the technology to ensure data security by embedding data in multimedia to achieve covert communication, copyright protection, integrity authentication, or leak traceability. Digital steganography and digital watermarking are the two most important branches of information hiding: the former is mainly used for covert communication and the latter is mainly for copyright protection. With the rapid development of computer vision and 3D scanning technology, 3D models, especially 3D meshes, are widely used in 3D games, virtual reality, film and television animation, and industrial production. The popularity of 3D mesh makes it a suitable carrier for covert communication on the one hand, and the object of intellectual property protection on the other hand. However, the published monographs and textbooks on steganography and watermarking usually introduce information hiding methods based on images, audio, and videos, and rarely involve 3D meshes. The existing literature on 3D mesh steganography and watermarking is scattered in journals or conference papers in graphics, multimedia security, artificial intelligence, and other fields. Therefore, it becomes difficult to have a global-oriented view for the basic technology and advances of 3D mesh information hiding. Fortunately, this monograph written by Hang et al. timely met the need for a quick understanding of 3D mesh information hiding.

This book introduces the typical methods of 3D mesh watermarking, steganography, and steganalysis. In particular, the deep learning-based 3D mesh watermarking framework and 3D print-scan-resistant watermarking methods are introduced, which are the most exciting and promising directions in this field. There is no doubt that this book will be an important reference for anyone who wants to understand information hiding in 3D meshes. 3D information hiding is the subject of Hang's doctoral dissertation, and several coauthors he invited have also been engaged in related fields for a long time. They have a deep understanding of the state of the art and trends of 3D mesh information hiding. It's great to see that after nearly 2 years of hard work, they finally got this book published.

Hefei, China   Nenghai Yu
August 2022

Foreword by Zhenxing Qian

Information hiding is an important research field of multimedia security, which has attracted much attention of scholars all over the world. In the past decades, many information hiding techniques have been developed for digital images with a clear illustration. However, these works cannot be used in 3D meshes directly, as the characteristic of 3D mesh is different. This book fills the gap by introducing the basic concepts of information hiding in image domain and then transferring into 3D meshes.

3D meshes are widely used to represent virtual surfaces and volumes. Numerous research papers on 3D steganography and watermarking have been published in proceedings of conferences and journals, such as IEEE Workshop on Information Forensics and Security, IEEE Transactions on Multimedia, and IEEE Transactions on Visualization and Computer Graphics. However, this new field is challenging to browse for a reader who is not involved in active research. This book aims to present some critical advances from a systematic view, which is suitable for a scientist who may not be an expert in data hiding.

For 3D mesh steganography, the readers can learn to define steganographic distortion of meshes, and use steg-codes to realize the minimization and combat the steganalysis. For 3D mesh watermarking, this book introduces not only the traditional robust watermarking in the digital domain but also the watermarking schemes for 3D printed objects combined with the emerging 3D printing technique. Therefore, the readers can get a quick overview of the information hiding technology in 3D meshes.

The authors of this book are experienced researchers on information hiding. The monograph is very well written and easy for reading. I think it should be an essential reference book for those interested in 3D mesh watermarking and steganography.

Shanghai, China Zhenxing Qian
August 2022

Preface

While I was working on scene composition problems at Simon Fraser University, I found that triangle meshes, one of the common 3D representations, are still the leading and stable representation across academia and industry. Despite other prevailing representations including point clouds, voxels, and implicit fields, I still believe the ultimate goal of 3D reconstruction and generation is meshes these days. I have always been impressed by new techniques like the popular neural rendering, differentiable rendering, and neural marching cube that facilitate the development of graphics and downstream applications like VR. The popularity of triangle mesh makes it a suitable carrier for covert communication as well as the object of intellectual property protection. As far as I'm concerned, the contents of related books covering watermarking and steganography are mostly 2D images related techniques. Thus, in late 2021, I decided to write a monograph on triangle mesh watermarking and steganography. My goal was to produce a book that is organized and self-contained, with sufficient preliminary materials and detailed proofs, so that the readers need not consult scattered literatures, be plagued by inconsistent notations, and be carried away from the central ideas by non-essential contents. Luckily, my former lab fellows, Kejiang Chen, Zehua Ma, Feng Wang, and my PhD supervisor Prof. Weiming Zhang were happy to join this work.

This task turned out to be very hard, as we had to work among our busy schedules. Eventually, we managed to have the first complete yet crude draft in August 2022. We are truly honored to have forewords from Prof. Nenghai Yu and Prof. Zhenxing Qian. While this book deprived us of all our leisure time in the past nearly 1 year, we still feel that our endeavor pays when every part of the book is ready. Hope this book is a valuable reference for the multimedia security and the graphics communities. This will be the highest praise for our work.

Burnaby, BC, Canada   Hang Zhou
Hefei, China   Kejiang Chen
Hefei, China   Zehua Ma
Hefei, China   Feng Wang
Hefei, China   Weiming Zhang
August 2022

Acknowledgments

The authors would like to thank all our collaborators and friends, especially: Weixiang Li, Yaofei Wang, Jiansong Zhang, Han Fang, and Qichao Ying for careful proofreading. The authors also thank Jingying Chen and Veena Perumal from Springer, who offered much assistance during the production of the book. This monograph is supported in part by the Natural Science Foundation of China under Grant 62102386, 62002334, 62072421, and 62121002.

Contents

About the Authors

Hang Zhou is an expert in the fields of 3D vision and graphics. He is currently a postdoctoral fellow at GrUVi, School of Computer Science, Simon Fraser University, Canada. He has received the best paper award of IJCAI workshop on safety and security of deep learning in 2021, outstanding doctoral dissertation of the Chinese Academy of Sciences in 2020, the President Scholarship of the Chinese Academy of Sciences in 2020, and Cyberspace Security Scholarship of China in 2018.

Kejiang Chen is an expert in the fields of information hiding. He is currently an associate researcher at the School of Cyberspace Science and Technology, University of Science and Technology of China. He has received the best student paper award of ACM workshop on Information Hiding and Multimedia Security in 2018, ACM SIGWEB CHINA outstanding doctoral dissertation in 2021, and Cyberspace Security Scholarship of China in 2019. He has published more than 30 papers about information hiding in journals and conferences.

Zehua Ma is now a PhD candidate at the Information Process Center and Key Laboratory of Electromagnetic Space Information (Chinese Academy of Science), School of Information Science and Technology, University of Science and Technology of China. His research interests include image watermarking, image processing, and 3D printing.

Feng Wang is now an engineer at Megvii. He graduated from the University of Science and Technology of China with a master's degree. His research interests include geometric analysis and computer vision.

Weiming Zhang is a leading expert in the fields of information hiding, multimedia security, and privacy-preserving data searching and analysis. He is currently a professor at the in Information Process Center and Key Laboratory of Electromagnetic Space Information (Chinese Academy of Science), School of Information Science and Technology, University of Science and Technology of China. He has published more than 200 papers in journals and conferences including TIT, TIFS, TIP, TVCG, TCOMM, TDSC, CVPR, ICCV, AAAI, INFOCOM, and ACM MM. He has received the first prize of Anhui natural science and the special prize for teaching achievement.

Acronyms

STC	Syndrome Trellis Code
SRM	Spatial Rich Model
SPAM	Subtractive Pixel Adjacency Matrix
SVM	Support Vector Machine
FDM	Fused Deposition Modeling
CLAHE	Contrast-Limited Adaptive Histogram Equalization
NIR	Near Infrared
PLA	Polylactic Acid
TVR	Tetrahedron Volume Ratio
VFA	Vertex Flood Algorithm
TSQ	Triangle Similarity Quadruple
TFA	Triangle Flood Algorithm
HMF	Histogram Mapping Function
BER	Bit Error Rate
FMM	Fast Marching Method
TSPS	Triangle Strip Peeling Symbol
PSP	Polygon Stencil Pattern
MDP	Mesh Density Pattern
WCV	Wavelet Coefficient Vector
D-WHT	Dirichlet Manifold Harmonics Transform
D-MHB	Dirichlet Manifold Harmonic Basis
NCE	Neighbor Couple Embedding
HD	Hausdorff Distance
QEM	Quadric Error Metric
MLP	Multi-Layer Perceptron
MSE	Mean Square Error
MEP	Macro Embedding Procedure
SNR	Signal-to-Noise Ratio
MLEP	Multi-Level Embedding Procedure
QIM	Quantization Index Modulation
TNT	Triangular Neighbor Table

AJS	Advanced Jumping Strategy
SSA	Symmetric Swap Algorithm
PCA	Principal Component Analysis
EMST	Euclidean Minimum Spanning Tree
SAC	Static Arithmetic Coding
PSNR	Peak Signal-to-Noise Ratio
MSDM2	Mesh Structure Distortion Measurement
LSB	Least Significant Bit
CD	Constant Distortion
FLDs	Fisher Linear Discriminants
OOB	Out-of-Bag
VND	Vertex Normal Distortion
GCD	Gaussian Curvature Distortion
MSBs	Most Significant Bits
STCs	Syndrome-Trellis Codes
SPCs	Steganographic Polar Codes
PLS	Payload-Limited Sender
PMF	Probability Mass Function
KLD	Kullback-Leibler Divergence
MEL	Maximum Expected Level
LFS	Local Feature Set
WCVs	Wavelet Coefficient Vectors
CSM	Cover Source Mismatch
BOSS	Break Our Steganographic System
CLS	Calibrated Least Squares
OEAP	Online Ensemble Average Perceptron
RRFS	Robustness and Relevance based Feature Selection
PCC	Pearson Correlation Coefficient
mRMR	Min-Redundancy and Max-Relevancy
DISR	Double Input Symmetrical Relevance
CMIM	Conditional Mutual Info Maximization
RFS	Relevance-based Feature Selection
SVM	Support Vector Machine
RBF	Radial Basis Function

Chapter 1
Introduction

Abstract In this chapter, we introduce the basic concept of information hiding, steganography, and watermarking.

1.1 Introduction of Multimedia Security

The popularity of the Internet and the rapid development of many businesses have penetrated into all fields of the economy and society. Social networks, online media, instant messaging, mobile Internet, and Internet of things have become the main value-added forms. The business mode of people to people communication has changed from a single voice to a rich and colorful multimedia data business, while users can enjoy the new digital life presented by multimedia at will. At present, multimedia represented by digital text, digital image, digital audio and video, and three-dimensional model has been more and more widely used. However, the convenient network environment also makes it easier to illegally occupy, copy, modify, and spread the infringement of unauthorized multimedia products. Therefore, how to implement effective copyright protection and content authentication for digital information in the network environment has become a hot and difficult point in the research and application of multimedia security, which has attracted extensive attention from the academic and business circles.

Because of the particularity of multimedia form, there are many practical problems in using traditional cipher to encrypt multimedia. In the early research, the traditional data encryption algorithm was directly used for multimedia encryption. However, due to the characteristics of large amount of multimedia information, high correlation between images and videos, and redundancy of data, the direct encryption method has many limitations such as large amount of calculation, delay, and power consumption. Therefore, multimedia security, a new direction of information security, came into being.

From the perspective of the life cycle of multimedia, multimedia exists in the application of multimedia in the forms of original format, multimedia content, multimedia processing, multimedia communication, and performance after it is generated from the sensor. At present, there are a variety of related security

H. Zhou et al., *Triangle Mesh Watermarking and Steganography*,
https://doi.org/10.1007/978-981-19-7720-6_1

issues focusing on various forms of multimedia in the public literature. Typical examples related to multimedia security include information hiding with multimedia as the carrier object, digital watermarking for copyright protection and tracking of multimedia content, multimedia forensics for authentication of multimedia originality, perceptual Hash for multimedia authentication, as well as multimedia privacy for the protection of multimedia sensitive content.

It can be seen that the emerging multimedia security research is booming. Compared with traditional information security, multimedia security is a new generation that is not mature. It also needs guidance of application demand, reasonable evaluation mechanism, mature theoretical model, open test data and metric system construction. Meanwhile, multimedia security still faces great challenges from scientific research and technology to reality.

1.2 Examples of Watermarking Application

In addition to the general characteristics of information hiding technology, digital watermarking technology also has its inherent characteristics and requirements. It embeds the secret information (digital watermark) containing the identification mark in the digital multimedia carrier to be protected (image, document, audio, video, etc.) through a certain algorithm, so that the digital multimedia carrier contains the functionality of additional information embedded. The embedding of the watermark information is not easily detected by human eyes and will not affect the use of the original carrier itself. Most importantly, it cannot be easily erased and destroyed. The most common application scenarios of digital watermarking are the authentication of copyright information and the tracking of leaked documents. When used for copyright protection, generally the watermark information contained in the original carrier is the identification information of the copyright owner, so that when a suspected infringing file with watermark information is found, the copyright authentication of the original file can be realized by extracting the watermark signal. When used for leak tracking, most of the embedded watermark information is the device number, time stamp, etc. When leaked files are circulated, the leaked device and leak time can be located according to the digital watermark in the leaked file, so as to further confirm the attribution of responsibility. Since 1954, digital watermarking technology has been extensively studied, but it was only used as a verification tool at that time and did not become a discipline. Until the early 1990s, Tirkel first proposed the term "water ark" as a watermarking term. Since then, digital watermarking technology has been regarded as a real research discipline. With the popularity of digital products and the popularization of digital storage, copyright disputes of private information are increasing, and the leaking incidents are also increasing. Not only has it attracted the attention of the academic world but also the favor of the business world. There have been many cases that illustrate the important role of digital watermarking. For example, in 2016, several Alibaba employees illegally "snap-buy" the company's customized mooncakes ahead of

Fig. 1.1 Screenshot of the original NSA classified document (left). Inverted image of the original NSA classified document part screenshot (right)

time using script transformation technology, but they were quickly investigated due to the circulation of screenshots of the webpage. The means of locating illegal employees is digital watermarking technology. Since there is an invisible digital watermark signal containing employee ID information on each web page, when the screenshot of the web page is circulated, the company can extract the corresponding ID information from the screenshot of the web page, so as to accurately locate the source of the leak to achieve accountability. For another example, in 2017, the secret documents of the US National Security Agency (NSA) were leaked, but as soon as the leak happened, the NSA arrested the leakers, and the key to accurately guiding the leakers was the information in the NSA documents. Invisible watermark.

As shown in Fig. 1.1, the NSA file contains an array of dot-shaped watermarks, which encode the information of different printing equipment and employee IDs, so that after the file is leaked, the relevant departments can retrieve the leaked printer, so as to carry out follow-up actions. Various cases show that digital watermarking is of great significance to the protection of multimedia copyrights at this stage.

1.2.1   Significance of Digital Watermarking for Multimedia Security

In the past decades, the development of multimedia technology and the popularization of the Internet have brought great convenience to people's information interaction. Compared with traditional media, digital media can guarantee high-precision, low-cost storage, reproduction, and distribution, hence digital media quickly replaces the status of traditional media. But this also brings about new information security problems: the production of copies of traditional media is very complicated, while the unauthorized copying of digital files is very easy. How to ensure a reasonable and standardized management of the property rights of digital files is an accompanying requirement for the development of multimedia technology. And digital watermarking is the most important way to solve such problems. Robustness and transparency are the most important performances of digital watermarking algorithms, both of which restrict each other but are indispensable. Robustness ensures the ability of digital watermarking technology to resist distortion, because in the traditional information transmission channel, the carrier file (such as image, document, etc.) is transmitted through the digital channel, and it is likely to undergo various processing methods during the transmission. Various distortions, such as compression, after which the readability of the carrier content may not be impaired, but the additional watermark signal may produce distortions. How to correctly extract the watermark signal from a distorted text is the key to protecting the copyright of the file. The transparency of the watermark is another important property to ensure the universality of the watermark algorithm and various carrier files. The existence of the watermark should not affect the visual quality of the original carrier or the normal use of the original carrier itself, which makes the watermark algorithm more widely used. Therefore, it is of great significance to develop the research of digital watermarking technology with high robustness and high transparency for the protection of multimedia copyrights.

With the popularization of smart mobile devices and the improvement of chip technology, the use of mobile phone cameras can easily record the contents of digital media to generate high-quality copies, and these copies are often spread through the network, further aggravating the loss of the original owner. How to deal with the information security problems in this network era is an important research direction.

1.2.2   Research Status of Image Watermarking Technology

As an important means of copyright protection and traceability of leaks and an important branch of information hiding technology, digital watermarking technology [1–9] has received great attention from research institutes at home and abroad. The digital watermarking algorithm of images and texts has also been a hot topic. As an accompanying technology of multimedia technology, the performance of digital watermarking technology is also updated with the popularization of intelligent devices and the diversification of information transmission methods. Here, this paper mainly takes images and document carriers as examples and focuses on the research status of algorithms at home and abroad in recent years.

The research on robust watermarking with digital image as carrier has a long history. Traditional image watermarking methods can be divided into two categories based on the distribution of the embedded coefficients: spatial domain coefficients [10] and transform domain coefficients [11, 12]. The spatial domain-based robust watermarking algorithm for digital images was also developed from the least significant bit (LSB) replacement algorithm in the early time. The least significant pixel that does not affect the visual quality of the image is added or subtracted by one to embed the message. After that, a digital watermarking scheme based on pixel histograms appeared. Coltuc et al. [13] proposed the idea of expressing watermarks using different distributions of image pixel histograms. By fine-tuning and replacing the distribution of spatial pixel histograms, it can well hide the watermark information in the image and produce less visual distortion. Xiang et al. [14] proposed a method to embed digital watermark according to the histogram group distance characteristics and realize the embedding of watermark by adjusting the number of histogram group distance elements.

The method based on transform domain coefficients is the research focus of digital watermarking algorithms in recent years. Common transforms include discrete cosine transform (DCT) [15–17], discrete Fourier transform (DFT) [18–20], and discrete wavelet transform (DWT) [21–23]. Bami et al. [24] earlier proposed a watermarking algorithm that utilizes the stability of DCT low-frequency coefficients to embed messages, JPEG compression, and other attacks. Sisaudia et al. [25] proposed a method based on DCT coefficients, which selects appropriate DCT coefficients for embedding through image texture to ensure the image quality requirements after embedding. At the same time, the stability of the intermediate frequency coefficient of DCT can also provide the corresponding robustness. Amiri et al. [23] proposed a digital watermarking algorithm based on DWT domain, which scrambles the watermark signal to be embedded and embeds it into the wavelet intermediate frequency signal of the original carrier image, so as to meet the requirements of robustness and visual quality at the same time. Fares et al. [26] proposed a digital watermarking algorithm based on DWT coefficients to protect the copyright of medical images. Through the embedding of intermediate frequency DWT coefficients, the compromise between the robustness of the algorithm and the visual quality is guaranteed. Kang et al. [27] proposed a DFT-based digital watermarking algorithm, which effectively embeds the information bits into the Fourier intermediate frequency component, thus ensuring the robustness of the algorithm to JPEG compression. The current mainstream approach is to realize the design of a digital watermarking algorithm through a combination of multiple frequency domain transformations. Al-haj et al. [28] proposed a robust digital watermarking algorithm that combines DCT and DWT transforms. The algorithm firstly decomposes the image carrier information through DWT transform, separates the stable low-frequency and medium-frequency signals, and embeds the DCT coefficients of this part of the signal. This scheme combines the advantages of DWT and DCT coefficients well and ensures the robustness of the algorithm and the visual quality of the embedded image.

Whether it is a digital watermarking algorithm based on the spatial domain or based on the transform domain, the watermark embedding scheme can be designed according to the characteristics of image processing distortion that need to be resisted, so as to generate a watermark that is robust to common image processing processes. However, the image distortion caused by the screen-shooting process is different from the common image processing process. The signal conversion between the screen cameras combines geometric distortion, sampling distortion, light source distortion, compression distortion, and other distortions; with the difference between the camera and the screen different distortions are produced, so traditional methods for image processing distortions are relatively limited in robustness to the screen capture process.

At present, some work has begun to design algorithms for the process of print scanning and print photography, which are similar to the screen photography process. Nakamura et al. [29, 30] designed a watermark template that is robust to printing and photographing. The embedding process of the watermark is realized by the method of template superposition. After the image is printed, the superimposed watermark signal is filtered out by a manually designed filter so as to realize the extraction of the message. Pramila et al. [31–34] proposed a watermarking method that utilizes the angle-encoded information of periodic images and introduced the Just Noticeable Difference model. By controlling the amplitude of the watermark, the watermark is superimposed in a weighted manner. It is embedded in the original image, and at the extraction end, the algorithm applies the idea of template matching to extract. Kang et al. [35] proposed a scheme based on log-polar coordinate mapping, which spread the watermark bit signal in a pseudo-random sequence and embedded it in the Fourier Merlin coefficient of the image in the form of an additive watermark. Robustness to geometric distortions that occur during print scanning is achieved. On this basis, Delgado-Guillen et al. [36] have updated and improved the correction scheme for perspective distortion in the process of printing and photographing.

Compared with the process of printing scanning and printing and taking pictures, the distortion introduced by the screen-shooting process is more complicated. At present, there are relatively few targeted digital watermarking algorithms, and the existing digital watermarking schemes cannot solve the problem of screen-shooting distortion very well. Awesome question. In 2014, the Camera program designed by Schaber et al. [37] simulated the process of screen shooting, including the more significant sampling distortion (moiré), light source distortion, and color distortion during screen shooting, which to a certain extent can be used as the basis for the analysis of screen distortion. In 2018, Guglemann et al. [38] proposed a screen watermarking scheme, which implements the embedding and extraction of messages by superimposing a layer of templates with different brightness in front of the screen. The brightness of the template is encoded as different messages.

1.2.3   Research Status of Digital Watermarking Technology Based on Deep Learning

The maturity of deep learning technology has also resulted in algorithms based on deep learning in various image processing fields. Similarly, the powerful capabilities of deep learning technology have also been applied to the field of digital watermarking. The two most successful deep learning tasks: image processing tasks [39] and image classification tasks [40] can correspond to the embedding and extraction processes in digital watermarking algorithms, respectively. The embedding process is to embed the digital watermark signal into the original image carrier in a certain way, while ensuring the consistency of the visual quality of the embedded image and the original carrier. This process is similar to the traditional image processing process, that is, both the generated images are required to have a similar visual sense to the label image. The extraction process of digital watermark is highly similar to the image classification task. It is filtered through layers of neural network to obtain high-dimensional features hidden in the image, so as to analyze the features. The difference is that image classification requires the neural network to learn the semantic features of the image itself, while watermark extraction requires the neural network to extract the hidden information features in the image. On the basis of deep learning, a partial end-to-end digital watermarking framework is proposed. Zhu et al. [41] proposed an information embedding network with an autoencoder structure. By jointly training the encoder, decoder, and anti-noise layer, the network can achieve adaptive embedding of messages and robustness against different attacks. In this, the main task of the encoder is to embed the digital watermark bits into the original carrier image in an inconspicuous way, thereby ensuring the visual consistency of the generated watermark image with the original carrier image. The function of the anti-noise layer is to add noise to the watermark image, so that the decoding end can better decode the distorted image. The task of the decoder is to correctly extract the embedded watermark signal from the distorted image. Through such a design, the embedding network and extraction network of the watermark can be effectively obtained, and the robustness to the over-distortion in the training process can be guaranteed at the same time. On the basis of this structure, Tancik et al. [42] proposed a noise layer to simulate the printing and photographing process. The image processing operation is defined by the formula, and then this processing is added to the overall training framework for adversarial training, so as to achieve the robustness of the printing and photographing process. In addition to an approximation scheme for non-quantifiable processes, Wengrowski et al. [42] also transformed non-quantifiable processes by means of neural network simulations. They established a screenshot image library, trained a screenshot simulation network to simulate the screenshot process through this image library, and added such a simulated network to the noise layer for adversarial training to achieve robustness to screenshot. Both of the above two methods simulate the non-steerable cross-media transmission process in a steerable way, so that the network can conduct targeted adversarial training, but there is a mismatch problem in the way of using network simulation. When the test phone and screen are not present in the training set, the robustness of the algorithm will be greatly reduced. In addition to the end-to-end network structure, in 2019, Liu et al. [43] used a two-stage deep neural network framework that achieved robustness to non-steerable processes. They initialized an end-to-end embedding network and extraction network in the first training session, while in the second training session, they used the embedding end initialized by the first session of the network combined with a real distortion attack to generate a batch of distorted images, and then exploited the decoder is augmented with batches of images to improve the performance of the decoder against this distortion. However, this method has a poor effect on screen distortion.

References

1. Ding, W., Ming, Y., Cao, Z. & Lin, C. A generalized deep neural network approach for digital watermarking analysis. *IEEE Transactions On Emerging Topics In Computational Intelligence.* (2021)
2. Zear, A. & Singh, P. Secure and robust color image dual watermarking based on LWT-DCT-SVD. *Multimedia Tools And Applications.* pp. 1–18 (2021)
3. Singh, R. & Ashok, A. An optimized robust watermarking technique using CKGSA in frequency domain. *Journal Of Information Security And Applications.* **58** pp. 102734 (2021)
4. Seo, J. & Yoo, C. Image watermarking based on invariant regions of scale-space representation. *IEEE Transactions On Signal Processing.* **54**, 1537–1549 (2006)
5. Lydia, E., Raj, J., Pandi Selvam, R., Elhoseny, M. & Shankar, K. Application of discrete transforms with selective coefficients for blind image watermarking. *Transactions On Emerging Telecommunications Technologies.* **32**, e3771 (2021)
6. Fares, K., Khaldi, A., Redouane, K. & Salah, E. DCT & DWT based watermarking scheme for medical information security. *Biomedical Signal Processing And Control.* **66** pp. 102403 (2021)
7. Sinhal, R., Jain, D. & Ansari, I. Machine learning based blind color image watermarking scheme for copyright protection. *Pattern Recognition Letters.* **145** pp. 171–177 (2021)
8. Li, Y., Wei, D. & Zhang, L. Double-encrypted watermarking algorithm based on cosine transform and fractional Fourier transform in invariant wavelet domain. *Information Sciences.* **551** pp. 205–227 (2021)
9. Hosny, K., Darwish, M. & Fouda, M. Robust color images watermarking using new fractional-order exponent moments. *IEEE Access.* **9** pp. 47425–47435 (2021)
10. Voloshynovskiy, S., Deguillaume, F. & Pun, T. Content adaptive watermarking based on a stochastic multiresolution image modeling. *2000 10th European Signal Processing Conference.* pp. 1–4 (2000)
11. Kundur, D. & Hatzinakos, D. A robust digital image watermarking method using wavelet-based fusion. *Proceedings Of International Conference On Image Processing.* **1** pp. 544–547 (1997)
12. Maheshwari, J., Kumar, M., Mathur, G., Yadav, R. & Kakerda, R. Robust digital image watermarking using DCT based pyramid transform via image compression. *2015 International Conference On Communications And Signal Processing (ICCSP).* pp. 1059–1063 (2015)
13. Coltuc, D. & Bolon, P. Robust watermarking by histogram specification. *Proceedings* 1999 International Conference On Image Processing (Cat. 99CH36348). **2** pp. 236–239 (1999)
14. Xiang, S., Kim, H. & Huang, J. Invariant image watermarking based on statistical features in the low-frequency domain. *IEEE Transactions On Circuits And Systems For Video Technology.* **18**, 777–790 (2008)
15. Lutovac, B., Daković, M., Stanković, S. & Orović, I. An algorithm for robust image watermarking based on the DCT and Zernike moments. *Multimedia Tools And Applications.* **76**, 23333–23352 (2017)
16. Horng, S., Rosiyadi, D., Li, T., Takao, T., Guo, M. & Khan, M. A blind image copyright protection scheme for e-government. *Journal Of Visual Communication And Image Representation.* **24**, 1099–1105 (2013)
17. Parah, S., Sheikh, J., Loan, N. & Bhat, G. Robust and blind watermarking technique in DCT domain using inter-block coefficient differencing. *Digital Signal Processing.* **53** pp. 11–24 (2016)
18. Urvoy, M., Goudia, D. & Autrusseau, F. Perceptual DFT watermarking with improved detection and robustness to geometrical distortions. *IEEE Transactions On Information Forensics And Security.* **9**, 1108–1119 (2014)
19. Solachidis, V. & Pitas, L. Circularly symmetric watermark embedding in 2-D DFT domain. *IEEE Transactions On Image Processing.* **10**, 1741–1753 (2001)

20. Cedillo-Hernandez, M., Garcia-Ugalde, F., Nakano-Miyatake, M. & Perez-Meana, H. Robust watermarking method in DFT domain for effective management of medical imaging. *Signal, Image And Video Processing.* **9**, 1163–1178 (2015)
21. Thakkar, F. & Srivastava, V. A blind medical image watermarking: DWT-SVD based robust and secure approach for telemedicine applications. *Multimedia Tools And Applications.* **76**, 3669–3697 (2017)
22. Hu, H. & Hsu, L. Collective blind image watermarking in DWT-DCT domain with adaptive embedding strength governed by quality metrics. *Multimedia Tools And Applications.* **76**, 6575–6594 (2017)
23. Amiri, T. & Moghaddam, M. A new visual cryptography based watermarking scheme using DWT and SIFT for multiple cover images. *Multimedia Tools And Applications.* **75**, 8527–8543 (2016)
24. Barni, M., Bartolini, F., Cappellini, V. & Piva, A. A DCT-domain system for robust image watermarking. *Signal Processing.* **66**, 357–372 (1998)
25. Sisaudia, V. & Vishwakarma, V. Copyright protection using KELM-PSO based multi-spectral image watermarking in DCT domain with local texture information based selection. *Multimedia Tools And Applications.* **80**, 8667–8688 (2021)
26. Kahlessenane, F., Khaldi, A., Kafi, R. & Euschi, S. A DWT based watermarking approach for medical image protection. *Journal Of Ambient Intelligence And Humanized Computing.* **12**, 2931–2938 (2021)
27. Kang, X., Huang, J., Shi, Y. & Lin, Y. A DWT-DFT composite watermarking scheme robust to both affine transform and JPEG compression. *IEEE Transactions On Circuits And Systems For Video Technology.* **13**, 776–786 (2003)
28. Al-Haj, A. Combined DWT-DCT digital image watermarking. *Journal Of Computer Science.* **3**, 740–746 (2007)
29. Nakamura, T., Katayama, A., Yamamuro, M. & Sonehara, N. Fast watermark detection scheme for camera-equipped cellular phone. *Proceedings Of The 3rd International Conference On Mobile And Ubiquitous Multimedia.* pp. 101–108 (2004)
30. Katayama, A., Nakamura, T., Yamamuro, M. & Sonehara, N. New high-speed frame detection method: Side Trace Algorithm (STA) for i-appli on cellular phones to detect watermarks. *Proceedings Of The 3rd International Conference On Mobile And Ubiquitous Multimedia.* pp. 109–116 (2004)
31. Pramila, A., Keskinarkaus, A. & Seppänen, T. Reading watermarks from printed binary images with a camera phone. *International Workshop On Digital Watermarking.* pp. 227–240 (2009)
32. Pramila, A., Keskinarkaus, A. & Seppänen, T. Toward an interactive poster using digital watermarking and a mobile phone camera. *Signal, Image And Video Processing.* **6**, 211–222 (2012)
33. Pramila, A., Keskinarkaus, A., Takala, V. & Seppänen, T. Extracting watermarks from printouts captured with wide angles using computational photography. *Multimedia Tools And Applications.* **76**, 16063–16084 (2017)
34. Pramila, A., Keskinarkaus, A. & Seppänen, T. Increasing the capturing angle in print-cam robust watermarking. *Journal Of Systems And Software.* **135** pp. 205–215 (2018)
35. Kang, X., Huang, J. & Zeng, W. Efficient general print-scanning resilient data hiding based on uniform log-polar mapping. *IEEE Transactions On Information Forensics And Security.* **5**, 1–12 (2010)
36. Delgado-Guillen, L., Garcia-Hernandez, J. & Torres-Huitzil, C. Digital watermarking of color images utilizing mobile platforms. *2013 IEEE 56th International Midwest Symposium On Circuits And Systems (MWSCAS).* pp. 1363–1366 (2013)
37. Schaber, P., Kopf, S., Wetzel, S., Ballast, T., Wesch, C. & Effelsberg, W. CamMark: Analyzing, modeling, and simulating artifacts in camcorder copies. *ACM Transactions On Multimedia Computing, Communications, And Applications (TOMM).* **11**, 1–23 (2015)
38. Gugelmann, D., Sommer, D., Lenders, V., Happe, M. & Vanbever, L. Screen watermarking for data theft investigation and attribution. *2018 10th International Conference On Cyber Conflict (CyCon).* pp. 391–408 (2018)

39. He, K., Zhang, X., Ren, S. & Sun, J. Deep residual learning for image recognition. *Proceedings Of The IEEE Conference On Computer Vision And Pattern Recognition*. pp. 770–778 (2016)
40. Zhu, J., Kaplan, R., Johnson, J. & Fei-Fei, L. Hidden: Hiding data with deep networks. *Proceedings Of The European Conference On Computer Vision (ECCV)*. pp. 657–672 (2018)
41. Tancik, M., Mildenhall, B. & Ng, R. Stegastamp: Invisible hyperlinks in physical photographs. *Proceedings Of The IEEE/CVF Conference On Computer Vision And Pattern Recognition*. pp. 2117–2126 (2020)
42. Wengrowski, E., Dana, K., Gruteser, M. & Mandayam, N. Reading between the pixels: Photographic steganography for camera display messaging. *2017 IEEE International Conference On Computational Photography (ICCP)*. pp. 1–11 (2017)
43. Liu, Y., Guo, M., Zhang, J., Zhu, Y. & Xie, X. A novel two-stage separable deep learning framework for practical blind watermarking. *Proceedings Of The 27th ACM International Conference On Multimedia*. pp. 1509–1517 (2019)

Chapter 2
Basic Concepts

Abstract In this chapter, we introduce the essential concepts of digital watermarking, steganography, and steganalysis. Besides, the format of 3D Mesh is presented.

2.1 Watermarking

2.1.1 Digital Watermarking

In essence, the digital watermarking system is actually a communication system, that is, the basic requirement it meets is to transmit a message between the embedder (sender) and the extractor (receiver) of the digital watermark. The basic framework of the digital watermarking system is shown in Fig. 2.1, which can be defined as a 9-element body $(\mathbf{M}, \mathbf{X}, \mathbf{W}, \mathbf{K}, G, E_m, A_t, D, E_x)$, where the definition of each dimension is listed as follows:

1. $\mathbf{M}$ represents the set composed of the original watermark information m.
2. $\mathbf{X}$ represents the set composed of the original cover x.
3. $\mathbf{W}$ represents the set composed of the watermark signal w to be embedded.
4. $\mathbf{K}$ represents the set of keys K required to generate the watermark signal.
5. G represents the algorithm for generating the watermark signal w to be embedded using the key K, the original watermark information M, and the original carrier x that may be included, that is,

$$w = G(m, x, K). \qquad (2.1)$$

6. E_m represents the algorithm to embed the digital watermark signal w into the original cover x, namely,

$$x^w = E_m(x, w), \qquad (2.2)$$

where x^w represents the signal after being embedded with the watermark.

H. Zhou et al., *Triangle Mesh Watermarking and Steganography*,
https://doi.org/10.1007/978-981-19-7720-6_2

Fig. 2.1 The basic framework of watermarking

7. A_t represents the possible attack distortion of the watermark, namely,

$$\hat{x}^w = A_t\left(x^w\right),\tag{2.3}$$

where $\hat{x}^w$ represents the signal after being attacked.

8. D represents the watermark detection algorithm, namely,

$$D\left(\hat{x}^w\right) = \begin{cases} 1 \ H_1 : \text{if } \hat{x}^w \text{ exists in } w \\ 0 \ H_0 : \text{otherwise} . \end{cases}\tag{2.4}$$

9. E_x represents the watermark extraction algorithm, namely,

$$\hat{w} = E_x(\hat{x}, K),\tag{2.5}$$

where $\hat{w}$ is the extracted watermark signal, which may require the participation of the watermark signal to be embedded or the participation of the original carrier.

2.1.1.1 Adaptive/Non-Adaptive Watermarking Systems

According to whether the original carrier itself is considered when the watermark is embedded, the watermarking systems can be divided into adaptive systems and non-adaptive systems. In a non-adaptive system, the embedding module of the watermark does not need to consider the characteristics of the carrier content itself and only needs to encode a watermark signal w into the cover x. For the adaptive system, the embedding of the watermark needs to consider the influence of the cover itself. By selecting the appropriate cover coefficients, the encoded watermark signal is added to the specific coefficients in some way, so as to achieve better visual quality or fidelity. The cost of adaptive embedding is the time for the cover-specific calculation. Therefore, how to balance the embedding efficiency and visual quality at the embedding end is a more concerning issue for digital watermarking.

2.1.1.2 Blind/Semi-blind/Non-blind Watermarking System

According to the type of information required by the watermark extraction end, watermarking systems can be divided into blind watermarking systems, semi-blind watermarking systems, and non-blind watermarking systems. The non-blind watermark system means that when extracting the watermark, the extraction end needs the participation of the original carrier. Specifically, the original carrier is used as the auxiliary information of the extractor to help the correct extraction of the watermark signal. The semi-blind watermarking system does not require the participation of the original carrier in the watermark extraction process but requires the original embedded watermark signal as auxiliary information for the watermark detection or extractor. The blind watermarking system can extract or detect the watermark signal without any auxiliary information. Most non-blind and semi-blind watermarking systems exist in the early digital watermarking algorithms. With the advancement and improvement of digital watermarking technology, most algorithms can achieve blind extraction. In practical applications, the application of blind extraction is also broader.

2.1.1.3 Evaluation Metric

To evaluate the performance of digital watermarking methods more reasonably, it is often necessary to define some suitable evaluation indicators to give quantitative conclusions. The two most important evaluation indicators of digital watermarking are visual quality (transparency) and robustness. Here we take image as instance to illustrate the evaluation meric.

Visual Quality Evaluation Generally, digital image quality assessment methods are roughly divided into two categories: subjective quality assessment (SQA) and objective quality assessment (OQA). SQA mainly refers to the subjective evaluation and scoring of the image quality by the subjects. OQA refers to using a certain quantifiable model to analyze and calculate the image to be evaluated and finally obtain a score to express the quality of the image.

Subjective Quality Assessment Method: The main method of image subjective quality assessment is to select a group of non-professional experts, and the number is generally not less than 20. Let them see test images in a specific environment, and the image display time is generally controlled within 10–30 min. Then let it evaluate the visual quality of the observed image according to their own subjective level (1 to 5 points). Generally speaking, 1 represents the worst visual quality, and 5 represents the best visual quality. Then, the scores of this batch of subjects are averaged to obtain the mean opinion score (MOS), and the obtained score is the final score of the subjective quality evaluation.

SQA is not only suitable for evaluating the quality of traditional paper images, but also for evaluating the quality of electronic images currently displayed on monitors. The obtained MOS can better reflect the visual perception of the image in the human eye to a certain extent. However, it should be noted that the subjective quality assessment method must provide a specific test environment because the human eye's perception of the image is easily affected by the environment.

Objective Quality Assessment Method: Objective quality assessment of images is a method that uses a specific model to simulate the human eye's assessment of image quality. Because the visual quality of an image is actually the most objective and real to the human eye, the result of the objective quality assessment needs to be as close as possible to the result of the subjective quality assessment. In the digital watermarking algorithm, the most commonly used is the objective quality assessment of the full reference image. The objective quality assessment of the full reference image refers to an evaluation calculation method that requires the participation of the original reference image in the evaluation calculation.

In watermarking algorithms, the two most commonly used algorithms are peak signal-to-noise ratio (PSNR) and structure similarity (SSIM). The formula for calculating the peak signal-to-noise ratio (PSNR) is as follows:

$$\text{PSNR} = 10 \cdot \log_{10}\left(\frac{\text{MAX}_x^2}{\text{MSE}}\right), \tag{2.6}$$

where

$$\text{MSE} = \frac{1}{mn}\sum_{i=0}^{m-1}\sum_{j=0}^{n-1}[x(i,\,j) - y(i,\,j)]^2, \tag{2.7}$$

where x and y denote the reference image and the image to be evaluated of size $m \times n$, respectively. MSE expresses the mean squared error between these two images. MAX is the maximum possible pixel value of the picture, and the calculation unit of PSNR is dB. The larger the value calculated by PSNR, the better the visual quality of the image to be evaluated. PSNR is a way of calculating the difference between each image, so the assessment of image content and structure may not be as accurate.

For this purpose, SSIM is generally calculated as a complement to the visual quality. The calculation of SSIM is based on the comparison of three quantities between the reference image and the image to be evaluated, namely luminance, contrast, and structure. For the reference image x and the to-be-evaluated image y, the calculation formulas for the corresponding contrast values of the three quantities are

$$l(x,\,y) = \frac{2\mu_x\mu_y + c_1}{\mu_x^2 + \mu_y^2 + c_1} \tag{2.8}$$

$$c(x,\,y) = \frac{2\sigma_x\sigma_y + c_2}{\sigma_x^2 + \sigma_y^2 + c_2} \tag{2.9}$$

$$s(x,\,y) = \frac{\sigma_{xy} + c_3}{\sigma_x\sigma_y + c_3}, \tag{2.10}$$

where μ_x, σ_x and μ_y, σ_y are the mean and variance of the content in $N \times N$ windows of images x, y, respectively. σ_{xy} is the covariance of the content in $N \times N$ windows of images x, y. c_1, c_2, and c_3 are constants, avoiding instability caused when the denominator is close to 0. Generally, $c_1 = (0.01L)^2$, $c_2 = (0.03L)^2$, where L is the range of pixel values. $c_3 = c_2/2$. Then the final SSIM is calculated as

$$\mathrm{SSIM}(x, y) = [l(x, y) \cdot c(x, y) \cdot s(x, y)]$$

$$= \frac{\left(2\mu_x\mu_y + c_1\right)\left(2\sigma_{xy} + c_2\right)}{\left(\mu_x^2 + \mu_y^2 + c_1\right)\left(\sigma_x^2 + \sigma_y^2 + c_2\right)}. \tag{2.11}$$

An $N \times N$ window is generally taken from the picture for sliding calculation, and finally, the average value is taken as the global SSIM.

Robustness Evaluation In the process of channel transmission, the watermarked image will be affected by channel distortion, so whether the watermark embedded in it can be accurately extracted after distortion determines the ability of the algorithm to resist distortion. For traditional digital channels, the general distortion includes traditional digital image processing distortion, such as JPEG compression, clipping, and filtering. The accuracy of watermark extraction is generally measured by two methods: bit error rate (BER) and normalized cross-correlation coefficient (NCC). For embedding a few bits of watermark, using BER to measure can intuitively see the extraction situation of the watermarking algorithm after being attacked. At the same time, using BER as a measurement indicator can also guide the error correction coding scheme that can be used in the watermark generation, so as to better improve the accuracy of information transmission. For the methods of embedding color or binary images as watermarks, NCC is mostly used as the evaluation indicator of robust performance. BER and NCC are calculated as follows:

$$\mathrm{BER} = \frac{\mathit{diff}\left(w, w'\right)}{N} \tag{2.12}$$

$$\mathrm{NCC} = \frac{\sigma_{\mathbf{W}, \widehat{\mathbf{W}}}}{\sigma_{\mathbf{W}}\sigma_{\widehat{\mathbf{W}}}}, \tag{2.13}$$

where N represents the length of the watermark sequence, and diff represents the number of bits between the extracted watermark w' and the original watermark w. $\sigma_{\mathbf{W}}$ represents the variance of the watermarked image, and $\sigma_{\mathbf{W}, \widehat{\mathbf{W}}}$ represents the covariance of the extracted watermarked image and the original watermarked image.

For digital meshes, operations including affine transform, vertex reordering, noise addition, and smoothing are the typical 3D mesh digital distortions:

- **Affine transform** (including translation, rotation, and scaling). These operations are basic techniques used to understand a 3D object by moving it or the camera, and they can be expressed by homogeneous transformation matrices.

- **Vertex reordering.** Reordering does not change the topology of the mesh; it changes only the storage layout of the vertices and gives them new indices. It is commonly used for mesh optimization efficiency [27], cache coherency [28], etc.
- **Noise addition.** Measured mesh models often contain noise, introduced by the scanning devices and digitization processes.
- **Smoothing.** The aim of this operation is to generally remove certain high-frequency information in the mesh.
- **Simplification.** This is carried out to transform a given 3D mesh into another complexity-reduced mesh with fewer faces, edges, and vertices.

2.1.2 Physical Watermarking

In the traditional watermarking, the distortion is caused by digital processes, such as image cropping, image noising, and rotation. Nowadays, there are some cross-media distortion in the physical world, such as camera capturing and 3D scanning. Here, we introduce several representative distortions in the physical environments.

2.1.2.1 Physical Distortion on Images

Print–Scan Distortion During the scanning process of 2D printing, the distortions that exist mainly include geometric transformation, color redistribution, and random noise. Geometric transformation is reflected in the offset of paper documents before and after printing and scanning, and color redistribution is reflected in that because the color spaces used by printers and display devices are not the same, and different color spaces will be approximated once, resulting in color difference. The random noise is due to the printing and scanning channels, and the noise of the instrument itself will produce similar noise processing to the image.

Print-Photography Distortion In the process of 2D printing photography, the main distortions are perspective distortion, illumination distortion, random noise, and JPEG compression distortion. Perspective distortion is different from geometric distortion. It is a three-dimensional distortion that converts the image from a regular quadrilateral into an irregular quadrilateral. The reason for this distortion is the different shooting angles of mobile phones, which will record images from different angles, resulting in different shooting pictures. When correcting for distortion, different degrees of interpolation are generated. Lighting distortion is due to the uncertainty of the shooting environment, which may affect the light and dark of the image or even cause overexposure. The random noise is similar to the random noise in the printing and scanning process, and it is also due to the channel of different devices, which has the effect of noise on the image itself. The JPEG compression distortion is the lossy compression distortion caused by the post-processing of the image by the mobile phone and saving it in JPEG format.

Screen-Shooting Distortion In the process of taking pictures on the screen, the main distortions are perspective distortion, light source distortion, and Moiré distortion. Perspective distortion is similar to the perspective distortion that exists during print photography. Distortion of light source refers to the distortion of ambient light when taking an image. Different from the process of printing and taking pictures, the screen itself is also a light source. This process shows the influence of two light sources on the image. Moiré distortion is a similar random pattern caused by the beat phenomenon between the screen display pixels and the mobile phone shooting pixels. Such patterns are unpredictable and difficult to accurately model and will have an irreversible overlay effect on the image.

2.1.2.2 Physical Distortion Resilient Image Watermarking

To resist the physical distortion, traditional image watermarking methods often embed watermarks in transform domain coefficients, commonly in the discrete cosine transform (DCT) domain [20], discrete wavelet transform (DWT) domain [21], and discrete Fourier transform (DFT) domain [22]. The insight of these methods is selecting element in a certain domain that is kept unchanged after these physical processes.

With the success of deep learning, recently, deep learning based watermarking frameworks [23–26] have been proposed. Generally, such frameworks contain an encoder, a noise layer, and a decoder. The encoder aims to embed the watermark message into the host image. The noise layer distorts the watermarked image to simulate physical distortions. The decoder tries to extract the watermark message from the distorted images. Based on the joint training of these three components, robustness to physical distortions that appear in the noise layer is greatly improved.

2.1.2.3 3D Physical Distortion and Watermarking

3D Print–Scan Distortion Like image, there are also some physical processes of 3D Mesh, e.g., 3D printing–scanning. During the 3D printing–scanning process, the distortions that exist mainly include geometric distortion, connectivity distortion, file distortion, and random noise. Geometric distortion mainly includes operations such as similarity transformation, noise, and smoothing. This type of distortion only modifies the geometric parameters (coordinate point positions) of the watermarked mesh. Connectivity distortion mainly includes operations such as clipping, simplifying, and remeshing. Among them, clipping refers to the loss of some local detail expressions due to the fact that the scanning beam cannot reach certain areas during the data sampling process of the 3D scanning of the printed model. In the processing after 3D scanning, the point cloud model will be simplified and meshed according to actual needs, which will bring about mesh simplifying distortion and remeshing distortion. File distortion refers to distortion caused by rearranging vertices or facets in a mesh description file. The random noise is due to the fact that after the printing

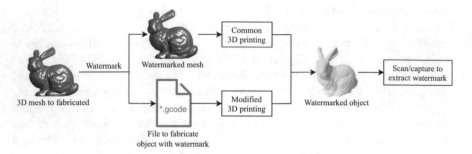

Fig. 2.2 The general framework of 3D Print–Scan Resilient Watermarking

and scanning channels, the noise of the instrument itself will produce similar noise processing to the restored 3D mesh model.

3D Print–Scan Resilient Watermarking This book focuses on 3D watermarking. Considering the increasing popularity of 3D printing technology, 3D printing resilient watermark schemes are needed to protect the copyright of 3D printed objects. The existing schemes can be divided into two categories, one is to embed the watermark on the digital 3D mesh to obtain the watermarked mesh and then 3D print it. The other category is to embed the watermark information on the 3D printed object through the 3D printing control file (e.g., G-code file). Finally, both categories of watermarks can be extracted by scanning or capturing the watermarked 3D printed object (Fig. 2.2).

2.2 Steganography

Steganography is an art that embeds secret message into innocent-look objects. The pursuit of stenography is making the stego object indistinguishable from the cover object. The development of steganography is largely benefited from the progress of steganographic coding. According to the development of coding, digital image steganography can be divided into three types:

- Constant Distortion Model: Assuming that the effects of modification on different elements are the same, it is the most basic distortion model. Under this coding model, the steganographer seeks to complete information embedding with minimal modification.
- Wet Paper Model: Divide the element into two parts, one is modifiable (called "dry spot") and the other is non-modifiable (called "wet spot," whose modification cost is "∞"); it is assumed that all dry point modifications have the same effect (which can be set to "1"), so the wet paper model is a "second-order distortion model."

- Multi-level Distortion Model: Different modification distortions are defined for different elements, that is, the impact of embedding can be quantified into any number of levels, which can be considered as an "adaptive distortion model." Filler et al. [1] proposed an STC (syndrome trellis codes) encoding method based on convolutional codes, which can approximate the upper bound of the embedding efficiency under the multi-level distortion model, also known as minimizing distortion steganography.

The minimizing distortion steganography model is the most widely studied steganographic model, and its mathematical model is described as follows: Given vector sequence $\mathbf{x} = (x_1, x_2, \ldots, x_n)$, distortion is introduced by modifying cover $\mathbf{x}$ into stego $\mathbf{y} = (y_1, y_2, \ldots, y_n)$, named $D(\mathbf{x}, \mathbf{y}) = D(\mathbf{y})$. Assume that the probability of modifying cover $\mathbf{x}$ into $\mathbf{y}$ is $\pi(\mathbf{y})$, the whole distortion can be defined as follows:

$$E_\pi(D) = \sum \pi(\mathbf{y})D(\mathbf{y}). \tag{2.14}$$

Minimizing distortion steganography is to minimize steganographic distortion under the condition of satisfying the secret message of embedding length L:

$$\min_\pi \ E_\pi(D) \tag{2.15}$$

$$\text{subject to} \quad H(\pi) = L, \tag{2.16}$$

where

$$H(\pi) = -\sum \pi(\mathbf{y}) \log \pi(\mathbf{y}). \tag{2.17}$$

According to the Lagrange multiplier method, the optimal solution of the above optimization problem can be obtained as

$$\pi_\lambda(\mathbf{y}) = \frac{1}{Z(\lambda)} \exp(-\lambda D(\mathbf{y})). \tag{2.18}$$

The corresponding relationship between the optimal probability distribution and distortion follows the Gibbs distribution [2], where $Z(\lambda)$ is the normalized factor:

$$Z(\lambda) = \sum \exp(-\lambda D(\mathbf{y})), \tag{2.19}$$

where λ is the Lagrange multiplier, $\lambda > 0$. In the steganography process, given cover and the corresponding distortion, λ is increased by $H(\pi)$. Given the message length L, we can get the value of λ by binary search.

When element modification operations are considered to be independent of each other, we call the distortion of changing $\mathbf{x}$ to $\mathbf{y}$ is additive, $D(\mathbf{y}) = \sum_i^n \rho_i(y_i)$. Here, we denote $\rho_i(y_i)$ as the distortion of modifying x_i to y_i. Taking ± 1 modification as an example, $I_i = \{x_i + 1, x_i, x_i - 1\}$, Eq. (2.18) can be rewritten as

$$\pi_i(y_i) = \frac{\exp(-\lambda \rho_i(y_i))}{\sum_{y_i \in I_i} \exp(-\lambda \rho_i(y_i))}, \quad i = 1, 2, \ldots, n. \tag{2.20}$$

When λ varies in $(0, +\infty)$, we can obtain the relationship curve between message length $H(\pi)$ and steganographic distortion $E_\pi(D)$, named rate-distortion curve. This curve is the theoretical bound for minimizing distortion steganography. Given the optimal embedding probability, we can obtain an upper bound on the theoretical rate distortion of embedding by simulating the embedding. In practical steganography, STC coding can embed secret information with performance approaching the upper bound of rate distortion.

2.2.1   Steganographic Coding

The multi-level distortion model is a natural extension of the early constant distortion model and the wet paper model, and the optimal embedding theory gives the optimal limit and its corresponding modified distribution. On the basis of the above content, this subsection introduces the most common adaptive steganographic coding algorithm for additive multi-level distortion model in the field of steganography.

2.2.1.1   Problem Formulation

Considering the binary case, suppose the secret message to be embedded is $\mathbf{m}$, the original cover is $\mathbf{x}$, and the stego sequence received by the receiver is $\mathbf{y}$. The basic idea of steganographic coding using matrix encoding is encoding the secret message in the syndrome so that the receiver can extract the message by calculating the syndrome $H\mathbf{y} = \mathbf{m}$, and the check matrix H here is the parity check matrix in channel coding. Let the set of solutions satisfying the above equation be

$$C(\mathbf{m}) = \left\{ \mathbf{z} \in \{0, 1\}^n \,\middle|\, H\mathbf{z} = \mathbf{m} \right\}, \tag{2.21}$$

where n is the length of the cover sequence. Then the goal of the minimize distortion embedding algorithm $Emb()$ is

$$Emb(\mathbf{x}, \mathbf{m}) = \arg \min_{\mathbf{y} \in C(\mathbf{m})} D(\mathbf{x}, \mathbf{y}), \tag{2.22}$$

where $D(\mathbf{x}, \mathbf{y}) = \sum_{i=1}^{n} \rho_i(x_i, y_i)$ represents the distortion of modifying x_i to y_i. Generally, $D(x_i, y_i) = 0$ when $x_i = y_i$.

2.2.1.2 Syndrome Trellis Coding

Since the matrix $\mathbf{H}$ used in steganographic coding is a parity matrix of channel coding, the steganographic coding is generally transformed from the decoding algorithm of channel coding. The syndrome trellis coding (STC) is transformed from convolutional code: its parity matrix $\mathbf{H}$ generally uses the truncated matrix of the parity matrix of convolutional code, and the encoding process is very similar to the Viterbi decoding algorithm of convolutional code. The general form of matrix $\mathbf{H}$ is as follows:

$$
H_{m \times n} = \begin{pmatrix}
\hat{h}_{1,1} \cdots \hat{h}_{1,w} & 0 & \cdots & 0 & \cdots & \cdots & \cdots & \cdots & \cdots & \cdots & 0 \\
\vdots & \ddots & \vdots & \hat{h}_{1,1} \cdots \hat{h}_{1,w} & 0 & \cdots & \cdots & \cdots & \cdots & \cdots & 0 \\
\hat{h}_{h,1} \cdots \hat{h}_{h,w} & \vdots & \ddots & \vdots & \cdots & 0 & \cdots & \cdots & \cdots & \cdots & 0 \\
0 & 0 & 0 & \hat{h}_{h,1} \cdots \hat{h}_{h,w} & \cdots & 0 & \cdots & \cdots & \cdots & \cdots & 0 \\
\vdots & \cdots & \cdots & \cdots & \cdots & \cdots & \cdots & \cdots & \cdots & \cdots & \vdots \\
0 & \cdots & \cdots & \cdots & \cdots & \cdots & \cdots & \hat{h}_{1,1} \cdots \hat{h}_{1,w} & 0 & \cdots & 0 \\
0 & \cdots & \cdots & \cdots & \cdots & \cdots & \cdots & \hat{h}_{2,1} \cdots \hat{h}_{2,w} & \hat{h}_{1,1} & \cdots & \hat{h}_{1,w}
\end{pmatrix} .
$$

$$(2.23)$$

It is formed by staggered arranging from upper left to lower right along the diagonal of a small $\widehat{H}_{h \times w}$ and truncating the lower right corner.

$$
\widehat{H}_{h \times w} = \begin{pmatrix}
\hat{h}_{1,1} & \cdots & \hat{h}_{1,w} \\
\vdots & \ddots & \vdots \\
\hat{h}_{h,1} & \cdots & \hat{h}_{h,w}
\end{pmatrix} .
$$

$$(2.24)$$

Operation Process The operation process of the STC algorithm can be described by the trellis diagram. The following is an example to intuitively and comprehensively introduce the composition of the trellis diagram and the operation process of the algorithm. Assume that the message to be embedded is $\mathbf{m}^T = \{110\}$, the cover is $\mathbf{x}^T = \{011010\}$, and the parity matrix $\mathbf{H}$ is as follows:

$$
\mathbf{H}_{3 \times 6} = \begin{pmatrix}
1 & 0 & 0 & 0 & 0 & 0 \\
1 & 1 & 1 & 0 & 0 & 0 \\
0 & 0 & 1 & 1 & 1 & 0
\end{pmatrix} .
$$

$$(2.25)$$

It can be seen that the small matrix used is

$$
\widehat{\mathbf{H}}_{2 \times 2} = \begin{pmatrix}
1 & 0 \\
1 & 1
\end{pmatrix} .
$$

$$(2.26)$$

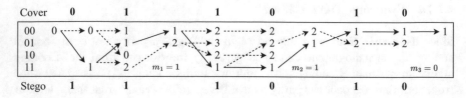

Fig. 2.3 Embedding path of syndrome trellis coding

Then the STC algorithm needs to find the stego $\mathbf{y}^T = (y_1, y_2, y_3, y_4, y_5, y_6)$ that minimizes distortion and also satisfies

$$\begin{pmatrix} 1\,0\,0\,0\,0\,0 \\ 1\,1\,1\,0\,0\,0 \\ 0\,0\,1\,1\,1\,0 \end{pmatrix} \begin{pmatrix} y_1 \\ y_2 \\ y_3 \\ y_4 \\ y_5 \\ y_6 \end{pmatrix} = \begin{pmatrix} 1 \\ 1 \\ 0 \end{pmatrix}. \tag{2.27}$$

Assume that constant distortion is used, and the trellis diagram of STC encoding for this situation is shown in Fig. 2.3.

The STC first divides the cover into $\frac{n}{w}$ sub-blocks, each of which determines the first digit of the secret message. In this example, $w = 2$, $n = 6$, so there are three sub-blocks, which are represented by the three blocks from left to right in Fig. 2.3.

Since the extractor has to do $\mathbf{Hy} = \mathbf{m}$, from the knowledge of matrix multiplication in linear algebra, for a certain component y_i of the vector $\mathbf{y}$, $y_i = 0$ means not taking the ith column of $\mathbf{H}$, and $y_i = 1$ means taking the ith column of $\mathbf{H}$, then in fact $\mathbf{Hy} = \mathbf{m}$ can also be written in the following form:

$$\mathbf{m} = \sum_{1 \le i \le n, y_i = 1} H_i, \tag{2.28}$$

where H_i represents the column i of the matrix $\mathbf{H}$, the addition is the ordinary vector addition, and the internal components are added on GF(2), that is, XOR operation. The STC runs from small to large according to i, corresponding to the matrix $\mathbf{H}$ running from left to right. Since the matrix $\mathbf{H}$ is only 1 in the small matrix $\widehat{\mathbf{H}}$ placed diagonally from the upper left to the bottom right, and the rest is 0, in fact, the STC can be considered to run from top left to bottom right.

The local syndrome on the left side of the figure corresponds to all $\{0, 1\}^h$, where h is the number of rows of the small matrix $\widehat{\mathbf{H}}$. Notably, the high bit of the local syndrome corresponds to the lower component in the column vector of $\widehat{\mathbf{H}}$, and the low bit corresponds to the upper component. This is because the STC proceeds from the upper left to the lower right of the matrix, and the column vector is determined first. Determine the upper bit in $\mathbf{m}$, and then the lower bit. After the operation of each sub-block is completed, the local syndrome needs to be shifted to the right to discard its determined low-order bits, so the low-order bits of the local syndrome correspond to the uppermost component in the column vector.

Now describe the specific running process of the algorithm:

1. The number marked on each node in the graph represents the distortion caused by taking the current path in the trellis graph. First, the initial distortion is 0, and the local syndrome of the initial state is 00. At this time, enter the first sub-block of the trellis graph; there are 2 options for the first bit of the sub-block; if 1 is taken, the first column 11 of $\widehat{\mathbf{H}}$ is added to the local syndrome. If the cover bit is 0, a distortion of 1 will be introduced; if it is set to 0, the first column 11 of $\widehat{\mathbf{H}}$ will not be added to the local syndrome. At this time, the local syndrome remains 00 and the distortion is 0. Considering the next bit, for the 00 state, if 1 is taken, the second column 10 of $\widehat{\mathbf{H}}$ is added to the local syndrome, and there is no distortion; if 0 is taken, the 00 state is maintained, and the distortion is 1. For the 11 state: take 1 and add the local syndrome to the second column 10 of $\widehat{\mathbf{H}}$ to get $10 \oplus 11 = 01$, and the distortion remains 1. Take 0 to keep the 11 state, and the distortion becomes 2. Since $m_1 = 1$, the local syndrome with the low bit of 1 should be taken, that is, 11 and 01. At this time, after fixing m_1, shift to the right to obtain new local syndromes 01 and 00, and start to enter the next one.

2. There are two states of 00 and 01 at the beginning of the second sub-block. First consider the 00 state: similar to the previous, if 00 is maintained, the distortion will become 2, and if 11 is maintained, the distortion will remain 1; for the 01 state: if 01 is maintained, the distortion will become 1. If 10 is maintained, the distortion remains at 2. Then go to the next bit: there are four starting states at this time, and the distortion introduced by each state transition is calculated in the same way as before. For each state, only one path with the least distortion is reserved. If there are multiple paths with the minimum distortion, then just keep one at random. In this way, the distortions corresponding to the states 00, 01, 10, and 11 are 2, 2, 2, and 1, respectively. Then, since $m_2 = 1$, 01 and 11 are retained and shifted right into the next sub-block.

3. The third sub-block also has two states of 00 and 01 at the beginning. At this time, it is the last sub-block, and only the first row of the matrix $\widehat{\mathbf{H}}$ is left, that is, it is not necessary to care about the high bits of the local syndrome. For the 00 state: if it takes 1, it becomes 01, the distortion remains 2; if it takes 0, it remains 00, and the distortion becomes 3; for the 01 state: if it takes 1, it becomes the 00 state, and the distortion remains 1, and if it takes 0, the distortion remains 1. Keep the 01 state and the distortion becomes 2. At this time, the minimum distortion for 00 is 1, and the minimum for 01 distortion is 2. Then go to the next bit, because the value in matrix $\mathbf{H}$ corresponding to the next bit is 0, so the state is directly maintained. The secret message bit corresponding to this sub-block is $m_3 = 0$, so it can only take the state of 00 and the distortion is 1.

4. Finally, the final path is determined from right to left according to the final state, and the bits of $\mathbf{y}$ determined at each step on the path are combined to obtain the final $\mathbf{y}^T = \{111010\}$.

For multi-level distortion models, just replace the weights of the corresponding edges in the trellis graph with the corresponding modified distortions.

Extending binary STC directly to multi-ary will increase the number of local syndrome states, and the computational complexity and memory consumption will increase dramatically. When the association between multiple layers can be optimized, multi-ary STC can be realized by multi-layer STC. This section introduces the DSTC (double-layered STC) algorithm [1], which implements ternary embedding through double-layer embedding, and can be similarly promoted for more multi-element cases.

First, the message capacity of the double-layer embedding is analyzed. y_i is used to denote the stego sample points integrated by all layers, and $y_i^{(l)}$ is used to represent the stego sample points of the lth layer. Then in the case of double layers, the information entropy of sample point x_i is

$$
H\left(P(y_i - x_i)\right) = H\left(P\left(y_i^{(1)} - x_i^{(1)}\right)\right) + H\left(P\left(y_i^{(2)} - x_i^{(2)}|y_i^{(1)} - x_i^{(1)}\right)\right).
$$
(2.29)

Since the embedding capacity is the entropy of the modified distribution, the chain rule for reusing entropy is as above. Then the embedding capacity of the first layer and the second layer is

$$
m_1 = \sum_i H\left(P\left(y_i^{(1)} - x_i^{(1)}\right)\right), m_2 = \sum_i H\left(P\left(y_i^{(2)} - x_i^{(2)}|y_i^{(1)} - x_i^{(1)}\right)\right).
$$
(2.30)

Embedding in one layer belongs to binary embedding. Assuming that the distortion introduced by no modification is 0, the optimal modification probability in the case of a known distortion function known from the optimal embedding theory is

$$
P\left(y_i = \bar{x}_i\right) = \frac{e^{-\lambda \rho_i(y_i = \bar{x}_i)}}{1 + e^{-\lambda \rho_i(y_i = \bar{x}_i)}}.
$$
(2.31)

If the optimal modification probability is known first, the distortion function is

$$
\rho_i(y_i = \bar{x}_i) = \ln\left(\frac{1 - P\left(y_i = \bar{x}_i\right)}{P\left(y_i = \bar{x}_i\right)}\right).
$$
(2.32)

The equation is very important in double-layer embedding because double-layer embedding needs to deduce the conditional probability from the probability of one layer to the conditional probability of another layer, and STC encoding requires the input to be distortion, so the conversion between distortion and probability is essential.

We take the LSB layer and the sub-LSB layer of the cover for embedding. Suppose that m-bit messages are to be embedded. At this time, the optimal embedding theory is used to solve the optimal distribution of ternary embedding π_i such that $m = \sum_i H(\pi_i)$, and set the probability of the y_i point corresponding to π_i to be $p_i^0, p_i^{-1}, p_i^{+1}$, respectively. Then first perform the embedding of the sub-LSB layer. Here, the probability is derived according to the state of x_i. We give $x_i^{(2)} x_i^{(1)} = 00$, the derivation process, and other cases can be derived in a similar way. For the secondary LSB layer, the second layer, $+1$ modification or no modification will not affect this layer, -1 modification will make it change, so there are

$$P\left(y_i^{(2)} - x_i^{(2)} = 0\right) = p_i^0 + p_i^{+1}, P\left(y_i^{(2)} - x_i^{(2)} \neq 0\right) = p_i^{-1}. \tag{2.33}$$

In this way, the optimal modification probability of the LSB layer is obtained. The utilization Eq. (2.30) can calculate the message capacity m_2 embedded in the layer, and the utilization Eq. (2.32) can obtain the distortion function in the case of the modification probability distribution, so that binary STC encoding can be used to embed the information of the secondary LSB layer.

Next, the conditional probability of the LSB layer is derived. When $y_i^{(2)} - x_i^{(2)} = 0$,

$$P\left(y_i^{(1)} - x_i^{(1)} = 0 | y_i^{(2)} - x_i^{(2)} \neq 0\right) = 0, \tag{2.34}$$

$$P\left(y_i^{(1)} - x_i^{(1)} \neq 0 | y_i^{(2)} - x_i^{(2)} \neq 0\right) = 1. \tag{2.35}$$

The number of messages embedded in this layer is $m - m_2$. With the modification probability, we can use Eq. (2.32) to calculate the distortion function and complete the embedding of the LSB layer with binary STC.

If the abovementioned method is directly used for embedding, there will be some problems: from observation Eq. (2.32), it can be seen that when the modification probability $P(y_i = \bar{x}_i) > 0.5$, the modified distortion at this point will take a negative value. Just as $P\left(y_i^{(1)} - x_i^{(1)} \neq 0 | y_i^{(2)} - x_i^{(2)} \neq 0\right) = 1$ in Eq. (2.35), then the modification distortion is $-\infty$. Here, the cover flip method is used to solve this problem, when modifying the probability $P(y_i = \bar{x}_i) > 0.5$, flip x_i such that $x_i = \bar{x}_i$. Then the modification probability becomes $P(y_i = \bar{x}_i) < 0.5$. Now, the distortion function will no longer be negative.

For Eq. (2.35), let $x_i^{(1)} = \bar{x}_i^{(1)}$, then the modification probability is 0, and the modification distortion is $+\infty$, meaning that the point turns to be a wet point.

2.2.2 Steganographic Distortion Design

Relating the embedded distortion of distortion functions to statistical detectability is an important open problem in modern steganography. There are two general categories that minimize statistical detectability. The first category attempts to preserve the distribution of the cover completely or approximately. It has a long history, from one-order to higher-order statistical. The second category, called the overall distortion-minimizing framework, also transforms the problem into a distortion function since it employs a general and almost perfect coding scheme STC to minimize a well-defined distortion function. When designing the distortion function, since the additive distortion function is relatively simple, the additive distortion function is often used, and some non-additive distortion functions can also be approximated by the additive distortion function. The additive distortion function can be expressed as the sum of the embedded distortion, which is measured by modifying the corresponding cover elements. Therefore, the steganographic task in the overall distortion-minimizing framework can be further simplified to the distortion assignment of cover elements. Li et al. summarized three heuristic distortion definition principles that can be used for the distortion allocation of cover elements, namely, the complexity priority principle, the spreading principle, and the clustering principle [3]. Before introducing the principle of distortion definition, let us define the priority. Cover elements are sorted in an order related to statistical detectability, and cover elements with lower statistical detectability after modification have higher priority. Obviously, we want the higher priority cover elements to be assigned smaller distortion values.

2.2.2.1   Distortion Definition Principle

Complexity First Principle   It requires unpredictable regions of the image to have high priority. It works on the principle that non-periodic textures and noisy regions are difficult to model, and the deviations in the steganalysis feature space caused by modifications of these regions are usually small and therefore not easy to detect. This rule has been generally adopted in previous content-adaptive steganography designs.

HUGO is the one of the earliest practical spatial distortion definition methods under distortion–minimization framework. The per-pixel distortion is calculated by the weighted sum of the differences between the feature vectors extracted from the cover image and the stego image by SPAM. The result of such a distortion scheme is that embedding changes typically occur in textured regions and along edges, rather than in smooth regions. Due to this content-adaptive property, HUGO is undetectable in SPAM-based machine learning steganalysis.

WOW speeds up distortion assignment by using weighted residuals of directional wavelet filters [6]. This method is based on the assumption that larger filter residuals indicate lower statistical detectability. In addition, it assigns the same distortion value to addition and subtraction operations, so it can employ binary or ternary embedding schemes. The concept of WOW is extended to S-UNIWARD, which slightly modifies the distortion function of WOW [7]. Under the powerful SRM steganalysis detection [8], both WOW and S-UNIWARD are more secure than HUGO.

Taking the distortion allocation scheme of S-UNIWARD as an example, the application of the principle of complexity priority is introduced here. A set of linear shift invariant filters whose kernel function is expressed as $\mathbf{K}^{(1)}$, $\mathbf{K}^{(2)}$, $\mathbf{K}^{(3)}$, and size is 16×16, composed of one-dimensional low-pass and high-pass filters h and g[4]:

$$\mathbf{K}^{(1)} = h \cdot g^T, \mathbf{K}^{(2)} = g \cdot h^T, \mathbf{K}^{(3)} = g \cdot g^T. \tag{2.36}$$

The kernel function is used to calculate the directional residual, i.e., the matrix of wavelet coefficients.

$$W^{(i)}(\mathbf{I}) = \mathbf{K}^{(i)} \otimes \mathbf{I}, i = 1, 2, 3, \tag{2.37}$$

where $\otimes$ represents the mirror padding convolution, which represents the smoothness of the spatial image $\mathbf{I}$. $W_{pq}^{(i)}(\mathbf{I})$ represents the element value at index (p, q) of the wavelet coefficient matrix obtained using the kernel function $K^{(i)}$, $p = 1, 2, \ldots, l_1, q = 1, 2, \ldots, l_2$, where l_1, l_2 are the width and height of the wavelet coefficient matrix. Defining $\mathbf{X}$ and $\mathbf{Y}$ to represent the spatial pixel matrix of the cover and the stego image, respectively. The distortion between the cover and stego images can be defined as the sum of the wavelet coefficient changes relative to the cover image

$$D(\mathbf{X}, \mathbf{Y}) \triangleq \sum_{k=1}^{3} \sum_{p,q} \frac{\left| W_{pq}^{(k)}(\mathbf{X}) - W_{pq}^{(k)}(\mathbf{Y}) \right|}{\varepsilon + \left| W_{pq}^{(k)}(\mathbf{X}) \right|}, \tag{2.38}$$

where $\epsilon \approx 10^{-15}$. If $\mathbf{X}$ and $\mathbf{Y}$ represent the DCT coefficient matrix of a JPEG image, we define $\mathbf{B}(k, l)$ to be an 8×8 matrix, and all elements are 0 excepting the element at (k, l), where $k, l = 1, 2, \ldots, 8$. The inverse transformation process of DCT is represented by J^{-1}. Due to the nature of mirror filling convolution $\otimes$, each 8×8 matrix block corresponds to a wavelet coefficient matrix with a size of 23×23.

$$\rho_{mn}^{(k,l)} = \sum_{i=1}^{3} \sum_{p=1}^{23} \sum_{q=1}^{23} \frac{\left| W_{pq}^{(i)} \left(J^{-1} \left(\mathbf{B}^{(k,l)} \right) \right) \right|}{\left| W_{pq}^{(i)} \left(J^{-1} \left(\mathbf{X}^{(k,l)} \right) \right) \right| + \sigma}, \tag{2.39}$$

where $\sigma = 2^{-6}$.

Spreading Principle It requires that the priority of two adjacent elements should not be very different. In other words, elements with high priority should diffuse their properties to their neighbors and vice versa. In this way, elements close to highly complex areas should have higher priority than elements close to less complex areas, even if both elements have the same precedence after applying the Complexity First Principle. The diffusion principle is simple and easy to understand but is ignored in

Fig. 2.4 Spreading Principle

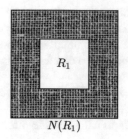 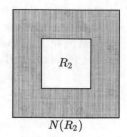

$N(R_1)$ $N(R_2)$

methods such as S-UNIWARD. In fact, the Spreading Principle can be used after the Complexity First Principle.

For example, there are two small regions in the image, denoted by R_1 and R_2, where they have the same content complexity level and the same priority according to the Complexity First Principle. Its adjacent regions are represented by $N(R_1)$ and $N(R_2)$, respectively, as shown in Fig. 2.4. Suppose the region $N(R_1)$ is more complex than $N(R_2)$, so based on the Complexity First Principle, the priority of the elements in $N(R_1)$ is higher than that of the elements in $N(R_2)$, and embedding information in R_1 will be better than embedding information in R_2. Therefore, we should assign higher priority to elements in R_1 compared to R_2, even though R_1 and R_2 have the same content complexity. When the spreading principle is applied, an element with a high modification probability will increase the modification probability of its neighbors and vice versa. In short, the spreading principle spreads priorities in the neighborhood. Essentially, the rule can be viewed as taking into account mutual embedded effects.

2.2.3 Deep Learning Based Steganography

ASDL-GAN [9] (Automatic Steganographic Distortion Learning Based on Generative Adversarial Networks) is the first method to automatically learn spatial image steganography using deep neural networks. The previous state-of-the-art spatial image steganography methods are all based on handcrafted. Early methods, such as HUGO, designed distortion for the features extracted by a steganalysis detector, and the generalization ability was not strong and easy to be detected. Subsequent methods such as S-UNIWARD [7] and HILL [10] are designed based on the principle of distortion definition and do not directly confront the detection of steganalysis, which shows the contradiction in the design of steganography distortion. With the emergence of CNN-based steganalyzers such as XuNet [11] and YeNet [12], the generalization detection ability and detection accuracy of steganalyzers have been continuously improved. ASDL-GAN adopts a generative adversarial network to simulate the competition between additive distortion steganography and a deep learning steganalyzer, so that both distortion generator and steganalysis detector can automatically learn image features through adversarial training, so as to obtain automatic steganographic distortion adapted to images. In recent years, on the basis of ASDL-GAN, various deep learning based steganographic distortion methods, such as UT-GAN [13], JS-GAN [14], SPAR-RL [15] and JEC-RL [16], have been proposed, which has become an important research direction in the field of steganography.

2.2.3.1 ASDL-GAN

ASDL-GAN adopts a minimal distortion framework in the additive case, using STC embeddings. The network is mainly composed of three parts: generator, analog embedder, and discriminator, as shown in Fig. 2.5. Among them, the generator is responsible for generating the steganographic modification probability of the cover image, that is, adaptive steganographic distortion; the simulator uses the modification probability to generate the modified value of the ternary embedding; and the discriminator adopts a convolutional neural network-based steganalyzer design for adversarial training.

(a) Generator

The generator of ASDL-GAN is divided into 25 groups. Each group contains convolutional layer, batch normalization layer (BN), and activation layer (ReLU or Sigmoid) and uses shortcut connection in the first 24 groups. To enhance the ability of feature learning, the output of the last group is a single feature map of the same size as the carrier image, where the elements represent the steganographic modification probability of the corresponding pixel, and the probability is limited by the activation function between 0 and 0.5. This chapter adopts the ternary embedding model, that is, a given pixel $x_{i,j}$ will be modified to $y_{i,j}$ with probability $p_{i,j}^{\phi}$ to $x_{i,j} + \phi$, where $\phi \in \{+1, -1, 0\}$, and a symmetric approximation to the modified probability, let $p_{i,j}^{+1} = p_{i,j}^{-1} = \frac{p_{i,j}}{2}$, $p_{i,j}^{0} = 1 - p_{i,j}$, so the embedding capacity corresponding to the entire cover image can be obtained

$$\textbf{capacity} = \sum_{i=1}^{H} \sum_{j=1}^{W} \left(-p_{i,j}^{+1} \log p_{i,j}^{+1} - p_{i,j}^{-1} \log p_{i,j}^{-1} - p_{i,j}^{0} \log p_{i,j}^{0} \right). \quad (2.40)$$

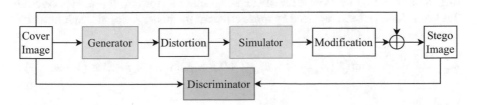

Fig. 2.5 The framework of ASDL-GAN

Fig. 2.6 The architecture of
simulator

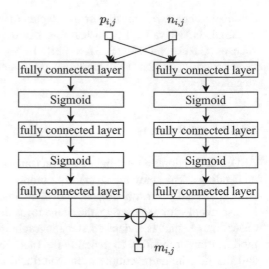

(b) Simulator

In order to obtain the stego image, it is also necessary to obtain the modified value
of the pixel from the pixel modification probability or modification distortion. In the
previous steganography scheme, the method of embedding simulator is generally
used. That is, the simulation modification $m'_{i,j}$ is obtained by given modification
probabilities $p_{i,j}$ and random numbers $n_{i,j}$:

$$m'_{i,j} = \begin{cases} -1, & \text{if } n_{i,j} < \frac{p_{i,j}}{2} \\ 1, & \text{if } n_{i,j} > 1 - \frac{p_{i,j}}{2} \\ 0, & \text{otherwise.} \end{cases} \tag{2.41}$$

But in the training process of GAN, the simulator should be differentiable to meet
the needs of back-propagation of gradients from the discriminator to the generator.
Obviously, Eq. (2.41) is non-differentiable as a step function. As an alternative,
ASDL-GAN adopts a TES activation function implemented with a miniature neural
network, which takes the modification probability and random number as input and
outputs the result of the modification of the ternary embedding, as shown in Fig. 2.6.

The modification is added to the pixel value of the cover element to load the stego
element. It is worth mentioning that in the follow-up development in the research
direction of neural network-defined steganographic distortion, the network-based
TES function has been replaced by more efficient methods. A double-tanh function
is proposed in UT-GAN [14]:

$$m'_{i,j} = -0.5 \times \tanh\left(\lambda\left(p_{i,j} - 2 \times n_{i,j}\right)\right) + 0.5 \times \tanh\left(\lambda\left(p_{i,j} - 2 \times \left(1 - n_{i,j}\right)\right)\right). \tag{2.42}$$

This differentiable function can simulate the modified value of the embedding
and also greatly reduces the time for iterative adversarial training of the network

because no pre-training is required. In addition, the convergence effect of the hyperbolic tangent function also exceeds that of the TES activation function, and most modified probability values can obtain the simulation modification results of ± 1. However, the hyperbolic tangent function has the problem that the absolute value of the gradient is very small when the modification deviation is small, and the gradient disappears easily. In the subsequent methods based on deep reinforcement learning, e.g., SPAR-RL [15], the gradient information is directly passed back to the generator (called the policy network in reinforcement learning), and the back-propagation process of the embedding simulator can be skipped, so the step function in Eq. (2.42) can be directly used to simulate the modified sampling, avoiding the disappearance of the gradient and making it easier for the network to converge.

(c) Discriminator

The design and development of CNN-based steganalyzers are presented in previous chapters. In the design of ASDL-GAN, XuNet is selected as the discriminator of GAN based on the dual consideration of detection performance and implementation efficiency. This module takes the cover-stego image pair as input to perform binary classification of images.

2.2.3.2 Training Strategy

(a) Design of Loss Function

Like all deep learning networks, the definition method of steganographic distortion based on deep learning also needs to design a loss function, iteratively train through optimization methods such as SGD and Adam to reduce the loss, and finally obtain a converged network model to adaptively generate the modification of the cover. According to the requirements of GAN confrontation training, the loss function of ASDL-GAN is designed as follows.

In order to make the TES activation function satisfy the step function in Eq. (2.42), the loss function of the pre-trained TES subnet is

$$l_{TES} = \frac{1}{H}\frac{1}{W}\sum_{i=1}^{H}\sum_{j=1}^{W}\left(m_{i,j} - m'_{i,j}\right)^2. \tag{2.43}$$

The goal of the discriminator is to distinguish the cover image from the corresponding stego image, and the loss function of such binary classification tasks is generally defined by cross-entropy. For a given image label y'_i and the discriminator output y_i, the loss function is calculated as follows:

$$l_D = -\sum_{i=1}^{2} y'_i \log y_i. \tag{2.44}$$

For the generator, the loss function is a weighted sum of two parts. One is the adversarial loss used to measure the detection ability of the resistant discriminator l_G^1, and the other loss l_G^2 is used to ensure that the generated secret image can carry a given message embedding rate q,

$$l_G^1 = -l_D \tag{2.45}$$

$$l_G^2 = (\textbf{capacity} - H \times W \times q). \tag{2.46}$$

(b) Training Process

Each process of the ASDL-GAN is shown in Fig. 2.5. Feed the cover image and message embedding rate to the generator and generate the modification probability. With the modification probability, the corresponding modified value is obtained by the embedding simulator. Then the modified value is added to the cover image to obtain the stego image. The stego image is fed into the discriminator to obtain the classification results, and the loss function is finally calculated from the classification result.

During each iteration, the network graph is run twice. For the first time, it is used to optimize the discriminator. Optimizers such as Adam use gradient descent to optimize the parameters of the discriminator to reduce the loss of the discriminator. The second time optimizes the generator parameters according to the generator loss. After several iterations of training, the network model tends to be stable, and the generator model with fixed parameters at this time can be used to generate modification probability.

2.3 Steganalysis

2.3.1 Handcrafted Feature Based Steganalysis

With the emergence of Least Significant Bit Matching (LSBM) and other methods, the early steganalysis methods based on simple statistical features such as chi-square statistics are no longer effective. Therefore, in order to achieve better steganalysis algorithms, researchers must analyze the image content more comprehensively and deeply, so as to design higher dimensional features, and then distinguish the stego image from the cover image through these features. Machine learning just provides a binary classification method that can accomplish this task. Therefore, high-dimensional feature detection algorithms based on machine learning came into being.

These algorithms extracts high-dimensional features from images, and then uses machine learning to classify them to determine whether an image is a cover image or a stego image. In general, it can be divided into three stages: feature extraction, training, and detection, as shown in Fig. 2.7.

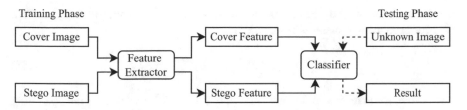

Fig. 2.7 Machine learning based steganalysis

In the stage of feature extraction, a high-dimensional feature that can reflect the content of the image from different angles is designed in advance, and then the respective features are extracted from the cover image and the stego image. In the training phase, the corresponding high-dimensional features are extracted from a large number of cover–stego image pairs and then thrown into the machine learning binary classification network for training, which is similar to the process of supervised learning. Finally, in the detection stage, high-dimensional features are extracted from the image to be tested, and then the trained classifier is used for detection to distinguish whether the image to be tested is a cover image or a stego image.

At present, commonly used high-dimensional features include adjacent pixel correlation features, statistical moment features, image quality measurement features, etc.; commonly used machine learning classifiers include support vector machines (SVM), neural networks, Bayesian networks, etc.

2.3.1.1 Subtractive Pixel Adjacency Matrix (SPAM)

For naturally captured images, there is a clear correlation between adjacent pixels. Based on the above observations on the correlation of neighborhood pixels, Pevny et al. proposed a spatial steganalysis method based on SPAM features. When steganography is performed on the cover image, the noise distribution of the cover signal will be changed, and the damage to the cover distribution will be reflected by the distribution of the pixel difference in the neighborhood. The SPAM method is based on this principle. In view of the destruction of the correlation of neighboring pixels by steganography, the difference values in different directions of the pixels are calculated, the statistical distribution features are extracted, and then features is processed by a nonlinear SVM (support vector machine).

First, the extraction of SPAM first-order features is introduced. Denote $\rightarrow$, $\leftarrow$, $\uparrow$, $\downarrow$, $\nwarrow$, $\searrow$, $\nearrow$, $\swarrow$ as the residuals of neighbor pixels in different directions, such as

$$D_{i,j}^{\rightarrow} = I_{i,j} - I_{i,j+1} \tag{2.47}$$

is the neighbor pixel difference in the horizontal direction from left to right. Then the corresponding transition probability is

$$M_{u,v}^{\rightarrow} = Pr\left(D_{i,j+1}^{\rightarrow} = u \middle| D_{i,j}^{\rightarrow} = v\right). \tag{2.48}$$

As before, truncating u and v such that $u, v \in [-T, T]$, where T is the truncating length. Similarly, $M_{u,v}^{\leftarrow}, M_{u,v}^{\uparrow}, M_{u,v}^{\downarrow}, M_{u,v}^{\nwarrow}, M_{u,v}^{\searrow}, M_{u,v}^{\nearrow}, M_{u,v}^{\searrow} M_{u,v}^{\swarrow}$ can be obtained. To reduce the total feature dimension and increase the robustness of the features, the features can be combined:

$$F_{u,v}^{+} = \frac{1}{4}\left(M_{u,v}^{\rightarrow} + M_{u,v}^{\leftarrow} + M_{u,v}^{\uparrow} + M_{u,v}^{\downarrow}\right) \tag{2.49}$$

$$F_{u,v}^{-} = \frac{1}{4}\left(M_{u,v}^{\searrow} + M_{u,v}^{\swarrow} + M_{u,v}^{\nwarrow} + M_{u,v}^{\nearrow}\right). \tag{2.50}$$

These $2K$ dimensional features are called first-order SPAM features. For the second-order SPAM feature, only the second-order transition probability needs to be considered,

$$M_{u,v,w}^{\rightarrow} = Pr\left(D_{i,j+2}^{\rightarrow} = u \middle| D_{i,j+1}^{\rightarrow} = v, D_{i,j}^{\rightarrow} = w\right). \tag{2.51}$$

2.3.1.2 Support Vector Machine (SVM)

In the SPAM feature-based steganalysis method, after the SPAM features are extracted, machine learning is used for classification, and the classifier used is the SVM. In machine learning, SVMs are supervised learning models and related learning algorithms that analyze data in classification and regression analysis. Given a set of training instances, each labeled as belonging to one or the other of the two classes, the SVM training algorithm creates a model that assigns new instances to one of the two classes, making it a non-probabilistic two metalinear classifier. The SVM model represents instances as points in space such that the mapping makes instances of individual classes separated by as wide a noticeable interval as possible. Then, map the new instances to the same space and predict the class they belong to based on which side of the interval they fall on.

2.3.1.3 Spatial Rich Models (SRM)

SPAM utilizes simple and a few filters to obtain the residual. More filters and statistical indicators lead to better detection ability. Fridrich et al. proposed steganalysis based on spatially rich model (SRM) [8].

SRM uses multiple submodels to extract more features. The so-called submodels are high-dimensional features obtained by residual calculation of images through different filtering methods. SRM uses a combination of multiple high-dimensional features to better characterize the destruction of multiple correlations by steganography on neighboring pixels.

The extraction of SRM features is generally divided into the following three steps:

1. Calculate residuals. The residual R is calculated by

$$R_{i,j} = \hat{X}_{i,j}(N_{i,j}) - cX_{i,j}, \tag{2.52}$$

where $N_{i,j}$ is the neighbor pixels of $X_{i,j}$, and $\hat{X}_{i,j}(N_{i,j})$ predict $cX_{i,j}$ through its neighbors.

2. Quantization and truncation. Quantize and truncate the above real residuals $R_{i,j}$

$$R_{i,j} \leftarrow trunc_T\left(round\left(\frac{R_{i,j}}{q}\right)\right), \tag{2.53}$$

where q is the quantization step size. For $x \in R$, the truncation function is defined as

$$trunc_T(x) = \begin{cases} x, & x \in [-T, T] \\ T\text{sign}(x), & x \notin [-T, T]. \end{cases} \tag{2.54}$$

The significance of the truncation operation is that, on the one hand, steganalysis is more interested in regions with strong correlation and small residuals; on the other hand, truncating the residuals is beneficial to reducing the dimension of the final extracted features.

3. Statistical co-occurrence matrix. The SRM feature is finally expressed as the fourth-order joint distribution form of truncated residuals under each submodel, that is, the joint distribution probability estimation of the residuals in 4 consecutive samples d_1, d_2, d_3, d_4 in the horizontal or vertical direction, where the horizontal direction is estimated as

$$C_d^{(h)} = \frac{1}{Z}\left|\{(R_{i,j}, \ R_{i,j+1}, \ R_{i,j+2}, \ R_{i,j+3})|R_{i,j+k-1} = d_k, k = 1, \ldots, 4\}\right|, \tag{2.55}$$

where Z is the total number of all occurrences, which serves as a normalization parameter such that

$$\sum_{d \in T_4} C_d^{(h)} = 1. \tag{2.56}$$

The co-occurrence matrix obtained in this way is the various high-dimensional features of the image, and the performance of the image in different aspects can be obtained by performing statistics on these co-occurrence matrices.

2.3.1.4   Ensemble Classifier

Unlike SPAM, the classifier used in the rich model is no longer a simple SVM, but an ensemble classifier. The so-called ensemble classifier is actually ensemble learning, by constructing and combining multiple learners to complete the learning task. A set of individual classifiers are first generated and then combined through a certain strategy to obtain the final result. By combining multiple learners, ensemble classifiers can often achieve better generalization performance than a single learner.

2.3.2   Deep Learning Based Steganalysis

Traditional steganalysis methods (such as SPAM [5] and SRM [8]) are obtained by professional researchers relying on their own prior knowledge and continuous heuristic attempts to calculate artificial heuristic features and then based on machine learning classifiers (such as SVM and ensemble classifier). For classification, these two steps are performed separately and cannot be optimized at the same time, so it is difficult to achieve a considerable state.

Recently, deep learning technology has developed vigorously and achieved great success in many fields (such as computer vision, natural language processing, and speech recognition), and scholars have also begun to combine steganalysis and deep learning. At present, the performance of deep learning based steganalysis has far surpassed traditional steganalysis methods.

2.3.2.1   The Transition from Traditional Steganalysis to Deep Learning Steganalysis

As shown in Fig. 2.8, the machine learning based steganalysis method can be divided into three steps: calculating the high-pass residual of the image, extracting

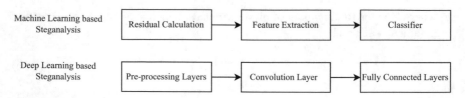

Fig. 2.8 Comparison between machine learning based steganalysis and deep learning based steganalysis

the features heuristically, and training the classifier. While in deep learning based steganalysis, the preprocessing layer, convolutional layer, and the fully connected layer are implemented, and the details are as follows:

(a) Residual calculation → preprocessing layer
    The residual is calculated to suppress the image content and enhance the steganographic signal to increase the signal-to-noise ratio in the steganalysis task. For example, pixel differences are calculated in SPAM, and various high-pass filters are used in SRM to calculate image residuals. In deep learning based steganalysis, a preprocessing layer is added to the front end of the network to improve the signal-to-noise ratio. The preprocessing layer is a convolutional structure, and some steganalysis networks (Ye-Net [12], Yedroudj-Net [17], Cov-Net [18], etc.) use high-pass filters in SRM to initialize these convolutional kernels, which can speed up network convergence. There are also some networks whose preprocessing layers are randomly initialized (such as SRNet [19]), which can prevent the network from falling into the artificially designed local optimal solution, but they require longer training time and are more prone to overfitting.

(b) Feature extraction → Convolutional layer
    Traditional steganalysis is based on prior professional experience and continuous heuristic attempts to obtain artificial heuristic features. The successful application of convolutional neural networks in the CV field illustrates that it can extract complex statistical dependencies from high-dimensional inputs.

(c) Classifier → Fully Connected Layer
    In traditional steganalysis, machine learning classifiers are trained after extracting features, such as SVM and ensemble classifiers. Deep learning usually uses one or more fully connected layers plus a softmax layer to achieve binary classification. Under the framework of deep learning, residual calculation, feature extraction, and classification will be optimized simultaneously as a whole framework, which solves the problem that traditional steganalysis two-stage optimization is difficult to achieve a heterogeneous equilibrium state.

2.3.2.2 Characteristics of CNN in the Field of Steganalysis

Steganalysis tasks are very different from computer vision tasks. Steganographic signals to be processed by steganalysis are usually not perceptible by the human perceptual system. In fact, in well-designed steganography algorithms, stego images are often not only visually, but also statistically very similar to cover images. Therefore, the feature representations of CNN-based steganalyzers should be very different from those in traditional CV tasks. In view of this, it is not difficult to find that using CNN directly in the CV domain to train steganalysis tasks usually fails to converge. Therefore, some custom designs specifically for steganalysis are needed to incorporate domain knowledge into the learning process of CNN-based steganalysis networks.

(a) Preprocessing layer

Unlike the CV task, the steganography process can be viewed as the process of adding an embedded signal with a very low signal-to-noise ratio to the cover image. The main function of the preprocessing layer is to improve the signal-to-noise ratio and facilitate network convergence. The two forms of the preprocessing layer have been introduced above and will not be repeated here.

(b) Truncated Linear Activation Function (TLU)

The shallow network output is relatively linear, and the steganographic signal is usually in the range of $[-1, 1]$. In order to suppress the image content and amplify the steganographic signal, a truncated linear activation function is used in the shallow layer of the network, which is defined as follows:

$$f(x) = \begin{cases} -T, & x < -T \\ x, & -T \le x \le T \\ T, & x > T, \end{cases} \tag{2.57}$$

where $T > 0$ is the parameter determined in the experiment.

(c) Selection channel awareness

According to the Kerckhoffs principle, to evaluate the security performance of a steganography algorithm, every element of the scheme except the secret key should be publicly declared. For image steganography, the steganalyzer can also estimate the probability that each pixel is modified when performing the embedding, the so-called selection channel awareness (SCA). Combined with knowledge of the selected channel, the performance of the steganalyzer for content-adaptive steganography schemes is expected to improve. SCA is combined with SRM feature sets, such as tSRM, maxSRM, and σSRM, to incorporate some statistical measures of embedding probability when computing the co-occurrence matrix or histogram of the corresponding residuals. However, for CNN models, there is no way to explicitly compute the co-occurrence matrix or histogram. Therefore, we have to find other ways to exploit the embedded probability.

In YeNet, the expected upper bound of the norm of ℓ_1 of the high-pass residual is used as the side information $\varphi(P)$. After derivation, $\varphi(P) = P * |K|$. K is the high-pass filter bank from SRM. There are also various forms of side information $\varphi(P)$. With the side information $\varphi(P)$, there are two easy ways to propagate $\varphi(P)$ throughout the network. One is to apply element-wise accumulation between $\varphi(P)$ and the output feature map of the first convolutional layer, and the other is to apply element-wise multiplication. Which one to use can be determined experimentally.

Figure 2.9 shows the structure of YeNet. For each convolutional layer, the input feature map is the output of the previous layer. The front end of the network removes the average pooling layer to prevent the steganographic signal from being erased. The structure in the dashed line exists only in the SCA version.

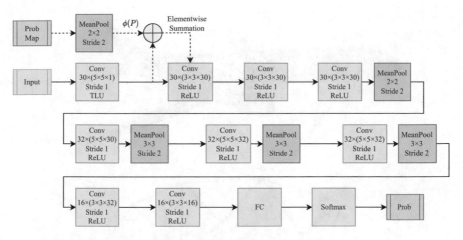

Fig. 2.9 The architecture of deep learning based steganalysis YeNet

2.4   Triangle Mesh

A mesh is a set of polygonal faces, and the goal is to form an approximation of a real 3D object. A polygonal mesh has three different combined elements: *vertices*, *edges*, and *faces*; a mesh can also be taken as the combination of *geometry connectivity*, where the *geometry* provides the 3D positions of all its vertices, and *connectivity*, which provides the information hidden between different adjacent vertices. Mathematically, a 3D polygonal mesh M containing V vertices and F faces can be formed as a set $M = \{\mathcal{V}, \mathcal{F}\}$, where

$$\begin{aligned}
\mathcal{V} &= \{v_i\}_{i=1,2,\dots,V}, \\
\mathcal{F} &= \{f_i\}_{i=1,2,\dots,F}, \quad f_i \in \mathcal{V} \times \mathcal{V} \times \mathcal{V}
\end{aligned} \tag{2.58}$$

in the Cartesian coordinate system and $\mathcal{F}$ is the face set. In addition, the edge set $\mathcal{E}$ is defined as

$$\mathcal{E} = \{e_i\}_{i=1,2,\dots,E}, \quad e_i \in \mathcal{V} \times \mathcal{V}. \tag{2.59}$$

The geometric embedding of a triangular mesh into $\mathbb{R}^3$ is determined by connecting the 3D position $\mathbf{p}_i$ to each vertex $v_i \in \mathcal{V}$ [29]:

$$\begin{aligned}
\mathcal{P} &= \{\mathbf{p}_1, \dots, \mathbf{p}_V\}, \\
\mathbf{p}_i &:= \mathbf{p}(v_i) = [x(v_i), y(v_i), z(v_i)]^T \in \mathbb{R}^3.
\end{aligned} \tag{2.60}$$

Users usually prefer a list of all mesh faces and arrange their respective component vertices in a certain circular order. Although this list contains redundant information, it can facilitate geometric and topological operations on a given mesh. Figure 2.10 shows an example of a 3D mesh, and Table 2.1 shows the corresponding

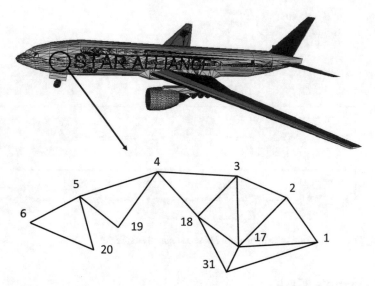

Fig. 2.10 An example of a 3D mesh (from the Princeton ModelNet dataset)

Table 2.1 Indexed face-set data structure for triangle meshes (Fig. 2.10)

Vertex list				Face list	
Index of vertex	x-axis	y-axis	z-axis	Index of face	Elements in each face
1	x_1	y_1	z_1	1	(17, 1, 2)
2	x_2	y_2	z_2	2	(3, 2, 17)
3	x_3	y_3	z_3	3	(4, 3, 18)
4	x_4	y_4	z_4	4	(5, 4, 19)
5	x_5	y_5	z_5	5	(6, 5, 20)
6	x_6	y_6	z_6	...	...
...	...	...	...	16	(31, 17, 1)
17	x_{17}	y_{17}	z_{17}	17	(18, 17, 31)
18	x_{18}	y_{18}	z_{18}	...	...
19	x_{19}	y_{19}	z_{19}	241	(17, 18, 3)
20	x_{20}	y_{20}	z_{20}	...	...
...	...	...	...	...	...
31	x_{31}	y_{31}	z_{31}	...	...
...	...	...	...	...	...

file formats. As shown in the enlarged view, the *degree* of a face is the number of its component edges, and the *valence* of a vertex is defined as the number of its incident edges. Faces are usually composed of triangles (triangle meshes), quadrilaterals (quads), or other simple convex polygons (n-gons). Since the triangle mesh is the current mainstream mesh, this chapter considers only triangle meshes.

2.4.1 Dataset

The **Princeton Segmentation Benchmark**[1] is a mesh segmentation dataset with 354 objects [30] splitting into 260 training cover objects and 94 testing cover objects. Given a steganographic algorithm, we generate the corresponding stego object of each cover object. Finally, we have 260 pairs of cover objects and corresponding stego for training and 94 pairs for testing.

The **Princeton ModelNet**[2] includes 12,311 mesh objects with 40 categories. 50% of the mesh objects are taken as the training cover set (6156), and the remaining are taken as the cover testing set (6155). Similarly, each object has the corresponding stego object, forming the training set or the testing set.

References

1. Filler, T., Judas, J. & Fridrich, J. Minimizing additive distortion in steganography using syndrome-trellis codes. *IEEE Transactions on Information Forensics and Security.* **6**, 920–935 (2011)
2. Filler, T. & Fridrich, J. Gibbs construction in steganography. *IEEE Transactions on Information Forensics and Security.* **5**, 705–720 (2010)
3. Li, B., Tan, S., Wang, M. & Huang, J. Investigation on cost assignment in spatial image steganography. *IEEE Transactions on Information Forensics and Security.* **9**, 1264–1277 (2014)
4. Pevny, T., Filler, T. & Bas, P. Using high-dimensional image models to perform highly undetectable steganography. *International Workshop on Information Hiding.* pp. 161–177 (2010)
5. Pevny, T., Bas, P. & Fridrich, J. Steganalysis by subtractive pixel adjacency matrix. *IEEE Transactions on Information Forensics and Security.* **5**, 215–224 (2010
6. Holub, V. & Fridrich, J. Designing steganographic distortion using directional filters. *2012 IEEE International Workshop on Information Forensics and Security (WIFS).* pp. 234–239 (2012)
7. Holub, V., Fridrich, J. & Denemark, T. Universal distortion function for steganography in an arbitrary domain. *EURASIP Journal on Information Security.* **2014**, 1–13 (2014)
8. Fridrich, J. & Kodovsky, J. Rich models for steganalysis of digital images. *IEEE Transactions on Information Forensics and Security.* **7**, 868–882 (2012)
9. Tang, W., Tan, S., Li, B. & Huang, J. Automatic steganographic distortion learning using a generative adversarial network. *IEEE Signal Processing Letters.* **24**, 1547–1551 (2017)
10. Li, B., Wang, M., Huang, J. & Li, X. A new cost function for spatial image steganography. *2014 IEEE International Conference on Image Processing (ICIP).* pp. 4206–4210 (2014)
11. Xu, G., Wu, H. & Shi, Y. Structural design of convolutional neural networks for steganalysis. *IEEE Signal Processing Letters.* **23**, 708–712 (2016)
12. Ye, J., Ni, J. & Yi, Y. Deep learning hierarchical representations for image steganalysis. *IEEE Transactions on Information Forensics and Security.* **12**, 2545–2557 (2017)
13. Yang, J., Ruan, D., Huang, J., Kang, X. & Shi, Y. An embedding cost learning framework using GAN. *IEEE Transactions on Information Forensics and Security.* **15** pp. 839–851 (2019)

---

[1] http://segeval.cs.princeton.edu/.

[2] http://modelnet.cs.princeton.edu/.

14. Yang, J., Ruan, D., Kang, X. & Shi, Y. Towards automatic embedding cost learning for JPEG steganography. *Proceedings of the ACM Workshop on Information Hiding and Multimedia Security*. pp. 37–46 (2019)

15. Tang, W., Li, B., Barni, M., Li, J. & Huang, J. An automatic cost learning framework for image steganography using deep reinforcement learning. *IEEE Transactions on Information Forensics and Security*. **16** pp. 952–967 (2020)

16. Tang, W., Li, B., Barni, M., Li, J. & Huang, J. Improving cost learning for JPEG steganography by exploiting JPEG domain knowledge. *IEEE Transactions on Circuits and Systems for Video Technology*. (2021)

17. Yedroudj, M., Comby, F. & Chaumont, M. Yedroudj-Net: An efficient CNN for spatial steganalysis. *2018 IEEE International Conference on Acoustics, Speech and Signal Processing (ICASSP)*. pp. 2092–2096 (2018)

18. Deng, X., Chen, B., Luo, W. & Luo, D. Fast and effective global covariance pooling network for image steganalysis. *Proceedings of the ACM Workshop on Information Hiding and Multimedia Security*. pp. 230–234 (2019)

19. Boroumand, M., Chen, M. & Fridrich, J. Deep residual network for steganalysis of digital images. *IEEE Transactions on Information Forensics and Security*. **14**, 1181–1193 (2018)

20. Ko, H., Huang, C., Horng, G. & Shiuh-Jeng, W. Robust and blind image watermarking in DCT domain using inter-block coefficient correlation. *Information Sciences*. **517** pp. 128–147 (2020)

21. Daren, H., Jiufen, L., Jiwu, H. & Hongmei, L. A DWT-based image watermarking algorithm. *IEEE International Conference on Multimedia and Expo, 2001. ICME 2001.*. pp. 80–80 (2001)

22. Urvoy, M., Goudia, D. & Autrusseau, F. Perceptual DFT watermarking with improved detection and robustness to geometrical distortions. *IEEE Transactions on Information Forensics and Security*. **9**, 1108–1119 (2014)

23. Mun, S., Nam, S., Jang, H., Kim, D. & Lee, H. Finding robust domain from attacks: A learning framework for blind watermarking. *Neurocomputing*. **337** pp. 191–202 (2019)

24. Ahmadi, M., Norouzi, A., Karimi, N., Samavi, S. & Emami, A. ReDMark: Framework for residual diffusion watermarking based on deep networks. *Expert Systems with Applications*. **146** pp. 113157 (2020)

25. Fang, H., Chen, D., Wang, F., Ma, Z., Liu, H., Zhou, W., Zhang, W. & Yu, N. TERA: Screen-to-Camera Image Code with Transparency, Efficiency, Robustness and Adaptability. *IEEE Transactions on Multimedia*. **24** pp. 955–967 (2021)

26. Cheng, Y., Ji, X., Wang, L., Pang, Q., Chen, Y. & Xu, W. mID: Tracing screen photos via Moiré patterns. *30th USENIX Security Symposium (USENIX Security 21)*. pp. 2969–2986 (2021)

27. S. M. Shontz and P. M. Knupp, "The effect of vertex reordering on 2D local mesh optimization efficiency," in *Proceedings of the International Meshing Roundtable*. Springer, 2008, pp. 107–124.

28. S. P. Sastry, E. Kulturssay, S. M. Shontz, and M. T. Kandemir, "Improved cache utilization and preconditioner efficiency through use of a space-filling curve mesh element- and vertex-reordering technique," *Engineering with Computers*, vol. 30, no. 4, pp. 535–547, 2014.

29. Botsch, M., Kobbelt, L., Pauly, M., Alliez, P. & Levy, B. Polygon Mesh Processing. (Taylor & Francis, 2010)

30. Chen, X., Golovinskiy, A. & Funkhouser, T. A benchmark for 3D mesh segmentation. *ACM Transactions on Graphics (Proc. SIGGRAPH), 28* (2009)

Chapter 3
3D Mesh Watermarking Techniques

Abstract In this chapter, we introduce 3D mesh watermarking techniques. These techniques mainly include traditional 3D mesh watermarking, deep learning based 3D mesh watermarking, 3D mesh watermarking against 3D print–scan attacks, and 3D mesh watermarking on the G-code file used in the 3D printing devices.

3.1 Early 3D Mesh Watermarking Against Digital Attacks

Early 3D mesh watermarking can be divided into two categories: spatial domain-based methods and transform domain-based methods.

3.1.1 Spatial Domain-Based 3D Mesh Watermarking

Spatial domain-based methods generally embed watermarks by performing a spatial domain analysis of the 3D mesh and directly modifying the X–Y–Z coordinates of the 3D mesh. A common problem for this class of algorithms is mesh synchronization. This is mainly because preprocessing operations such as vertex grouping need to be performed on both the original 3D mesh and the watermarked 3D mesh. When local areas of the mesh are modified, the grouping is changed, making the grouping at the extraction stage and embedding stage inconsistent. In the subsequent extraction of the watermark information, the extracted watermark information is also changed because the mesh is not synchronized. even now, there is no valid solution to the mesh synchronization problem.

3.1.1.1 LSB-Based Method

A simple method to embed the watermark in the spatial domain is the least significant bit (LSB) algorithm, and thus the watermark bit can be embedded by simply replacing the LSB of the vertex coordinates. Zhou et al. [1] proposed an algorithm for adaptive information hiding on 3D meshes. The algorithm designs a distortion function based on vertex normals and embeds bit information based on this function for multiple bit planes of vertex coordinates. This method is not robust to multiple attacks such as noise addition and smoothing and can be easily erased by noise.

3.1.1.2 Similarity-Based Method

The triangle similarity quadruple (TSQ) algorithm defines the similarity triangle in the mesh as the watermark embedding primitive and then embeds the watermark information into it. Based on the property of similarity triangles, it is resistant to geometric attacks, but not to mesh reconstruction attacks. The tetrahedron volume ratio (TVR) algorithm is applied to tetrahedral meshes. It uses the ratio of tetrahedron volume to embed watermarked information, which has a high information capacity, but is less resistant to many attacks such as vertex reordering, mesh simplification, and remeshing. The vertex flood algorithm (VFA) requires a number of triangular meshes to be selected in the 3D mesh model, and then the watermark is embedded by modifying the distance from the center of gravity of the triangular mesh to each vertex of the triangular mesh. The triangle flood algorithm (TFA) also involves selecting a number of triangle meshes and then adjusting and modifying the height of each triangle mesh to embed the watermark information for the other triangle meshes adjacent to the selected triangle mesh. Histogram mapping is also a common spatial domain watermarking algorithm. The algorithm requires histogram statistics and grouping of 3D mesh vertices, and the data is embedded into each histogram. The algorithm is resistant to a variety of geometric attacks but is not as resistant to cropping attack and noise addition attack.

3.1.1.3 Statistical Embedding-Based Method

Cho et al. [17] proposed a 3D mesh watermarking algorithm based on histogram mapping. It embeds the watermark by modifying the distance distribution between the mesh vertices and the mesh center. Before embedding, the mesh vertices are grouped into K bins based on the distance distribution to the center, and the distances of each bin are subsequently normalized within the bin. At the embedding process, the mean or the variance of the vertex distances for each bin is calculated and adjusted according to whether the watermarked bits are 0 or 1. This algorithm performs well in terms of robustness against a wide range of attacks but is more sensitive to noise addition attacks and cropping attacks.

For a 3D mesh with N vertices, the mesh center $\mathbf{o} = \{x_o, y_o, z_o\}$ is first calculated:

$$\mathbf{o} = \frac{\sum_{i=1}^{N} A(v_i)\mathbf{v}_i}{\sum_{i=1}^{N} A(v_i)}, \tag{3.1}$$

where $A(v_i)$ represents the area of all faces containing vertex v_i, and $\mathbf{v}_i = (x_i, y_i, z_i)$ denotes the Cartesian coordinates of vertex v_i. The Cartesian coordinates can be converted into the corresponding spherical coordinates:

$$
\rho_i = \sqrt{(x_i - x_o)^2 + (y_i - y_o)^2 + (z_i - z_o)^2}
$$

$$
\theta_i = \tan^{-1} \frac{y_i - y_o}{x_i - x_o} \tag{3.2}
$$

$$
\phi_i = \cos^{-1} \frac{z_i - z_o}{\sqrt{(x_i - x_o)^2 + (y_i - y_o)^2 + (z_i - z_o)^2}}.
$$

$\rho_i, i = \{1, 2, ..., N\}$, represents the distribution of vertex norms. Note that the distribution is invariant to similarity transformations such as rotation, translation, and scaling. To divide the distribution into K bins, we obtain the minimum norm ρ_{min} and the maximum ρ_{max}. The kth bin $\mathbf{B}_k$ is defined as follows:

$$
\mathbf{B}_k = \{\rho_{k,j} | \rho_{min} + \frac{\rho_{max} - \rho_{min}}{K} \cdot (k - 1) < \rho_i < \rho_{min} + \frac{\rho_{max} - \rho_{min}}{K} \cdot k\},
$$

$$
1 \leq k \leq K, 1 \leq i \leq N. \tag{3.3}
$$

Then the vertex norms in each bin are normalized into $[0, 1]$:

$$
\tilde{\rho}_{k,j} = \frac{\rho_{k,j} - \min_{\rho_{k,j} \in B_k}\{\rho_{k,j}\}}{\max_{\rho_{k,j} \in B_k}\{\rho_{k,j}\} - \min_{\rho_{k,j} \in B_k}\{\rho_{k,j}\}}. \tag{3.4}
$$

Considering a continuous random variable X which is uniformly distributed in $[0, 1]$, we can easily calculate the expectation of X:

$$
E(X) = \int_0^1 x dx = \frac{1}{2}. \tag{3.5}
$$

As the vertex norms are normalized, we can shift the vertex norms to change the mean $\tilde{\mu}_k$ of each bin based on the watermark bit w_k:

$$
\tilde{\mu}_k = \begin{cases} 1/2 + \alpha & \text{if } w_k = +1 \\ 1/2 - \alpha & \text{if } w_k = -1, \end{cases} \tag{3.6}
$$

where α is the strength factor to balance the robustness and imperceptibility. For the vertex norms, we can design a mapping function as

$$
Y = X^n, 0 < n < +\infty. \tag{3.7}
$$

Therefore, we can employ the mapping function to modify the mean of kth bin as
Algorithm 1:

Algorithm 1: The algorithm [17] by modifying the mean of each bin

---

Data: Vertex norms $\{\tilde{\rho}_{k,j}\}$, watermark bit w_k, the vertex number for the bin is M_k, the step
for modifying n_k is δ_n.
Result: Modified vertex norms:$\{\tilde{\rho}'_{k,j}\}$

1 Initialize the parameter $n_k = 1$;
2 Shift the normalized vertex norms as $\tilde{\rho}'_{k,j} = (\tilde{\rho}_{k,j})^{n_k}$, $j = 1, ..., M_k$;
3 **if** $w_k = +1$ **then**
4 $\quad$ Calculate the mean of $\tilde{\rho}'_{k,j}$:$\tilde{\mu}'_k = \frac{1}{M_k} \sum_{j=0}^{M_k} \tilde{\rho}'_{k,j}$;
5 $\quad$ **while** $\tilde{\mu}'_k < 1/2 + \alpha$ **do**
6 $\quad\quad$ $n_k = n_k - \delta_n$;
7 $\quad\quad$ Shift the normalized vertex norms as $\tilde{\rho}'_{k,j} = (\tilde{\rho}_{k,j})^{n_k}$, $j = 1, ..., M_k$;
8 $\quad$ **end**
9 **else**
10 $\quad$ **while** $\tilde{\mu}'_k > 1/2 - \alpha$ **do**
11 $\quad\quad$ $n_k = n_k + \delta_n$;
12 $\quad\quad$ Shift the normalized vertex norms as $\tilde{\rho}'_{k,j} = (\tilde{\rho}_{k,j})^{n_k}$, $j = 1, ..., M_k$;
13 $\quad$ **end**
14 **end**
15 Return $\{\tilde{\rho}'_{k,j}\}$.

After the modification for each bin, we can convert the normalized vertex norms
$\{\tilde{\rho}'_{k,j}\}$ into Cartesian coordinates. First inversely normalize the normalized vertex
norms:

$$\rho'_{k,j} = \tilde{\rho}'_{k,j} \cdot \left(\max_{\rho_{k,j} \in B_k} \{\rho_{k,j}\} - \min_{\rho_{k,j} \in B_k} \{\rho_{k,j}\} \right) + \min_{\rho_{k,j} \in B_k} \{\rho_{k,j}\}. \tag{3.8}$$

Then the spherical coordinates are transformed into Cartesian coordinates:

$$x'_i = \rho'_i \cos \theta_i \sin \phi_i + x_o$$
$$y'_i = \rho'_i \sin \theta_i \sin \phi_i + y_o \tag{3.9}$$
$$z'_i = \rho'_i \cos \phi_i + z_o.$$

For the watermark extraction, a similar procedure is implemented. As the
normalized vertex norms $\{\tilde{\rho}''_{k,j}\}$ are also acquired, we can calculate the mean $\tilde{\mu}''_k$
of vertex norms for each bin, and then the hidden watermark bit w''_k is extracted:

$$w''_k = \begin{cases} +1 \text{ , if } \tilde{\mu}''_k > \frac{1}{2}, \\ -1 \text{ , if } \tilde{\mu}''_k < \frac{1}{2}. \end{cases} \tag{3.10}$$

The watermark bit can also be hidden into the mesh by modifying the variance of each bin rather than the mean. And the similar watermarking algorithm is implemented during this process.

Bors and Luo [18] extended the statistical watermark embedding method to the preservation of the mesh surface. The surface preservation function includes the distance from the vertices shifted to the original surface by watermarking, the distance to the surface of the watermarked object, and the actual vertex shift.

The first function $\mathbf{f}_1$ is defined for measuring the distance of watermarked vertex to the original surface as

$$
\mathbf{f}_1 = \left\{
\begin{array}{c}
< (\hat{\mathbf{v}}_i - \mathbf{v}_i), \, \mathbf{n}_1 > \mathbf{n}_1 \\
\cdots \\
\cdots \\
\cdots \\
< (\hat{\mathbf{v}}_i - \mathbf{v}_i), \, \mathbf{n}_l > \mathbf{n}_1
\end{array}
\right\},
\tag{3.11}
$$

where $\hat{\mathbf{v}}_i$ denotes the coordinates of watermarked vertex $\hat{v}_i$, $< \cdot, \cdot >$ denotes the dot product, and $\mathbf{n}_l, l = 1, ..., \mathcal{N}_{v_i}$ represents the normal vector of the triangular facets connected with the vertex v_i.

The second function $\mathbf{f}_2$ defines the distortion of the watermarked vertices with respect to the updated surfaces as

$$
\mathbf{f}_2 = \left\{
\begin{array}{c}
< (\hat{\mathbf{v}}_i - \mathbf{v}_i), \, \hat{\mathbf{n}}_1 > \hat{\mathbf{n}}_1 \\
\cdots \\
\cdots \\
\cdots \\
< (\hat{\mathbf{v}}_i - \mathbf{v}_i), \, \hat{\mathbf{n}}_l > \hat{\mathbf{n}}_1
\end{array}
\right\},
\tag{3.12}
$$

where $\hat{\mathbf{n}}_l, l = 1, \ldots, \mathcal{N}_{v_i}$ represents the normal vector of the updated triangular facets connected with the vertex v_i.

The last function $\mathbf{f}_3$ measures the Euclidean distance between original vertices and watermarked vertices:

$$
\mathbf{f}_3 = \hat{\mathbf{v}}_i - \mathbf{v}_i.
\tag{3.13}
$$

The cost function for optimization is defined as $\mathbf{F} = \lambda_1 \mathbf{f}_1^\mathsf{T} \mathbf{f}_1 + \lambda_2 \mathbf{f}_2^\mathsf{T} \mathbf{f}_2 + \lambda_3 \mathbf{f}_3^\mathsf{T} \mathbf{f}_3$. And $\lambda_1 + \lambda_2 + \lambda_3 = 1$. The cost function is minimized using the Levenberg–Marquardt optimization [19, 20] in a spherical coordinate system. The spherical coordinates can be acquired using Eq. (3.34). In this optimization problem, the watermarked vector $\Phi_i = (\hat{\phi}_i, \hat{\theta}_i)$ is considered to be modified, while $\hat{r}_i$ is fixed. Using the Taylor expansion can linearize the given problem:

$$
\mathbf{F}(\Phi + h) = \mathbf{F}(\Phi) + \mathbf{J}h.
\tag{3.14}
$$

The Jacobian matrix $\mathbf{J}$ is calculated as

$$\mathbf{J} = \begin{pmatrix} \frac{\partial \mathbf{F}^{\mathrm{T}}}{\partial \hat{\phi}} \\ \frac{\partial \mathbf{F}^{\mathrm{T}}}{\partial \hat{\theta}} \end{pmatrix}, \tag{3.15}$$

where $\hat{\phi}$ and $\hat{\theta}$ denote the watermarked spherical coordinates. The optimal step h_k is calculated at each iteration k, and the updated vector Φ_{k+1} can be calculated as

$$\Phi_{k+1} = \Phi_k + h_k, \tag{3.16}$$

where h_k is acquired by using the Levenberg–Marquardt optimization to solve the following equation:

$$(\mathbf{J}_k{}^{\mathrm{T}}\mathbf{J}_k + \mu_k\mathbf{I})h_k = \mathbf{J}_k{}^{\mathrm{T}}\mathbf{F}_k, \tag{3.17}$$

where μ_k represents the damping factor.

Rolland et al. [21] analyzed blind optimized watermarking using a histogram mapping function (HMF) that relatively improves robustness against attacks such as noise addition, quantization, smoothing, etc. The vertex positions of the triangular mesh were adjusted using radial distances to embed the payload with minimal distortion. The scheme performs an iterative embedding process by continuously measuring the bit error rate (BER) until the BER reaches 0 or the maximum iteration set for the maximum iteration.

In summary, since the method is based on statistical shifting, it is robust to additive noise attacks, Laplacian smoothing attacks, and mesh simplification attacks.

Wang [8] treats the endings of floating-point numbers as unsigned integers and uses the XOR operator to perform numerical operations. The operation is stable. The embedding parameter achieves good performance in terms of invisibility and detection of unauthorized accesses. The watermark strength is controlled by eliminating causality by prohibiting most vertex adjacencies. The method successfully detects harmful operations such as noise addition, face modification, and model remeshing but fails to filter out some harmless operations such as model transformation.

Ai and Zhou [9] identified future points in rapidly changing regions of a 3D mesh model as Varonoi patches. This Varonoi patch was converted to a range image using a reference square plane that could be embedded in a secret. The length of the watermark, the number of feature points, and the embedding strength are adaptive according to the geometric complexity of the 3D model. The robust and blind watermarking scheme based on intrinsic 3D shape descriptors proposed by Wang [10] uses shape descriptors as analytical and continuous geometric volume moments. The global volume moments measure the normalized input mesh as a canonical and robust spatial pose. Luo [11] proposed the Fast Marching Method (FMM), a distance metric to embed the watermark. By varying the mean and variance of the geodesic distances, vertex displacement using the FMM ensures less surface distortion.

Singh [12] changed the size of the vertex specification to embed a watermark. A point cloud model is computed for each vertex norm to overcome robustness to reordering file attacks. The watermark is embedded by modifying the vertex length and the watermark bits are repeatedly embedded to produce a watermark model that is invariant to rotation, scaling, and reordering attacks. Wu and Cheung [13] embed the secret by slightly changing the vertex position, while the mesh topology remains unchanged and is robust to translations, rotations, and uniform scaling.

Molaei [14] generates patches by identifying mask triangles and embeds the watermark into the patches using Reed–Solomon block error correction codes. The watermark is extracted from a normalized model that classifies the face. The secret binary, grayscale, and color image watermarks were tested to provide better performance in terms of distortion. Yang [15] analyzed steganalysis attacks against grid-based watermarking and variance-based watermarking proposed by Cho [17]. Using the steganalysis algorithm, both mean and variance were grouped into 2 clusters, where embedding was performed in a k-histogram bin. The Batacharya distance [16] normality tests and t-tests were performed to improve the embedding process. In place of Cho's two bin, a three-bin embedding is proposed, which results in lower distortion than the two-bin approach.

3.1.1.4   Other Methods

Ohbuchi et al. [2] present a 3D mesh watermarking scheme for copyright protection, theft detection, and 3D polygon model inventory. The watermark data is embedded into 3D polygonal models by modifying either their vertex coordinates or their topology connections. Based on the fundamentals of watermarking 3D models, some embedding algorithms are proposed, such as TSQ algorithm, TVR algorithm, triangle strip peeling symbol (TSPS) sequence embedding algorithm, polygon stencil pattern (PSP) algorithm, and mesh density pattern (MDP) embedding algorithm. Some of the graphical elements that change during the geometric embedding process are the coordinates, the length of the line area, and the volume of the polygon. Other embedding primitives created for 3D polygon models are topological and quantitative arrangements, each of which requires initial conditions to initiate the arrangement. These arrangements include local, global, or subscripted local arrangements. Similarly, the topology of the model can be modified during embedding. The parameters of the vertex normals must be defined for the analysis of the embedding process to reduce degradation effects. TSQ techniques are invariant to translations, rotations, and uniform scaling but cannot withstand coordinate randomization, re-gridding, and other disturbances. Similarly, TVR is invariant to affine transformations but fails with respect to projection transformations, coordinate randomization, re-gridding, and other disturbances.

Wyvill et al. [3] proposed to extend the automatic blending in an implicit surface modeling system. As automatic blending has been widely applied in the implicit surface modeling system, the range of models should also be extended. To allow arbitrary compositions of models, a hierarchical structure is proposed, which is called as BlobTree. The warping, blending, and Boolean operators are treated in the same way, and polygonizer and ray tracing are the two algorithms used to traverse this structure. Some examples are analyzed using some interesting models to show their good performance.

In the system, models are defined by expressions which combine implicit primitives and operators. Operators are listed as union $\cup$, intersection $\cap$, difference $-$, blend $+$, super-elliptic blend $\diamond$, and warp w. The work defines the BlobTree as $\mathcal{T}$. A node in the tree is denoted as $\mathcal{N}$. And the left tree and the right tree are referred to as $\mathcal{L}(\mathcal{N})$ and $\mathcal{R}(\mathcal{N})$. Thus each node can create a field, defined as $f(\mathcal{N})$. The three operators can be defined as follows:

Boolean operator:

$$
\begin{aligned}
f_{A \cup B} &= \max(f_A, f_B), \\
f_{A \cap B} &= \min(f_A, f_B).
\end{aligned}
\tag{3.18}
$$

The difference operator can be defined as $f_{A-B} = f_{A \cap (-B)}$.
Blending operator:

$$
f_{A \diamond B} = \left(f_A^n + f_B^n \right)^{\frac{1}{n}}.
\tag{3.19}
$$

Warp operator:

$$
f_i(x, y, z) = g_i \circ d_i \circ w_i(x, y, z).
\tag{3.20}
$$

Benedens et al. [4] proposed a geometry-based watermarking method for 3D models. The watermark bit is embedded by varying the normal distribution values, and the robustness to randomization, remeshing, and simplification can be achieved.

Wagner et al. [5] proposed two variations of a robust watermarking method for polygonal meshes. And the carrier meshes can be with arbitrary topological connections. The watermarking method can resist similarity transformation such as translation, scaling, rotation, and their combinations. A simple watermarking algorithm was first proposed. Considering a mesh $\mathcal{M} = \{\mathcal{P}, C\}$, where $\mathcal{P}$ denotes the vertex set and C denotes the connection information,

$$
\begin{aligned}
\mathcal{P} &= \{\mathbf{p}_i\}_{i=1,\ldots,n}, \mathbf{p}_i = (x_i, y_i, z_i), \\
C &= \{\{i_k, j_k\}\}_{k=1,\ldots,m}, 0 \leq i_k \leq n, 0 \leq i_k \leq n.
\end{aligned}
\tag{3.21}
$$

The vertex set S_i connected with vertex $\mathbf{p}_i$ can be defined as

$$S_i = \{j | \{i, j\} \in C\}, i = 1, ..., n. \tag{3.22}$$

To achieve the translation-invariant watermarking method, the normal vector of vertex $\mathbf{p}_i$ is defined:

$$\mathbf{n}_i = \frac{1}{|S_i|} \sum_{j \in S_i} (\mathbf{p}_j - \mathbf{p}_i). \tag{3.23}$$

The basic algorithm is executed as follows. First we need to calculate the discrete normal vector length d:

$$d = \frac{1}{n} \sum_{i=1}^{n} ||\mathbf{n}_i||. \tag{3.24}$$

Then the vector length is transformed to an integer:

$$n_i = round \left(\frac{c}{d} ||\mathbf{n}_i|| \right). \tag{3.25}$$

The watermark bit is defined by the function $f(v)$:

$$w_i = round \left(2^b f \left(\frac{1}{||\mathbf{n}_i||} \mathbf{n}_i \right) \right). \tag{3.26}$$

In the final step of embedding stage, the new vector can be acquired, respectively,

$$\mathbf{n}_i' = \frac{n_i d}{c} \frac{\mathbf{n_i}}{||\mathbf{n}_i||}. \tag{3.27}$$

And the new point coordinates $\mathbf{p}_i'$ can be computed based on the following equation:

$$\mathbf{n}_i' = \frac{1}{|S_i|} \sum_{j \in S_i} \left(\mathbf{p}_j' - \mathbf{p}_i' \right). \tag{3.28}$$

In the above algorithm procedure, a translation-invariant watermarking method can be implemented. To ensure robustness against affine transformation, we need to make some improvements. First the center of the 3D model is computed as

$$\bar{\mathbf{p}} = \{\bar{x}, \bar{y}, \bar{z}\} = \frac{1}{n} \sum_{i=1}^{n} \mathbf{p}_i. \tag{3.29}$$

Then we can acquire a new matrix:

$$V = \begin{pmatrix} x_0 - \bar{x} & y_0 - \bar{y} & z_0 - \bar{z} \\ x_1 - \bar{x} & y_1 - \bar{y} & z_1 - \bar{z} \\ \dots & \dots & \dots \\ x_n - \bar{x} & y_n - \bar{y} & z_n - \bar{z} \end{pmatrix} \tag{3.30}$$

$$A = n(V^\mathrm{T}V)^{-1}. \tag{3.31}$$

Then the affine transformation-invariant p-norm can be defined as

$$\|\mathbf{p}\|_p = (x \; y \; z) A \begin{pmatrix} x \\ y \\ z \end{pmatrix}, \mathbf{p} = (x, y, z). \tag{3.32}$$

Benedens et al. [6] proposed a new robust non-blind algorithm based on direct free-form deformations. And this algorithm can be applied to smooth meshes. In the implementation process, low-frequency deformations are generated to embed the watermark bit. To ensure the robustness against affine transformation attacks, a new registration method was proposed, which is implemented before the watermark extraction.

Zafeiriou et al. [7] proposed two novel methods for 3D mesh watermarking, with one immune to similarity transformations and the other robust against geometric attacks and mesh simplification. To ensure the robustness against translation attack and rotation attack, the 3D mesh is rotated to the z-axis of the Cartesian coordinate system and the center is translated to the origin before the embedding and extracting process. The watermark bit is embedded by modifying the r coordinate of the corresponding (r, θ, ϕ) spherical coordinate system. The first method uses the principle object axis (POA) as the watermarking tool. For a 3D mesh object with vertices $\mathbf{V}^c$, $\mathbf{u}_i^c = (x_i, y_i, z_i)$ denotes the Cartesian coordinate of the ith vertex, and $\mathbf{u}_i^s = (r_i, \theta_i, \phi_i)$ denotes the corresponding coordinate in the spherical system. Some descriptions are defined as follows:

The object is translated so that its center is located on the origin of the Cartesian coordinate system. The mass center $\mathbf{k}^c$ of a 3D model can be computed:

$$\mathbf{k}^c = \frac{1}{N(\mathbf{V}^c)} \sum_{i=1}^{N(\mathbf{V}^c)} \mathbf{u}_i^c. \tag{3.33}$$

To achieve the robustness against rotation attack, the principal axis of 3D mesh is aligned. Specifically, the principal axis is the eigenvector that corresponds to the greatest eigenvalue of covariance matrix C. By the principal axis alignment, the 3D mesh can be rotated to the fixed direction. For the conversion to spherical coordinates, it can be defined as

$$r_i = r\left(\mathbf{u}_i^s\right) = \sqrt{x_i^2 + y_i^2 + z_i^2},$$

$$\theta_i = \theta\left(\mathbf{u}_i^s\right) = arccos\left(\frac{z_i}{r_i}\right), \qquad (3.34)$$

$$\phi_i = \phi\left(\mathbf{u}_i^s\right) = arctan\left(\frac{y_i}{x_i}\right).$$

For the watermark generation, a label for every vertex $\mathbf{u}_i^s$ is first assigned: $l(\mathbf{u}_i^s) \in \{-1, 0, 1, 2\}$. Then two sequences are generated: $\theta_i^w \in [0, \pi]$, $w_i \in \{-1, 1\}$, $i = 1, ..., N_w$. And $\Theta^w = \{\theta_i^w\}$ denotes the set of θ_i^w, which is the corresponding angle for watermark bit w_i. For watermark embedding, it is performed by modifying the r component according to

$$r^w\left(\mathbf{u}_i^s\right) = \begin{cases} r\left(\mathbf{u}_i^s\right) & \text{if } l\left(\mathbf{u}_i^s\right) = 0, 2 \\ g_1\left(\mathbf{u}_i^s\right) & \text{if } l\left(\mathbf{u}_i^s\right) = 1 \\ g_2\left(\mathbf{u}_i^s\right) & \text{if } l\left(\mathbf{u}_i^s\right) = -1. \end{cases} \qquad (3.35)$$

The embedding functions are given by

$$g_1\left(\mathbf{u}_i^s\right) = f(a_1) H\left(\mathbf{u}_i^s\right), \qquad (3.36)$$

$$g_2\left(\mathbf{u}_i^s\right) = f(a_2) H\left(\mathbf{u}_i^s\right), \qquad (3.37)$$

where a_1 and a_2 are the constants and $H(\mathbf{u}_i^s)$ is the local neighborhood operation of the vertices around vertex $\mathbf{u}_i^s$. Specifically, the neighborhood operator H is defined as

$$H\left(\mathbf{u}_i^s\right) = \frac{1}{n} \sum_{j=1}^{n} r\left(\mathbf{v}_j^s\right), \qquad (3.38)$$

where $\{\mathbf{v}_j^s\}$ denotes the vertex set connected with $\mathbf{u}_i^s$ and $n = N(\{\mathbf{v}_j^s\})$. For the watermark extraction, it can be implemented based on

$$d\left(\mathbf{u}_i^s\right) = \begin{cases} 1 & \text{if } r\left(\mathbf{u}_i^s\right) - H\left(\mathbf{u}_i^s\right) > 0 \\ -1 & \text{if } r\left(\mathbf{u}_i^s\right) - H\left(\mathbf{u}_i^s\right) < 0. \end{cases} \qquad (3.39)$$

The second method uses sectional principal object axis (SPOA) as the basic tool for 3D mesh watermarking. Define the set $\mathbf{I}(\Theta_j) = \{\mathbf{u}_i^s : \mathbf{u}_i^s \in \mathbf{V}^s, \theta(\mathbf{u}_i^s) \in \Theta_j\}$, where $\Theta_j \subset \Theta$ is the selected set for a range of θ angles. For each vertex in $\mathbf{I}(\Theta_j)$, the difference $d_r(\mathbf{u}_i^s)$ is formed:

$$d_r\left(\mathbf{u}_i^s\right) = r\left(\mathbf{u}_i^s\right) - H\left(\mathbf{u}_i^s\right). \qquad (3.40)$$

Assuming that d_r follows the Gaussian distribution with the variance σ^2 and zero mean, we can define the corresponding variance estimators:

$$\hat{\sigma}_l^2 = \frac{1}{N(\{d_r : d_r < 0\}) - 1} \sum_{d_r < 0} d_r^2, \tag{3.41}$$

$$\hat{\sigma}_r^2 = \frac{1}{N(\{d_r : d_r > 0\}) - 1} \sum_{d_r > 0} d_r^2. \tag{3.42}$$

And $\hat{\sigma}^2$ can be estimated via $\hat{\sigma}_l^2, \hat{\sigma}_r^2$.

For the watermark generation, the interval $[0, \pi]$ is first divided into L intervals $\Theta_j, j = 1, ..., L$. And every interval Θ_j is assigned with a label $w_j = l(\Theta_j) \in \{-1, 0, 1\}$. Given a label $l(\Theta_j)$, we can embed the watermark by modifying the r component of vertices of $\mathbf{I}(\Theta_j)$:

$$\mathbf{R}^w(\mathbf{I}^w(\Theta_j)) = \begin{cases} \mathbf{R}(\mathbf{I}(\Theta_j)) & \text{if } l(\Theta_j) = 0 \\ \mathbf{G}_1(\mathbf{I}(\Theta_j)) & \text{if } l(\Theta_j) = 1 \\ \mathbf{G}_2(\mathbf{I}(\Theta_j)) & \text{if } l(\Theta_j) = -1, \end{cases} \tag{3.43}$$

where $\mathbf{R}$ denotes the vector of the corresponding r components and $\mathbf{G}_1$ and $\mathbf{G}_2$ represent the embedding functions. For watermark detection, the detection ratio is formed as

$$d(\Theta_j) = \begin{cases} \frac{N(\mathbf{I}_r^w(\Theta_j))}{N(\mathbf{I}^w(\Theta_j))} & \text{if } l(\Theta_j) = 1 \\ \frac{N(\mathbf{I}_l^w(\Theta_j))}{N(\mathbf{I}^w(\Theta_j))} & \text{if } l(\Theta_j) = -1. \end{cases} \tag{3.44}$$

3.1.2 Transform Domain-Based 3D Mesh Watermarking

The spectral watermarking scheme embeds data into any coefficients of the harmonic, multiscale transform, frequency space, and geometric wavelet transform. The geometry of the 3D triangular grid model is changed according to the spreading coefficients. The embedded watermark introduces a distortion that can be globally distributed to achieve low distortion. To improve efficiency, the watermark is embedded by modifying the wavelet coefficients at multiple resolution levels. Laplace spectral schemes are also evaluated where secrets are embedded by modifying the magnitude of spectral variants like Haar wavelets and by compressing to increase the embedding strength. Spherical harmonic coefficients are modified to support both blind and non-blind schemes and to improve embedding capabilities. These algorithms resist various attacks such as simplification, rotation, translation, noise, smoothing, scaling, and some of these works also resist cropping attacks. Most watermarking schemes in the spectral domain are vulnerable to geometric rotations.

3.1.2.1 Laplacian Transform-Based Methods

Cayre et al. [22] proposed to use spectral decomposition to achieve watermarking 3D meshes. Laplacian operator is used to analyzing 3D meshes in this work. For a 3D mesh with N vertices and E edges, the $N \times N$ Laplacian matrix L can be defined as

$$L(i, j) = \begin{cases} 1, & \text{if } i = j, \\ -\frac{1}{|\mathcal{N}_i|}, & \text{if } j \in \mathcal{N}_i, \\ 0, & \text{otherwise}, \end{cases} \tag{3.45}$$

where $\mathcal{N}_i$ denotes the vertex set which is connected with vertex v_i and $|\cdot|$ denotes the cardinal number. The eigenvalues $e_i, 0 \leq i \leq N - 1$, and the corresponding eigenvectors $\mathbf{B}_i, 0 \leq i \leq N - 1$, are calculated by the matrix decomposition:

$$Diag(e_1, e_2, ..., e_{N-1}) = B^{-1}LB. \tag{3.46}$$

The coefficients (P, Q, R) can be obtained with the input vertices (X, Y, Z):

$$\begin{aligned} P &= BX, \\ Q &= BY, \\ R &= BZ. \end{aligned} \tag{3.47}$$

During watermark embedding, the corresponding coefficients are adjusted with respect to the bit "0" or "1." Then the watermarked vertices are constructed via inverse transform:

$$\begin{aligned} X &= B^{-1}P, \\ Y &= B^{-1}Q, \\ Z &= B^{-1}R. \end{aligned} \tag{3.48}$$

The power spectrum of the 3D mesh can be defined as the sum of squares of (P, Q, R). For each vertex $v_i, i = 1, 2, ..., N$, the corresponding power spectrum S_i is (Fig. 3.1)

$$S_i = ||P_i||^2 + ||Q_i||^2 + ||R_i||^2. \tag{3.49}$$

The watermark bit can be embedded by randomly modify the relationship between the vectors P, Q, and R. First the three coefficients can be sorted into

$$(P, Q, R) \rightarrow (C_{min}, C_{mid}, C_{max}) \tag{3.50}$$

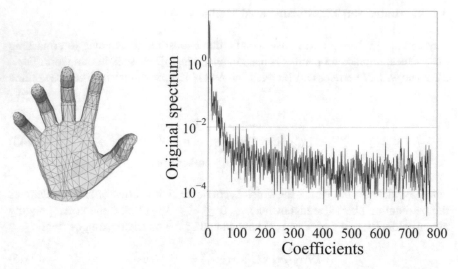

Fig. 3.1 Hand [38] and its power spectrum (ordered with respect to the corresponding eigenvalues of matrix decomposition operator)

with

$$
\begin{cases}
C_{min} = \min(P_i, Q_i, R_i), \\
C_{mid} = \mathrm{mid}(P_i, Q_i, R_i), \\
C_{max} = \max(P_i, Q_i, R_i).
\end{cases}
\tag{3.51}
$$

The interval $\Delta = (C_{max} - C_{min})$ is divided into two equal intervals: $W_0 = (C_{min}, C_{min} + \Delta/2)$ and $W_1 = (C_{max} - \Delta/2, C_{max})$. For watermark embedding, if the bit is "0", the C_{mid} is expected to be located in the W_0 subset. If C_{mid} lies in the W_1 subset, we flip it to meet the requirement. The flipping distance is divided by a factor $k = 10$, and then C_{mid} is flipped into the W_0 subset. If the bit is "1," C_{mid} is expected to lie in the W_1 subset. To guarantee the visual imperceptibility, the embedding operation starts at the medium frequency coefficients (Fig. 3.2).

For the watermark extracting, the similar process is implemented on the watermarked 3D mesh. And the extracted watermark bit is judged according to the location of C_{mid}:

$$
w_i = \begin{cases}
0 \text{ if } C_{mid} \in (C_{min}, C_{min} + \Delta/2) \\
1 \text{ if } C_{mid} \in (C_{max} - \Delta/2, C_{max}).
\end{cases}
\tag{3.52}
$$

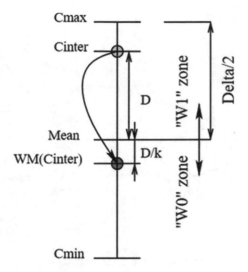

Fig. 3.2 Watermark embedding in the case of "0" commitment

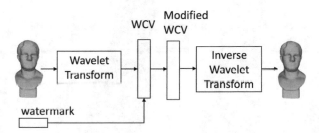

Fig. 3.3 Outline of the embedding process of the wavelet-based watermarking method. WCV represents the wavelet coefficient vector

3.1.2.2 Wavelet Transform-Based Methods

Wang et al. [23] proposed a hierarchical watermarking framework for semiregular 3D meshes [24]. The proposed framework is based on wavelet transform, and three kinds of watermarks are proposed: a geometrically robust watermark for copyright protection, a high-capacity watermark for carrying a large amount of auxiliary information, and a fragile watermark for content authentication. Specially, the three watermarks are embedded in the different appropriate resolution levels in the wavelet decomposition: the robust watermark is embedded with the lowest resolution, the fragile watermark is embedded with the highest resolution, and the high-capacity watermark is inserted into several intermediate levels (Fig. 3.3).

Figure 3.4 illustrates one iteration of wavelet transform on a 3D mesh. A group of four triangles is merged into one coarse triangle and three of six initial vertices. Then we calculate the wavelet coefficient vectors as the prediction errors for the other three vertices. In each iteration, the 3D mesh can be converted into a coarser

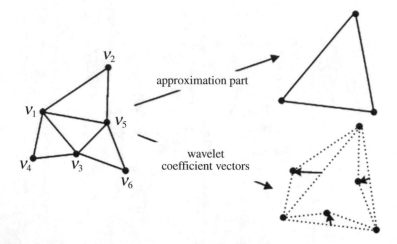

Fig. 3.4 Illustration of one iteration of the wavelet decomposition

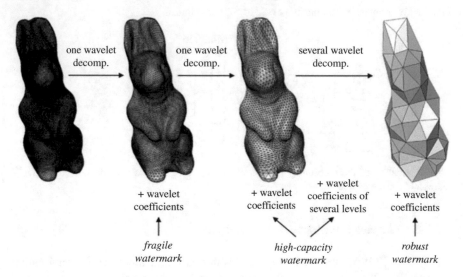

Fig. 3.5 The proposed hierarchical watermarking framework

3D mesh and some WCV can be generated. With these coefficients, the watermark bits can be inserted into the mesh. With different levels of coefficients, there are different watermark applications as shown in Fig. 3.5.

The three kinds of watermarking algorithms can be summarized as follows:

Zaid et al. [25] achieved high embedding capacity using metadata insertion in the grid quantized wavelet coefficients. Robust quantization is performed to regularize the irregular wavelet coefficients so that they are invariant to uniform scaling, resulting in good robustness to clipping attacks, especially in smaller grid regions, with high embedding rates through low distortion.

Algorithm 2: Blind and robust watermark embedding procedure [23]

---

1 Do wavelet analysis of the original 3D mesh until the coarsest level ;
2 Do descending sort of all the edges in this level according to their lengths ;
3 Calculate the average length l_{av} of the edges and fix the WCV norm quantization step as l_{av}/ϵ_{rob} ;
4 **for** *each edge in the descending sort* **do**
5 | Calculate the norm of its associated WCV ;
6 | Quantize this norm according to step 2 by using the scalar Costa quantization scheme ;
7 **end**
8 Do mesh reconstruction until the level where the high-capacity watermark is to be embedded.

Algorithm 3: Blind and high-capacity watermark embedding procedure [23]

---

1 Do wavelet synthesis after robust watermark embedding until a certain appropriate level ;
2 Do descending sort of all the edges in this level according to their lengths ;
3 Calculate the average length l_{av} of the edges and fix the WCV norm quantization step as l_{av}/ϵ_{rob} ;
4 Divide the edges in several ordered groups of E edges according to their length sorting ;
5 **for** *each ordered edge group* **do**
6 | Translate the $\lfloor \log_2(G!) \rfloor$ bits in the watermark sequence to a corresponding permutation ;
7 | **for** *each descending sorted edge in the current group* **do**
8 | | Substitute the norm of its associated WCV according to step 3 in order to assign it to an expected norm residue order in the desired permutation ;
9 | | Modify the new norm by applying a compensation scheme similar to step 2 and by introducing a dither signal generated by using secret K_{hc} ;
10 | **end**
11 **end**
12 Do mesh reconstruction until the second densest level where the fragile watermark is to be embedded.

Algorithm 4: Fragile watermark embedding procedure [23]

---

1 Do wavelet synthesis after robust and high-capacity watermark embeddings until level 1 ;
2 Generate two pseudorandom dither signals t_{θ_k} and t_{r_k} by using secret keys K_θ and K_r ;
3 Construct two lookup tables giving correspondences between vale ranges of the geometric ratio gr_k and the pseudorandom dither signals t_{θ_k} and t_{r_k} ;
4 **for** *each edge e_k^1 in this resolution level* **do**
5 | Do symbol-preserving SCS quantization for θ_k with the established lookup table between gr_k and t_{θ_k} ;
6 | Do SCS quantization for r_k with the lookup table between gr_k and t_{r_k}, so that the two quantized values imply the same symbol s_k ;
7 **end**
8 Do one iteration of wavelet synthesis in order to obtain the watermarked dense mesh $\hat{M}_0$.

Hamidi et al. [26] proposed a blind robust 3D mesh watermarking scheme for copyright protection based on wavelet transform. The watermark bits are inserted into the low frequency of WCV norms. And the edge normal norms are chosen to synchronize the watermark bits.

In the watermark embedding process, the wavelet decomposition is first applied to initialize mesh $\mathcal{M}_0$ until the coarsest level mesh $\mathcal{M}_J$. Then the edges in this level are sorted in descending order according to the norm of edge normals. Note that the normal $\mathbf{n}_{1,2}$ of edge e_1 is the average of the two normals $(\mathbf{n}_1, \mathbf{n}_2)$ of the two vertices (v_1, v_2). The sorted edges are listed as e_1^J, e_2^J, etc. And the associated wavelet coefficient vectors are denoted as WCV_1^J, WCV_2^J, etc. The watermark bits are embedded by quantifying the WCV norms using scalar Costa scheme and the quantization step Q_S is fixed to N_{av}/λ. A random code is established for each WCV norm by

$$\beta_{x_i, t_{x_i}} = \bigcup_{l=0}^{1} \left\{ u = z \cdot Qs + l \cdot \frac{Q_S}{2} + t_{x_i} \right\}, \tag{3.53}$$

where z in $\mathbb{Z}^+$, $l \in \{0, 1\}$ denotes the watermark bit and t_{x_i} is an additive pseudo-random dither signal generated using a secret key K. We use $\beta_{WCV_i}^J$ to denote the code which is nearest to WCV_i^J, which implies the correct watermark bit. Then the quantized value $WCV_i'^J$ is calculated as

$$WCV_i'^J = \|WCV_i^J\| + 1/2 \left(\beta_{WCV_i^J} - \|WCV_i^J\| \right). \tag{3.54}$$

After the quantization process, the dense mesh can be reconstructed using the modified WCVs. The average edge normal norms of all edges in the coarsest-level are chosen as synchronizing primitives.

In the watermark extracting process, the wavelet transform is also applied to the watermarked mesh until the coarsest level. Then the edge order is reestablished and the codebook is reconstructed. Finally, the nearest codeword to the WCVs is found to acquire the watermark bits. The watermark embedding and extracting algorithms are described as follows:

Algorithm 5: Watermark embedding [26]

---

1 Do the wavelet analysis of the original mesh until the coarsest-level ;
2 Sort in descending order the edges in the coarsest level according to their normal norms in this level ;
3 Calculate the average norm N_{av} of edge normals in this level and set the WCV norm quantization step as N_{av}/λ ;
4 Calculate the norms of the WCVs and quantize them according to step 3 using scalar Costa quantization scheme, keeping the same order of edges ;
5 Do mesh reconstruction starting from the modified WCV norms in order to obtain the watermarked dense semi-regular mesh.

Algorithm 6: Watermark extracting [26]

---
1 Do the wavelet analysis of the watermarked mesh until the coarsest-level ;
2 Reestablish the edge order according to the norm of normals of edges in this level ;
3 Calculate the quantization step and reconstruct the codebook ;
4 Extract the watermark bits by looking for the nearest codeword in the codebook.

3.1.2.3   Parameter Transform-Based Methods

Liu et al. [27] proposed a blind spectral two-way watermarking framework for 3D meshes with parametric information. The watermarking framework includes a geometric method and a texture method. The original 3D mesh with texture can be decomposed into a geometric mesh G, a texture image I, and a parametric mesh T. The correspondence between G and $\mathcal{T}$ can also be constructed as $M : \mathcal{T} \to G$.

In the geometric method, the input 3D model is handled as geometric coordinate functions (X, Y, Z) defined over parametric domain $\mathcal{T} \subset \mathbb{R}^2$. The embedding and extracting algorithms are described as follows:

(1) Preprocessing. Find the pair $vt_m, vt'_m \in T$, which have the longest distance between points in T, and rotate the 3D model to make the line connecting vt_m and vt'_m aligns with the v axis.

(2) Cutting analysis domain and resampling. Some parameters are used to control this process: cutting factor $0 < c_u, c_v < 1$ and resampling density $d_u, d_v \in \mathbb{N}$. The operations are listed as (a) build the bounding box of rotated mesh $\mathcal{T}_R$ with the center c_b, the width w_b, and the height h_b. (b) Build a rectangle area with the center c_b, the width $c_u \cdot w_b$, and the height $c_v \cdot h_b$. Then tile the rectangle as shown in Fig. 3.6. And the rectangle region that completely falls in T is selected for embedding. (c) Resample each selected region using a mesh with the resolution of $d_u \times d_v$. The new regular mesh is denoted as $\mathcal{T}_Q \subset \mathbb{R}^2$. (d) Build three geometric functions (X_Q, Y_Q, Z_Q) for $\mathcal{T}_Q$ and the intermediate 3D surface patch $\mathcal{M}_Q$ can be created.

Fig. 3.6 Cutting analysis domain

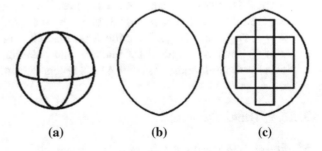

(a)   (b)   (c)

(3) Spectral analysis. D-WHT is used to transform X_Q, Y_Q, Z_Q. With D-MHB, $\{H^j\}, j = 1, ..., m$, can be used to analyze any scalar function as

$$x_d = x - x_h, \tilde{x}_j \quad = x_d^T D H^j = \sum_{i=1}^{|G|} x_i D_{i,i} H_i^j, \tag{3.55}$$

where $x = [x_1, x_2, ..., x_{|G|}]^T$ denotes the vector form of X_Q, x_h is the harmonic function, and D denotes the "mass" matrix. The inverse D-MHT (I-DMHT) can be used for transforming the spectral coefficients to geometric coordinates:

$$x_i = \sum_{j=1}^{m} \tilde{x}_j H_i^j + x_{h,i}. \tag{3.56}$$

(4) Bit embedding and extraction. The watermark bits are embedded by manipulating the spectral coordinates $\{\tilde{x}_i, \tilde{y}_i, \tilde{z}_i\}$ using NCE [28]. The rotation-invariant spectrum can be defined as $e_i = \sqrt{\tilde{x}_i^2 + \tilde{y}_i^2 + \tilde{z}_i^2}$. Then the middle frequency components can be divided into $|k|$ groups with $\{g_i = \{e_{d_o ff+2i}, e_{d_o ff+2i+1}\}\}, i = 0, ..., |k|-1$. For each group, the watermark bit $k[i]$ can be embedded by the following modification:

$$\begin{cases} e'_{i,0} \leq e'_{i,1} \cdot (1 - f_t), & \text{when } k[i] = 0, \\ e'_{i,0} \geq e'_{i,1} \cdot (1 + f_t), & \text{when } k[i] = 1, \end{cases} \tag{3.57}$$

where f_t is the parameter to balance the robustness and imperceptibility. The watermark extraction can be defined as

$$\begin{cases} k'[i] = 0 \text{ when } e_{i,0} < e_{i,1}, \\ k'[i] = 1 \text{ when } e_{i,0} > e_{i,1}. \end{cases} \tag{3.58}$$

(5) Reconstruction. According to the modified spectral descriptors, the watermarked 3D mesh $\mathcal{M}_w$ can be reconstructed. First, using I-DMHT to recreate the watermarked intermediate model $\mathcal{M}_{Q,w}$ by the modified coordinate functions $X_{Q,w}, Y_{Q,w}$, and $Z_{Q,w}$. Then the watermarked coordinate functions X_w, Y_w, and Z_w can be acquired by linearly interpolating $X_{Q,w}, Y_{Q,w}$, and $Z_{Q,w}$. Finally, the watermarked model $\mathcal{M}_w$ is reconstructed.

3.1.2.4 Other Methods

Medimegh [29] partitioned the grid into regions based on salient points extracted using a robust prominence detector based on the automatic diffusion function (ADF). The watermark is embedded statistically into each region by modifying the magnitude according to the watermark bits and the average value of each bin. This scheme achieves a HD of approximately 10–3 when embedded in 16 bits and has better robustness and good imperceptibility.

For the preliminaries, the Heat Kernel Diffusion Process and Geodesic Distance are introduced. The heat kernel has the following spectral decomposition:

$$K_t(x, y) = \sum_{n=0}^{\infty} \exp(-\lambda_n t) h_n(x) h_n(y), \tag{3.59}$$

where h_n denotes the associated eigenfunctions corresponding to λ_n. The geodesic distance $T_O(x, y)$ between points x and y is the shortest length over all continuous paths determined by the geodesic curve $\gamma(t)$.

$$T_O(x, y) = \min_{\gamma(t) \in O} \int_O^P \sqrt{\gamma'(t)^T H(\gamma(t)) \gamma'(t)} dt. \tag{3.60}$$

Then the Auto Diffusion Function can be defined as

$$ADF_t(x) = K\left(x, x, \frac{t}{\lambda_2}\right) = \sum_{n=0}^{\infty} exp\left(-t\frac{\lambda_n}{\lambda_2}\right) h_n^2(x). \tag{3.61}$$

The local extrema prove to be the interest points in a 3D model. Let $P = \{p_1, p_2, ..., p_m\}$ be an ensemble of salient points. The Voronoi cell $VC(p_i)$ of the site p_i can be defined explicitly as follows:

$$VC(p_i) = \{q \in M \| d(p_i, q) \le d(p_j, q), \forall i \neq j\}. \tag{3.62}$$

The geodesic Voronoi diagram (GVD) of P is the union of all Voronoi cells:

$$GVD(P) = \overset{m}{\underset{i=1}{\cup}} VC(p_i). \tag{3.63}$$

The proposed watermarking method also embeds the watermark bit into normalized histograms $\mathcal{H} = \{\mathcal{H}_1, \mathcal{H}_2, ..., \mathcal{H}_m\}$, which is derived from different Voronoi cells. For watermark embedding and extracting, this method follows the similar procedure as Cho et al. [17].

Narendra [30] used Weber's law to generate a fingerprint 3D model from a host 3D model. The secret watermark was embedded into the host 3D model using an intensity factor based on inverse colony optimization recognition. This method achieves a high embedding rate and better robustness to basic attacks.

The vertex coordinates are first grouped into 3×3 blocks, and then the watermark bit is generated by the following equation:

$$W(x_i, y_i) = \sum_{x=1}^{m/3} \sum_{y=1}^{3} \arctan\left(\sum_{n=0}^{m-1} \frac{\delta_n - \delta_i}{\delta_i}\right). \tag{3.64}$$

The fingerprint 3D model is embedded by linearly interpolating between the original center value i_c and watermark vertices w_c:

$$W_m = \sum_{x=1}^{m/3} \sum_{y=1}^{3} (1 - \alpha) * w_c + \alpha * i_c. \tag{3.65}$$

And the watermark can be extracted by the following equation:

$$W_e = \sum_{x=1}^{m/3} \sum_{y=1}^{3} \frac{1}{\alpha} W - \frac{1 - \alpha}{\alpha} W_m. \tag{3.66}$$

3.2 Deep Neural Network-Based 3D Mesh Watermarking

Wang et al. [31] proposed deep learning based methods for 3D mesh watermarking. Compared with traditional methods, deep learning based methods can provide a more general framework and achieve more universal robustness. Considering the diversities of topologies of 3D meshes, deep learning based methods can be divided into two categories: deep watermarking for template-based 3D meshes [32] and deep watermarking for topology-agnostic 3D meshes [37].

3.2.1 Deep Template-Based Watermarking for 3D Morphable Models

A 3D mesh can be defined as M= (V,F), where V denotes vertices and F denotes faces. For 3D morphable models, they usually share a fixed topology and the same number of vertices. And we define watermark capacity as C bits.

3.2.1.1 Preliminary: Chebyshev-Based Spectral Convolution

The convolution operator in the spatial domain can be defined as a Hadamard product in the Fourier domain. To achieve the convolution on 3D mesh, we can use the equivalent operation in the transform domain of 3D mesh by the normalized Laplacian matrix L [25]. Considering the expensive computation, we use the Kth order Chebyshev polynomials $T_k(x)$ to approximate the spectral convolution:

$$g_\theta(L) = \sum_{k=0}^{K-1} \theta_k T_k(L). \tag{3.67}$$

For a 3D mesh with N vertices, we can regard it as a graph with N nodes. And the connections between nodes indicate the edges of the mesh. For the l-layer feature $f_i^l \in \mathbb{R}^N$ of ith channel, we can compute the next layer feature $f_i^{l+1} \in \mathbb{R}^N$:

$$f_i^{l+1} = \sum_{i=0}^{F_{in}-1} g_{\theta_{i,j}}(L) f_i^l. \tag{3.68}$$

3.2.1.2 Watermark Embedding and Extracting

We employ two sub-networks to achieve watermarking embedding and extracting, respectively. In order to increase the receptive field and capture the features with multiple scales, we construct a hierarchical architecture. We employ the mesh sampling operation proposed by Ranjan et al. [33] to change the scale. For vertices with the shape of $N_{in} \times 3$, we use the transformation matrix $Q \in \mathbb{R}^{N_{in} \times N_{out}}$ to change vertices to N_{out}. For the down-sampling process, we calculate the matrix via QEM [33]. And for the up-sampling, we seek the nearest triangle for each vertex and calculate the interpolation weights $\tilde{v} = w_1 v_1 + w_2 v_2 + w_3 v_3 (s.t. w_1 + w_2 + w_3 = 1)$ to acquire the up-sampling matrix.

As shown in Fig. 3.7, we use Encoder and Decoder to denote the embedding sub-network and extracting sub-network, respectively. The input of Encoder module is input mesh $\mathcal{M}_{in}$ and input watermark $wm_{in} \in [0, 1]^C$. Encoder first encodes the input watermark by MLP. Then the input vertices V_{in} and the encoded watermark are concatenated and fed into the U-Net-based network. The output of the Encoder is the watermarked mesh $\mathcal{M}_{wm}$. The Decoder module is responsible for training to extract the watermark message $\mathbf{wm}_{ext}$ from the watermarked mesh. We define the targeted problem as

$$\min_{\Theta_{enc}, \Theta_{ext}} \quad ||\mathbf{wm}_{ext}, \mathbf{wm}_{in}||_2^2,$$

$$\text{s.t.} \quad |\mathcal{M}_{wm} - \mathcal{M}_{in}| < \epsilon, \tag{3.69}$$

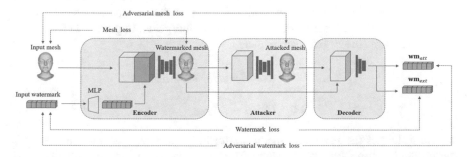

Fig. 3.7 The proposed watermarking network includes three modules: Encoder, Attacker, and Decoder

where ϵ defines the maximum of modifications on the input mesh, and $\theta_{enc}, \theta_{dec}$ denote the network parameters for both modules. Thus we can define the watermark loss $\mathcal{L}_{wm}$ as

$$\mathcal{L}_{wm} = \frac{1}{C}||\mathbf{wm}_{ext}, \mathbf{wm}_{in}||_2^2, \tag{3.70}$$

where C denotes the watermark capacity. For the measure of imperceptibility, although there are many measures of grid distortion, this work defines grid loss based on MSE (Mean Square Error) in consideration of the convenience of network optimization:

$$\mathcal{L}_M = \frac{1}{V}\sum_{i=1}^{V}||\mathbf{v}_{in,i} - \mathbf{v}_{wm,i}||_2^2, \tag{3.71}$$

where $\mathbf{v}_{in,i}$ and $\mathbf{v}_{wm,i}$ represent the coordinate vectors for input vertex v_{in} and watermarked vertex v_{wm} and V denotes the number of mesh vertices.

3.2.1.3 Adversarial Training

DNNs are vulnerable to adversarial examples [34]: when some imperceptible modifications are added into a targeted carrier, the classifier may produce false result. A similar phenomenon also happens in our network: we find that when the watermarked mesh $\mathcal{M}_{wm}$ is attacked by some tiny perturbations, such as Gaussian noise addition, the extracted message changes a lot. In actual application scenarios, the watermarked meshes may suffer from many agnostic attacks, so we need to improve the robustness of our method as much as possible.

Adversarial training was first proposed by Goodfellow et al. [35] as a method to enhance the generative quality of the targeted network. Luo et al. [36] proposed to use an adversarial network to train against the watermarking network. Inspired by this, in our context, we can employ an adversary which is responsible for both training against watermarking modules and enhancing the robustness. Thus, we design the Attacker module which is responsible for adding some subtle perturbations on the watermarked mesh $\mathcal{M}_{wm}$ and generating the attacked mesh $\mathcal{M}_{att}$. We define the targeted problem as

$$\max_{\Theta_{att}} \quad ||Ext(\mathcal{M}_{att}), \mathbf{wm}_{in}||_2^2,$$
$$\text{s.t.} \quad |\mathcal{M}_{att} - \mathcal{M}_{wm}| < \delta, \tag{3.72}$$

where δ defines the maximum of the perturbation and Θ_{att} denotes the network parameters for the Attacker module. The maximization problem guarantees the antagonistic contradiction with the main network. To train the Attacker module, we define the adversarial mesh loss $\mathcal{L}'_M$ and the adversarial watermark loss $\mathcal{L}'_{wm}$ for the Attacker module as

$$\mathcal{L}'_{wm} = \frac{1}{C}||\mathbf{wm}_{att}, 1 - \mathbf{wm}_{in}||_2^2, \tag{3.73}$$

$$\mathcal{L}'_M = \frac{1}{V}\sum_{i=1}^{V}||\mathbf{v}_{in,i} - \mathbf{v}_{att,i}||_2^2, \tag{3.74}$$

where $\mathbf{wm}_{att} = Ext(\mathcal{M}_{att})$ denotes the watermark extracted from attacked mesh. To make the distinction, $\mathbf{wm}_{ext}$ only denotes the extracted watermark from the watermarked mesh $\mathcal{M}_{wm}$. We minimize the adversarial training loss for the Attacker module:

$$\mathcal{L}_{att} = \lambda'_M\mathcal{L}'_M + \lambda'_{wm}\mathcal{L}'_{wm}, \tag{3.75}$$

3.2.1.4 Network Training

Figure 3.7 shows the proposed network architecture. Similar to the Attack module, we define the adversarial watermark loss $\mathcal{L}''_{wm}$ for the main network as

$$\mathcal{L}''_{wm} = \frac{1}{C}||\mathbf{wm}_{att}, \mathbf{wm}_{in}||_2^2. \tag{3.76}$$

Thus we minimized the loss $\mathcal{L}_w$ for the Encoder module and the Decoder module:

$$\mathcal{L}_W = \mathcal{L}_{wm} + \lambda_M\mathcal{L}_M + \lambda''_{wm}\mathcal{L}''_{wm}. \tag{3.77}$$

During training, we set $\lambda_{wm} = 1, \lambda'_{wm} = 0.001, \lambda''_{wm} = 0.5, \lambda_M = \lambda'_M = 8$. We alternately train the main network and adversarial network, with details shown in Algorithm 1. We use the Adam [29] algorithm to update the network parameters with the learning rate lr. Note that we only need the main network for embedding and extracting process in the inference stage, so adversarial training does not introduce extra computation costs in this stage.

Algorithm 7: Network training

Data: Mesh dataset $\{\mathcal{M}_i\}_{i=1}^{O}$
Result: Network parameters:$\Theta_{enc}, \Theta_{ext}, \Theta_{att}$
1 Initialize the network parameters, max_steps, step = 0 ;
2 while step < max_steps **do**
3 $\mathcal{M}_{in}$ = Random Selection from $\{\mathcal{M}_i\}_{i=1}^{O}$;
4 $\mathbf{wm}_{in}$ = Random Generation ($\{0, 1\}^C$) ;
5 $\mathcal{M}_{wm} = Enc(\mathcal{M}_{in}, \mathbf{wm}_{in})$;
6 $\mathcal{M}_{att} = Att(\mathcal{M}_{wm})$;
7 $\mathcal{M}_{ext} = Ext(\mathcal{M}_{wm})$;
8 $\mathcal{M}_{wm} = Ext(\mathcal{M}_{att})$;
9   Calculate $\mathcal{L}_W, \mathcal{L}_{att}$;
10   Update $\Theta_{att} = \Theta_{att} - -lr * \text{Adam}(\mathcal{L}_{att})$;
11   Update $\Theta_{enc} = \Theta_{enc} - -lr * \text{Adam}(\mathcal{L}_W)$;
12   Update $\Theta_{ext} = \Theta_{ext} - -lr * \text{Adam}(\mathcal{L}_W)$;
13 end
14 Return $\Theta_{att}, \Theta_{enc}, \Theta_{ext}$

3.2.2 Deep Watermarking for Topology-Agnostic 3D Models

3.2.2.1 Topology-Agnostic GCN

Due to the possible attacks, watermarked meshes cannot simply be treated as template-based meshes. Even original meshes can also be non-template-based in the actual scenario. To represent these meshes, we employ isotropic filters to compose our convolution operation, with a fixed w_j in Eq. (3.78) for each neighboring vertex:

$$f_i^{l+1} = \phi \left(w_0 f_i^l + \sum_{j \in \mathcal{N}(i)} w_1 f_j^l \right). \tag{3.78}$$

During training, we find our network converges slowly. We analyze this phenomenon for two reasons: randomly generated watermark bits in each iteration step and different connectivity for each vertex. To speed up training and ensure convergence, we apply the degree normalization in GCN and design the Graph-Conv+BatchNorm+ReLU block as the main component of our network. We first define our GraphConv operation (Fig. 3.8):

$$f_i^{l+1} = w_0 f_i^l + w_1 \sum_{j \in \mathcal{N}(i)} \frac{1}{|\mathcal{N}(i)|} f_j^l, \tag{3.79}$$

where $| \cdot |$ denotes the cardinal number, indicating the vertex degree. Different from previous GCNs in generative tasks, the topology for each 3D mesh is agnostic. For each mesh with its own topology, topology-agnostic GCN needs

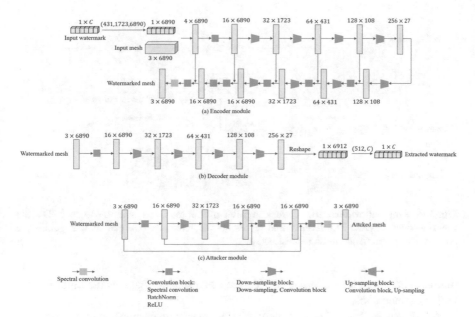

Fig. 3.8 Proposed network architecture

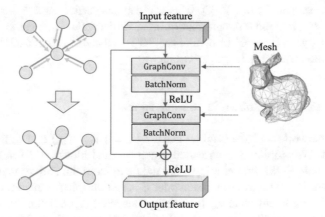

Fig. 3.9 Graph residual block. The dashed line represents that the mesh is utilized for querying the adjacent vertices in GraphConv operation

to search the neighboring vertices for every vertex. For every mini-batch data, we employ the batch normalization operation to normalize the feature from the output of GraphConv. Then we define the graph residual block consisting of two GraphConv+BatchNorm+ReLU blocks with a short connection [39], as shown in Fig. 3.9. For the initial block of the embedding sub-network and extracting sub-network, the input feature is the 3D coordinates of vertices and outputs 64-dim

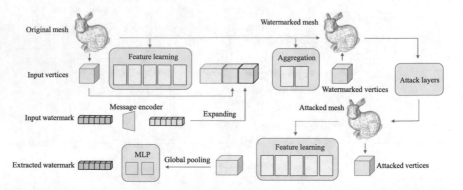

Fig. 3.10 Proposed watermark network architecture for training an end-to-end deep 3D mesh watermarking network. The dashed line represents the reference information that guides the convolution operation and mesh reconstruction

feature. For other blocks, the output feature has the same shape as the input feature with 64 dimensions.

As shown in Fig. 3.10, our network includes a watermark embedding sub-network, attack layers, and a watermark extracting sub-network. In the network, we define a 3D mesh as $M = (\mathcal{V}, \mathcal{F})$, where $\mathcal{V}$ denotes vertices and $\mathcal{F}$ denotes faces. And we use N_{in} to denote the number of input vertices. For each vertex $i \in \mathcal{V}$, we use $\mathbf{v}_i = [x_i, y_i, z_i]^{\mathrm{T}} \in \mathbb{R}^3$ to denote the 3D coordinates in the Euclidean space. And we define watermark length as C bits.

3.2.2.2 Watermark Embedding Sub-Network

In this sub-network, we take original mesh $M_{in} = (\mathcal{V}_{in}, \mathcal{F}_{in})$ and watermark $\mathbf{w}_{in}$ as the input. We employ five cascaded graph residual blocks to form the feature learning module $\mathbf{F}$. We first employ this module to learn the feature map F_{in} from input vertices $\mathcal{V}_{in}$. The watermark encoder $\mathbf{E}$ is responsible for encoding the input watermark into a latent code $\mathbf{z}_w$ by a fully connected layer. Then the latent code $\mathbf{z}_w$ is expanded along the number of vertices to align the vertices. After expanding, the latent code is concatenated with input vertices $\mathcal{V}_{in}$ and the mesh feature F_{in} and then fed into the aggregation module $\mathbf{A}$. In the last block of $\mathbf{A}$, there is a branch that applies an extra GraphConv layer and outputs the 3D coordinates of watermarked vertices $\mathcal{V}_{wm}$. The aggregation module $\mathbf{A}$ includes two graph residual blocks and outputs the 3D coordinates of mesh vertices. According to the original mesh M_{in} and watermarked vertices $\mathcal{V}_{wm}$, the watermarked 3D mesh M_{wm} can be constructed. Note that the symmetric function *Expanding* is used to align the vertices and the watermark feature, making the embedding process invariant to the reordering of input vertices, which may be very practical in the actual scenario.

3.2.2.3   Attack Layers

To guarantee the adaptive robustness to specific attacks, we train our network with attacked meshes. In this work, we mainly consider representative attacks (including cropping, Gaussian noise, rotation, and smoothing) and integrate them into attack layers. Note that we can integrate different attacks as the attack layers, according to the actual requirements.

Rotation   We rotate the 3D mesh in three dimensions with the rotation angle randomly sampled in every dimension. We use θ to denote the rotation scope and the rotation angle in each dimension is randomly sampled: $\theta_x, \theta_y, \theta_z \sim U[-\theta, \theta]$. Then we rotate $\mathcal{V}_{wm}$ with the corresponding angle for every dimension in the Euclidean space.

Gaussian Noise   We employ a zero-mean Gaussian noise model, sampling the standard deviation $\sigma_g \sim U[0, \sigma]$ to generate random noise to 3D meshes. We generate $noise \sim \mathcal{N}(0, \sigma_g{}^2)$ and attach it on the 3D coordinates of watermarked vertices.

Smoothing   The Laplacian smoothing model [40] is employed to simulate the possible smoothing operation. For the watermarked mesh $\mathcal{M}_{wm} = (\mathcal{V}_{wm}, \mathcal{F}_{wm})$, we first calculate the Laplacian matrix $\mathbf{L} \in \mathbb{R}^{N_{in} \times N_{in}}$ and use $\alpha_s \sim U[0, \alpha]$ to control the level of Laplacian smoothing. For the coordinate matrix $\mathbf{V}_{wm} \in \mathbb{R}^{N \times 3}$ of watermarked vertices $\mathcal{V}_{wm}$, we calculate the coordinate matrix $\mathbf{V}_{att}$ of attacked vertices $\mathcal{V}_{att}$ as

$$\mathbf{V}_{att} = \mathbf{V}_{wm} - \alpha_s \mathbf{L} \mathbf{V}_{wm}. \tag{3.80}$$

Cropping   We simulate this attack by cutting off a part of the mesh. We first normalize the vertices in a unit square and search for the two farthest points in the negative quadrant and the positive quadrant, respectively. Then we connect two points and simulate using a knife cutting perpendicular to the line. So that we can cut off the part of the mesh, with β to control the minimum ratio of the reservation. $\beta_c \sim U[\beta, 1]$ is used to denote the actual ratio of the reservation at each cropping operation.

   During training, we set the hyperparameters as follows: $\theta = 15°, \sigma = 0.03, \alpha = 0.2, \beta = 0.8$. Besides four attacks, we also integrate one identity layer which does not have any attack, to ensure the performance when no attack is suffered. During training, we randomly select one attack as the attack layer in each mini-batch. Then we can generate the attacked mesh $\mathcal{M}_{att} = (\mathcal{V}_{att}, \mathcal{F}_{att})$ after the watermarked mesh $\mathcal{M}_{wm} = (\mathcal{V}_{wm}, \mathcal{F}_{wm})$ passes through the attack layer. Figure 3.11 shows the original and attacked meshes under different attacks. With the differentiable attack layers, we can jointly train our embedding sub-network and extracting sub-network and update the parameters simultaneously.

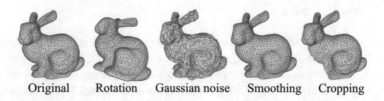

Fig. 3.11 Stanford Bunny model and its attacked meshes

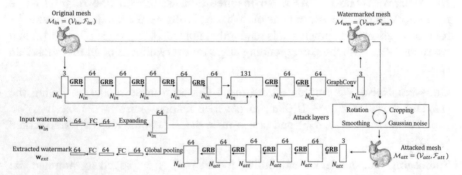

Fig. 3.12 The detailed illustration of the proposed network. The dashed line represents the reference information for the mesh reconstruction. Note that all graph convolution operations are also guided by the corresponding mesh

3.2.2.4   Watermark Extracting Sub-Network

We design a straightforward structure to extract the watermark. For the attacked vertices $\mathcal{V}_{att}$, we first employ the same feature learning module **F** to acquire the feature map F_{no}. Followed by the global average pooling layer and a two-layer fully connected layer (MLP), the extracted watermark $\mathbf{w}_{ext}$ is obtained. The symmetric function *Global pooling* aggregates information from all vertices, which can also guarantee the variance under the vertices reordering attack (Fig. 3.12).

3.2.2.5   Loss Function

To train the network, we define some loss functions. MSE loss is first employed for constraining the watermark and mesh vertices:

$$l_w(\mathbf{w}_{in}, \mathbf{w}_{ext}) = \frac{1}{C}||\mathbf{w}_{in} - \mathbf{w}_{ext}||_2^2, \tag{3.81}$$

$$l_m(\mathcal{M}_{in}, \mathcal{M}_{wm}) = \frac{1}{N_{in}} \sum_{i \in \mathcal{V}_{in}} ||\mathbf{v}_i - \mathbf{v}_{i'}||_2^2, \tag{3.82}$$

where i' denotes the paired vertex of vertex i in the watermarked mesh $\mathcal{M}_{wm}$.

l_m can constrain the spatial modification on mesh vertices as a whole. Yet the local geometry smoothness is also supposed to be guaranteed, as it greatly affects the visual perception of human eyes [41]. The local curvature can reflect the surface smoothness property [42]. For 3D meshes, the local curvature should be defined based on the connection relations. As shown in Fig. 3.13, we use $\theta_{ij} \in [0°, 180°]$ to represent the angle between the normalized normal vector $\mathbf{n}_i$ for vertex i and the direction of neighboring vertex j. We can find that the vertex's neighboring angles represent the local geometry. For each vertex i in the mesh $\mathcal{M}$, we define the vertex curvature as

$$cur(i, \mathcal{M}) = \sum_{j \in \mathcal{N}_i} \cos(\theta_{ij}), \tag{3.83}$$

where

$$\cos(\theta_{ij}) = \frac{(\mathbf{v}_j - \mathbf{v}_i)^{\mathrm{T}} \mathbf{n}_i}{||\mathbf{v}_j - \mathbf{v}_i||_2}. \tag{3.84}$$

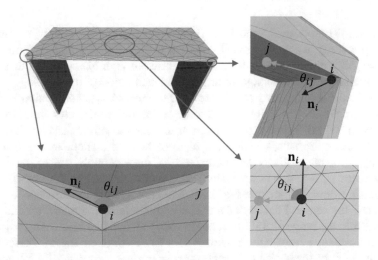

Fig. 3.13 This is a 3D model of a desk. In the bottom right figure, the desktop is flat and the normal vector $\mathbf{n}_i$ is perpendicular to the local area. For each $j \in \mathcal{N}_i$, $\theta_{ij} = 90°$. The bottom left figure and the top right figure are the convexity and concavity of the desk, respectively, with $\theta_{ij} > 90°$ and $\theta_{ij} < 90°$

To guarantee the local curvature consistency between original 3D mesh $\mathcal{M}_{in}$ and watermarked 3D mesh $\mathcal{M}_{wm}$, we define the curvature consistency loss function:

$$l_{cur}(\mathcal{M}_{in}, \mathcal{M}_{wm}) = \frac{1}{N_{in}} \sum_{i \in \mathcal{V}_{in}} ||(cur(i, \mathcal{M}_{in}) - cur(i', \mathcal{M}_{wm}))||_2^2. \qquad (3.85)$$

The combined objective is employed in the network: $\mathcal{L} = \lambda_1 l_w + \lambda_2 l_{cur} + \lambda_3 l_m$. By default, $\lambda_1 = \lambda_2 = 1$ and $\lambda_3 = 5$.

3.3   3D Mesh Watermarking Techniques Against 3D Print–Scan Attacks

With the development of the 3D printing content industry, there may be copyright issues with 3D meshes and 3D printed objects, for example, rescanning 3D printed objects to illegally obtain the original 3D mesh. However, the 3D print–scan process introduces considerable distortions, which means that 3D mesh watermarking in most digital domains becomes no more effective. And techniques illustrated in this subsection hope to resist the distortion of the 3D mesh during the 3D printing and scanning process, so as to achieve traceability and copyright protection.

3.3.1   Layering Artifact-Based Watermark

Hou et al. [47] proposed a robust and blind watermarking scheme, which protects content not only when sharing 3D models in the digital world but also when converting 3D digital content to analog content through 3D printing. To achieve this, they first proposed an algorithm for blind estimation of the printing direction from the analysis of layering artifacts as their watermark synchronization method.

Layer thickness and print orientation are the main attributes that affect the accuracy of 3D printed objects, and adding material to different layers inherently causes layering artifacts, which are typical of layered manufacturing. Generally speaking, layering artifacts are perceived as imperceptible noise, yet Hou et al. use them as a template for watermark synchronization to design watermark synchronization algorithms; see Fig. 3.14. Specifically, before watermark extraction, they rotate the scanned data $\mathbf{M}$ of the layered manufacturing model around the z-axis with θ in the range [0, 180) to generate the rotated model $\mathbf{M}_\theta$. Then, project $\mathbf{M}_\theta$ onto the xz-plane to obtain the thickness map $\mathbf{P}_\theta$. To measure the thickness of $\mathbf{M}_\theta$, the depth map of the backside is subtracted from the depth map of the front side. The depth map $\mathbf{P}_f$ of the front side is calculated using the z-buffer algorithm. The z-axis of $\mathbf{M}_\theta$ is inverted and the backside is rendered to obtain the depth map $\mathbf{P}_b$. Then, $\mathbf{P}_b$ is subtracted from $\mathbf{P}_f$ to obtain the thickness map $\mathbf{P}_\theta$. Then, to emphasize

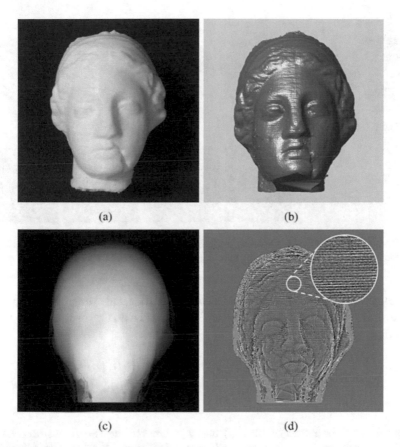

Fig. 3.14 The process of obtaining layering artifacts from the scanned model. (**a**) The 3D printed Venus model, (**b**) the scanned model $\mathbf{M}_\theta$, (**c**) the thickness map $\mathbf{P}_\theta$, and (**d**) the enhanced layering artifacts $\mathbf{P}'_\theta$ by filtering

the presence of periodic properties in the layering artifacts, a high-pass filter and histogram thresholding is applied to $\mathbf{P}_\theta$ to obtain an enlarged $\mathbf{P}'_\theta$ of the traces of the layering artifacts.

If the input scan data is a model of a layered fabrication, the corresponding artifact contains specific strong periodicity that can be analyzed using the 2D discrete Fourier transform; see Fig. 3.15. Performing a 2D Fast Fourier Transform (FFT), the magnitude is calculated as follows:

$$\mathbf{F}_\theta(u, v) = H\left(\left|\mathcal{F}\left(\mathbf{P}'_\theta(x, y)\right)\right|\right), \tag{3.86}$$

where u and v are the frequency variables of x and y. $\mathcal{F}(\cdot)$ denotes the 2D FFT. $H(\cdot)$ is the filter for the Butterworth high-pass filtering to remove the significant low frequency components. Then, $\mathbf{F}_\theta(u, v)$ is converted to polar coordinates $\mathbf{F}_\theta(r, \phi)$. Then, they apply the threshold-based peak detector reported in [46] to search for

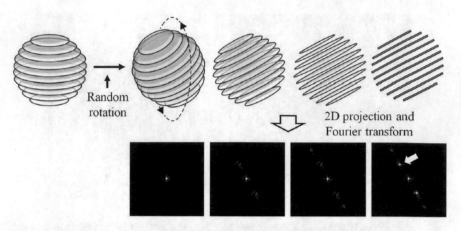

Fig. 3.15 Considering that the layering artifacts are periodic, the correctness of the recovered rotation angle can be determined by the peak response in the Fourier frequency domain

candidate local maxima (peaks n times larger than the local average amplitude) and obtain a set of locations $\mathcal{P}_0^\theta$ for the candidate peaks. Then, the maximum magnitude peak ϱ_θ is selected, satisfying that

$$\begin{cases} \text{pos}(\varrho_\theta) = (r_0, \varphi_0) = \underset{(r,\varphi)\in\mathcal{P}_0^\theta}{\text{argmax}} \ (\mathbf{F}_\theta(r, \varphi)) \\ \text{mag}(\varrho_\theta) = \mathbf{F}_\theta (r_0, \varphi_0) , \end{cases} \tag{3.87}$$

where θ is in the range of $[0, 180)$ and $\mathcal{P}_0^\theta$ denotes the set of positions of the candidate peaks. pos and mag denote the position and magnitude values of peak ϱ_θ. ϱ_θ denotes the maximum peak position of the rotating model $\mathbf{M}_\theta$, and the magnitude of ϱ_θ indicates the size of the layering artifact. Finally, they estimate the global maximum point of $\mathbf{F}_\theta(r, \phi)$ by solving the optimization problem.

$$\hat{\theta} = \underset{\theta}{\text{argmax}} \ (\text{mag} \, (\varrho_\theta)) , \tag{3.88}$$

where $\hat{\theta}$ denotes the value of the degree of rotation.

The binary watermark pattern $\mathbf{w}$ of length l_w is generated using a watermark key and a pseudo-random generator. And the watermark embedding formula is as follows:

$$\rho_i' = \rho_i + \alpha \, (v_i) \cdot \Psi \, (\varphi_i), \tag{3.89}$$

where $1 \leq i \leq V$ and $\alpha(\cdot)$ is the watermark strength function. The spread spectrum signal Ψ is synthesized as a sinusoidal signal in the frequency band

$[f_s + 1, f_s + l_w]$ as follows:

$$\Psi(\varphi_i) = \sum_{m=1}^{l_w} \mathbf{w}_m \cdot \sin\left(2\pi \varphi_i (m + f_s) + \phi_{i,l}\right), \tag{3.90}$$

where f_s is the value of the minimum frequency band and $\phi_{i,l}$ is a phase parameter for imperceptibility.

The watermark detection is based on the correlation between the spectral domain of the scanned mesh and the reference pattern generated by the watermarked key. Then, the embedded data are decoded based on the positions of the correlation peaks. The subvector $\mathbf{M}^*$ is chosen from $\mathbf{M}'$ as follows:

$$\mathbf{M}^*(m) = \mathbf{M}'(m + f_s), \tag{3.91}$$

where $1 \leq m \leq l_w$, f_s and l_w are the starting frequency and length of the embedded watermark, respectively. Then, we calculate the detector response using normalized correlation as follows:

$$\text{corr}\left(\mathbf{w}, \mathbf{M}^*\right) = \frac{(\mathbf{w} - \overline{\mathbf{w}}) \cdot \left(\mathbf{M}^* - \overline{\mathbf{M}}^*\right)}{\|\mathbf{w} - \overline{\mathbf{w}}\| \cdot \left\|\mathbf{M}^* - \overline{\mathbf{M}}^*\right\|}. \tag{3.92}$$

In summary, this method has well visual quality, and have robustness to various distortions, including the distortions in 3D printing, scanning and reprinting process, and small amount of cropping. Yet it has a low watermark capacity (1 bit).

3.3.2   Geodesic Distance-Based Local Watermark

Chen et al. [45] used geodesic distance to design a robust 3D printing–scanning process invariant to uniquely identify the model, determine and locate the watermark embedding region, and then locally embed the watermark. To synchronize the watermark, a special tracking signal is embedded into the model synchronously. In the extraction process, for the model after the 3D printing scanning process, they use the model residual to detect the watermark.

The flowchart of their proposed algorithm is shown in Fig. 3.16. First, a bipolar watermark sequence $\mathbf{w}$ of length l_w is generated using a private key. Then, the net load signal $p(x)$ can be expressed as

$$p(x) = \sum_{i=1}^{l_w} w_i \cdot \cos(2\pi x(i + f_s)), \tag{3.93}$$

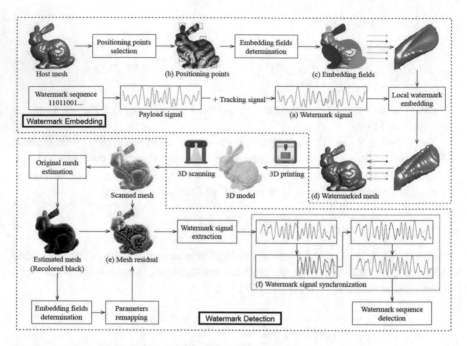

Fig. 3.16   The workflow of the proposed watermark algorithm

where $x \in [0, 1]$ and f_s is the minimum frequency band. According to Fourier's theorem, the watermark sequence $\mathbf{w}$ is embedded in the frequency band $[f_s + 1, f_s + l_w]$ of $p(x)$. For watermark localization, a centrosymmetric tracking signal $t(x) = -\sin(x/10)$ is added to the center of the symmetric watermark signal $p(x)$; see Fig. 3.16a.

The localization point locations are estimated by the geodesic distance function ϕ, and then the watermark signal $f(x)$ is embedded locally and repeatedly around each localization point; see Fig. 3.16b and c. Defining the vertices in this embedding domain as $\mathcal{V} = \{v_i\}_{i=1,2,...,N}$, the watermark embedding operation modifies the position $\mathbf{p}_i$ in the normal direction:

$$\mathbf{p}'_i = \mathbf{p}_i + \beta \cdot f(\tilde{\phi}(v_i)) \cdot \mathbf{n}(v_i), \tag{3.94}$$

where $\mathbf{n}(v_i)$ is the normal vector of v_i, $f(\cdot)$ is the watermark signal function, and β is the watermark strength. $\tilde{\phi}(\cdot)$ is the normalization in $\mathcal{V}$.

In the extraction process, for the 3D scanner scan to obtain the digital mesh $\mathcal{M}$, the smoothed $\mathcal{M}$ is used as the estimation $\mathcal{M}'$ of the original mesh (Fig. 3.16e). Similar to the inverse process of the embedding process, for each vertex v_i, the modification between $\mathcal{M}'$ and $\mathcal{M}$ can be estimated as

$$\Delta(v_i) = (\mathbf{p}'_i - \mathbf{p}_i) \cdot \mathbf{n}(v'_i). \tag{3.95}$$

Based on the resampling of the geodesic distance function ϕ', the residuals can be transformed to the watermarked signal $g(x)$. Considering the translation and scaling distortions occurring in the 3D print–scan process, the tracking signal is used to synchronize the watermark signal. Specifically, as shown in Fig. 3.16f, when they flip the extracted signal, the centrosymmetry of the tracking signal makes it have an intersection with itself, whose position could be used to estimate the parameters of translation and scaling recovery. Finally, the watermark signal is transformed to the Fourier domain, and the value at $[f_s + 1, f_s + l_w]$ is the extracted watermark sequence.

In summary, their local watermarking scheme takes into account the performance of low-resolution 3D printing and scanning devices, but still only has a 1-bit watermark capacity.

3.3.3   Spectral Subspace-Based Watermark

Yamazaki et al. [50] propose a method for extracting watermarks from 3D printed objects created from 3D mesh data with watermarks. They use an informed watermarking algorithm that requires the original 3D mesh as well as the watermark to extract the suspect watermark from the suspect 3D object. Both the embedding and extraction steps can only be performed by the owner of the original 3D mesh who has full access to the secret data, and it is assumed that the owner has access to the 3D print to obtain a 3D scan of the surface.

Given a suspicious 3D printed object, the surface model is acquired by a vision sensor. If the object consists of smooth and convex surfaces, the entire shape model can be accurately acquired by standard modeling methods such as [53]. A watermark can then be extracted from this shape model by registering the scanned data to the original 3D mesh and resampling it to a homogeneous 3D mesh [51, 52]. However, it is impractical to reconstruct the entire 3D shape if the object has complex structures, holes, and voids, e.g., objects with concave surfaces and holes lead to inaccurate surface reconstruction; see Fig. 3.17. This large geometric error makes it

Fig. 3.17 Original 3D mesh, printed and scanned 3D mesh, and reconstructed 3D mesh (from left to right). Compared to the original mesh, the reconstructed 3D mesh has a large distortion in the hole and void part

difficult to extract the watermark. In addition, watermark extraction requires that the original mesh and the reconstructed mesh have the same topology. During 3D scan reconstruction, resampling makes it difficult for the 3D mesh to maintain a specific topology, which leads to geometric errors.

To solve the above problem, the authors propose to use a linear combination of a small number of shape bases to represent the 3D mesh and reconstruct the shape by estimating the coefficients in the subspace. To compute the spectrum of the 3D mesh, they first do an eigenvalue decomposition of the Laplace matrix derived from the connectivity of the mesh vertices. The Laplace matrix used is the Kirchhoff matrix K proposed and defined by Bollabás [54] as

$$K = D - A,$$

where D is a diagonal matrix whose diagonal element d_{ii} indicates the degree of the vertex i, and A is an adjacency matrix of the polygonal mesh whose elements a_{ij} are 1 if vertices i and j are connected by an edge, and otherwise 0.

For a 3D mesh M composed of n vertices, its Kirchhoff matrix has size $n \times n$, whose eigenvalue decomposition is represented as

$$K = U \Lambda U^T,$$

where Λ is a diagonal matrix composed of the eigenvalues in ascending order and U is a unitary matrix whose columns represent normalized eigenvectors. Then, the spectrum of the mesh could be obtained by projecting the 3D coordinates of vertices to the linear space spanned by the eigenvectors. All the eigenvalues are non-negative, and the smallest c eigenvalues of K are equal to zero, where c is the number of connected components in M from the nature of the Laplacian matrix.

In their method, a watermark is embedded in and extracted from each element of 3D coordinates independently. Defining x be an n-vector of the vertex coordinates of the mesh in one dimension, then the spectral decomposition and reconstruction are defined, respectively, by

$$s = U^T x \quad \text{and}$$

$$x = U s,$$

where $s = (s_1, \ldots, s_n)^T$ is a vector of spectrum. Then, watermark is embedded to the spectral coefficients corresponding to non-zero eigenvalues. The watermark is an m-vector $w = (w_1, \ldots, w_m)^T$ composed of random numbers $w_k \in [-1, 1]$ sampled from an i.i.d. Gaussian distribution with mean zero and variance one. A 3D mesh M is watermarked by modulating a set of spectral coefficients chosen by an injection $\sigma : \{1, \ldots, m\} \to \{c + 1, \ldots, n\}$ as

$$s'_j = \begin{cases} (1 + \epsilon w_k) s_j & j = \sigma(k) \\ s_j & j \notin \text{Image}(\sigma), \end{cases}$$

where ϵ is a parameter to control the strength of the watermark. A watermarked mesh $\mathcal{M}'$ is created by replacing the vertex coordinates x with $x' = Us'$ and repeating the above operation for all three dimensions.

Algorithm 8: Reconstruct a mesh from a scan

---

1 Reconstruct(S^*)
2 $S^* \longleftarrow S$
3 **repeat**
4 | $x^* \leftarrow U_{s^*}$
5 | $\mathcal{M}^* \longleftarrow$ CreateMesh(x^*)
6 | $T \leftarrow$ SimilarityICP $\left(S^*, \mathcal{M}^*\right)$
7 | $s^* \leftarrow$ SpectralICP $\left(TS^*, \mathcal{M}^*\right)$
8 | $\Delta \leftarrow$ Distance $\left(TS^*, \mathcal{M}^*\right)$
9 **until** Δ *is converged*;
10 Return $\mathcal{M}^*$

After the above watermarked mesh is 3D printed, define S^* as the 3D scanned point cloud. Then, they propose an algorithm for generating $\mathcal{M}^*$ homologous to $\mathcal{M}$, by reconstructing the 3D mesh from S^* in the spectral domain. Its algorithm is summarized in Algorithm 8, where a variant of the iterative closest point (ICP) [55] technique is used.

Once a suspect 3D mesh $\mathcal{M}^*$ homologous to $\mathcal{M}$ is obtained, they could obtain a suspect watermark by inverting the embedding process. Define $s^* = \left(s_1^*, \ldots, s_n^*\right)^T$ as the spectrum of $\mathcal{M}^*$, and then the suspect watermark $w^* = \left(w_1^*, \ldots, w_m^*\right)^T$ could be calculated by

$$w_k^* = \frac{s_{\sigma(k)}^* - s_{\sigma(k)}}{\epsilon S_{\sigma(k)}} \quad k \in \{1, \ldots, m\}.$$

Because the distribution of w_k^* is unknown, a non-parametric correlation known as Spearman's r is adopted as

$$r = \frac{\sum_i \left(R_i - \bar{R}\right)\left(R_i^* - \bar{R}^*\right)}{\sqrt{\sum_i \left(R_i - \bar{R}\right)^2}\sqrt{\sum_i \left(R_i^* - \bar{R}^*\right)^2}},$$

where R_i and R_i^* are, respectively, the rank of w_k and w_k^* among the other inliers and $\bar{R}$ and $\bar{R}^*$ are, respectively, the average of R's and R^*'s. The correlation r is turned into a probabilistic answer using the standard statistical analysis. Finally, they compute the probability P_{fp} that the correlation of w^* with a randomly generated watermark w would be as high as the observed r, using Student's t-test.

In summary, they present a framework for extracting watermarks from 3D printed objects and discuss the cases of holes in the original mesh. But the watermarking method is non-blind because the extraction process requires the original mesh.

3.3.4 Surface Norm Distribution-Based Watermark

Delmotte et al. [58] propose a novel blind watermarking algorithm for 3D printed objects, which could embed data in a 3D printed object and retrieve it by 3D scanning without the original mesh. Moreover, the proposed method allows avoiding shape degradation by subdividing the bin of the histogram and improving the robustness of bin localization by introducing a bin margin.

The proposed method is based on the vertex-parametric watermarking algorithm, but the authors have made some improvements to make it applicable to 3D printed scanned scenes. Since the vertex norm watermarking algorithm is invariant to translation, rotation, rescaling, and vertex connectivity, designing a 3D printing scan watermark based on it will have a great advantage. However, the first thing that needs to be considered in the application is the desynchronization attack due to the resampling of 3D printed scans. The vertex specification watermarking algorithm can be briefly described as follows.

For a 3D mesh, each vertex on it can be represented by spherical coordinates (p_i, θ_i, ϕ_i), where p_i is the vertex's parametric number, i.e., the distance to the center, and (θ_i, ϕ_i) is the orientation angle. By obtaining all the vertex norms, we can get the histogram of the parametric distribution, as shown in Fig. 3.18. Then, we can embed a bit of information by modifying the distribution of parametric in a bin range. Specifically, the modification makes the mean of the distribution to the left or right of the bin center, respectively, to represent the code "0" or "1." Since the modified parametric distributions do not exceed the boundaries of their original bin and the directions (θ_i, ϕ_i) remain unchanged, the perturbation to the original mesh is small.

To avoid the resampling problem, Delmotte et al. calculate the probability density function of the surface norm over the whole surface, i.e., the distance between the

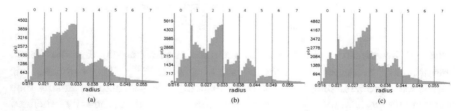

Fig. 3.18 Distribution of vertex norms from the bunny model, each vertical line represents the border of a bin. One bit of data is encoded by shifting the mean to the left or right side of the bin. (**a**) Original distribution, (**b**) after the watermarking process, (**c**) after the print simulation

surface and the center of gravity. The surface norm obtained by this calculation method is less affected by resampling in the absence of degeneracy in the mesh shape. Specifically, to calculate the average value for each bin, each triangle is subdivided so that each sub-triangle is contained in only one bin. Then the average of the vanes of the three vertices of each triangle within a bin is taken, multiplied by the area of that triangle, and divided by the total area of all triangles within a bin. This method of approximation has a very small error when the triangles are far enough from the center of gravity of the 3D mesh relative to their size.

In addition, there is a technical issue to consider. Since bin partitioning is performed periodically by the distance to the center of gravity, some bins are populated by a large surface of the model, while other bins are populated by only a small surface. This causes some of the bins to contain much less surface than others, such as the bins on the left and right of Fig. 3.19. To obtain a more uniform distribution of surfaces and reduce the effect of hard-to-watermark areas parallel to the center vector, they subdivide each bin and combine equally spaced sub-bins into a new bin; see Fig. 3.19. Finally, the center of the 3D mesh is computed using a moment-based center estimate that has been shown to be more resistant in the 3D printing environment [47].

$$c = (\bar{x}, \bar{y}, \bar{z}) = \frac{(M_{100}, M_{010}, M_{001})}{M_{000}}, \qquad (3.96)$$

where M_{pqr} denotes the pth, qth, and rth order volume moments of the mesh.

In the watermark extraction process, the model is first centered using the method of moments described in the previous section. Then they subdivide each triangle so

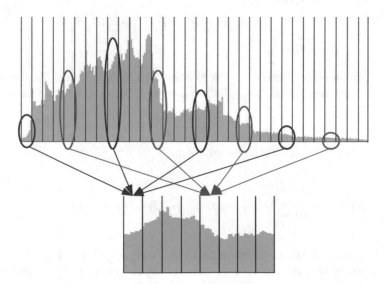

Fig. 3.19 Fusion of multiple non-consecutive bins to get a more uniform histogram

that it is completely contained in a single sub-bin, whose boundaries are calculated by the following equation:

$$
\begin{cases}
\# \text{subBin} & = N * N_d + 2 * b \\
\text{subBinSize} & = \frac{\text{maxNorm} - \text{minNorm}}{\# \text{subBin}} \\
\text{minBound}[j] & = \min \text{Norm} + (j + m) * \text{subBin Size} \\
\text{maxBound}[j] & = \min \text{Norm} + (j + 1 - m) * \text{sub BinSize} ,
\end{cases}
\tag{3.97}
$$

where j is the index of the sub-bin. To calculate the area of the triangle, the following formula is used:

$$
\text{Surf}(A, B, C) = \frac{|\overrightarrow{AB} \times \overrightarrow{AC}|}{2},
\tag{3.98}
$$

where A, B, and C are the three vertex coordinates of the triangle. Then they define the function

$$
f_j(X) = \frac{X - \text{minBound}[j]}{\text{maxBound}[j] - \text{minBound}[j]},
\tag{3.99}
$$

which remaps the norm X inside the sub-bin j to the range $[0,1]$. Then they calculate the total area $S[j]$ and the average norm $\mu[j]$ in each sub-bin:

$$
S[j] = \sum_{(A,B,C) \in \text{Tri}[j]} \text{Surf}(A, B, C)
$$

$$
\mu[j] = \sum_{(A,B,C) \in \text{Tri}[j]} f_j \left(\frac{\|A\| + \|B\| + \|C\|}{3} \right) \frac{\text{Surf}(A, B, C)}{S[j]}
\tag{3.100}
$$

where A, B, and C are the coordinates of a vertex, and $\text{Tr}\,i[j]$ is the list of triangles included in the range $[\text{minBound}[j], \text{maxBound}[j]]$. Then, they merge the sub-bins into the bins:

$$
S'[i] = \sum_{j=1}^{N_d} S[i + j * N + b]
$$

$$
\mu'[i] = \frac{1}{S'[i]} \sum_{j=1}^{N_d} \mu[i + j * N + b] * S[i + j * N + b].
\tag{3.101}
$$

And finally they obtain the watermark signal by $w[i] = (\mu'[i] > 0.5)$.

In summary, they present a blind watermarking algorithm for 3D printed objects that extracts watermarks with high accuracy even in the presence of some printing and scanning errors. Moreover, the method uses a rotation-invariant approach to avoid the orientation synchronization step and thus has fewer constraints than previous work. However, the watermarking method that modifies vertices along the normal direction is imperceptible on natural shape meshes but causes strong visual distortion on CAD files, which can only be embedded using lower intensities.

3.3.5   Shape-Based Watermark

Yamamoto et al. [59] argue that the method of expressing information by embedding cavities inside 3D printed objects is not robust to rescanning–printing attacks. To solve this problem, they proposed a watermarking method that embeds information into the external shape of the object. When an attacker wants to change or remove the information embedded in an object, the attacker must change the external shape of the object.

In this work, the proposed method embeds information into the external shape of a 3D printed object at specific multiple locations, and it is crucial to share the embedded locations between the embedding and extracting ends. First, the authors define a pseudo rotation axis of the 3D object, which is determined by the external shape of the 3D printed object only, in order to synchronize the coordinate system of the 3D object between the embedding end and the extraction end. Specifically, the pseudo rotation axis is the axis of rotation when the 3D object is approximated as a rotating body. Considering that any axis of the 3D object can be chosen as the rotation axis to rotate the 3D object, this results in a different planar projection of the 3D object. As shown in Fig. 3.20, the image area of a parallel projection on a projection plane parallel to the axis may change with rotation. The ratio of the maximum value of the image area to the minimum value of the image area is called the ratio of change for the axis, and its minimum value is 1. They define the pseudo rotation axis of a 3D object as follows: the axis with the smallest ratio of change for the axis is the pseudo rotation axis of the object.

After the pseudo rotation axis is determined, an observation coordinate system is established with the pseudo rotation axis as the z-axis. Define l as the length of the object's axis. Then the intersection of the z-axis with the object is $(x, y, z) = (0, 0, 0)$ and $(x, y, z) = (0, 0, l)$. Then the 3D object is sliced with $2n + 1$ planes at uniform intervals between the plane $z = 0$ and the plane $z = l$; see Fig. 3.21. Consider the cross-section of the object in the ith cutting plane ($i = 1, 2, ..., 2n+1$) and define its pseudo-radius as the maximum of the distances from the z-axis to the points in the cross-section as the pseudo-radius in the cutting plane.

The embedding end first measures the axis length l and the pseudo-radius r_i ($1 \leq i \leq 2n + 1$) and then obtains the characteristic quantity f_j ($1 \leq j \leq n + 1$). The characteristic quantity of the object ($f_1, f_2, ..., f_{n+1}$) is defined as follows:

- f_1: the ratio of r_{n+1} (the pseudo radius in the center cutting plane) to l
- f_2: the ratio of max (r_n, r_{n+2}) (the larger value between the radii of the cutting planes that are adjacent to the center cutting plane) to l

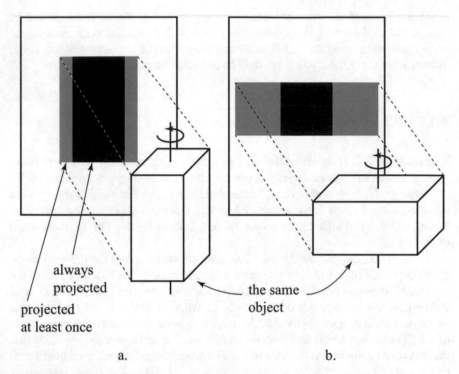

Fig. 3.20 Schematic diagram of the ratio of change for the axis. (**a**) has a smaller ratio of change than (**b**), so its rotation axis is defined as a pseudo rotation axis

- f_3: the ratio of max (r_{n-1}, r_{n+3}) to l
- ...
- f_{n+1}: the ratio of max (r_1, r_{2n+1}) to l

The ratio to l is used to ensure the robustness against a scaling attack on the object.

Then, the value of the feature quantity f_1 is converted to a normalized floating-point binary representation. Let $b_1, b_2, \ldots$ be the binary representation of the significant digits of f_1. The modified f_1' is obtained by embedding k bits starting from the dth highest significant bit. Similarly, the modified feature quantities $(f_1', f_2', \ldots, f_{n+1}')$ are obtained by modifying $f_2, f_3, \ldots, f_{n+1}$ to embed the rest of the information. The modified pseudo-radius in the central cutting plane r_{n+1}' is obtained by $r_{n+1}' = l \cdot f_1'$. The rest modified pseudo-radius $(r_1', r_2', \ldots, r_{2n+1}')$ could be obtained by the same process. Finally, 3D coordinates are modified using a scale factor to uniformly scale the surrounding coordinates to avoid obtrusive visual distortions.

The extraction process could be basically executed by performing the embedding process in reverse. After determining the pseudo rotation axis, a coordinate system is selected and the axis length l is measured. A planar cut model using $2n + 1$ perpendicular to the z-axis is used and the pseudo-radius in each plane is measured,

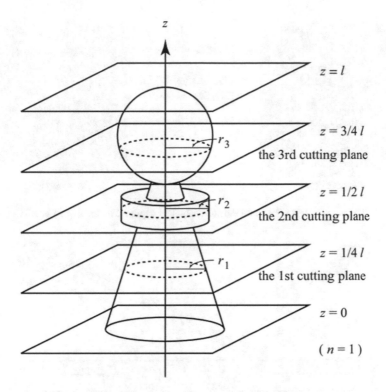

Fig. 3.21 Schematic diagram of the cutting plane in the watermark extraction process

and then the feature quantities are calculated and converted to a normalized floating-point binary representation. Finally, the embedded message is obtained by reading bits from the sth to the $s + k$th bits of the binary significant digit of each feature quantity.

In summary, the advantage of the proposed scheme is that the attacker cannot change the information embedded in the object without changing the external shape of the object. However, the scheme requires high-precision 3D printing and scanning equipment.

3.3.6 Air Pockets-Based Watermark

Li et al. [44] proposed AirCode, a method for embedding messages in 3D printed objects using a set of carefully designed air pockets located below the surface of the object. AirCode has good imperceptibility because the air pockets expressing the message only affect the scattered light transmission from the lower surface, and this small difference is imperceptible to the naked eye. However, it can be detected by computational imaging methods.

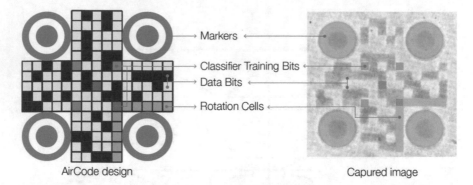

Fig. 3.22 The layout design (left) and the corresponding captured image (right) of AirCode

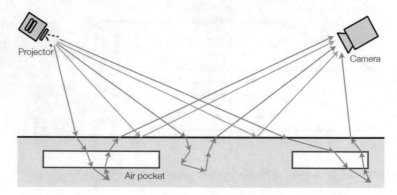

Fig. 3.23 The diagram of subsurface scattering. Air pockets beneath the 3D printed object result in a difference between the direct component (green) and the global component (orange) of the light reflection

The data is first encoded using an error correction scheme and then transformed into a designed 2D barcode; see Fig. 3.22. This barcode has four concentric circular markers and some rotation cells (green ones in Fig. 3.22) around the bottom right marker for the rotation restoration in the barcode detection process. Moreover, some known bits are also placed on the barcode, where the blue cells are always filled to represent bit "1" and the orange cells are always empty to indicate "0." These bits could improve the robustness of the decoding step further. This 2D barcode is then thickened and used as air pockets beneath the flat surface of the 3D model. After the 3D printing process, the AirCode is embedded in it.

To read the AirCode, they used subsurface scattering from a translucent 3D printed object to detect air pockets. As shown in Fig. 3.23, light that is directly reflected by the surface (green) represents the direct component and the light that enters the surface and scatters in it before leaving the surface (orange) produces the global component. And they utilized the computational imaging method [43] to separate the global and direct components of light transmission using structured light patterns projected by a projector. First, a checkerboard illumination pattern is illuminated multiple times with sweeping, producing one image each time. The illumination source is set as red in order to have a longer wavelength, resulting in a longer mean free path within the scattering medium and a sharper global component image. Then, in the image sequence, they calculate the maximum and minimum values for each pixel, resulting in two images L^+ and L^-. The direct and global component images can then be estimated by

$$
\begin{aligned}
L_d &= L^+ - \frac{\alpha}{1-\alpha} L^-, \\
L_g &= \frac{L^-}{1-\alpha},
\end{aligned}
\tag{3.102}
$$

where α is the percentage of projector pixels activated in the sweeping.

Then, based on the circular locators of AirCode, they use an ellipse detector to locate AirCode from the global component images. Based on these locators, the perspective transformation parameters are estimated and AirCode is recovered as a square. Finally, based on the design method of the AirCode pattern, the messages in it can be decoded in reverse.

In summary, AirCode provides an unobtrusive way to embed user-specified information into physical objects that are labeled as they are created during the manufacturing process without any post-processing. This allows AirCode to be used in a variety of scenarios such as metadata embedding, robotic grasping, and watermarking. But the extraction process of AirCode takes a couple of minutes and requires multiple devices to work together. In addition, printing distortions from consumer-grade 3D printers can also interfere with AirCode extraction.

3.4   3D Physical Watermarking on 3D Printed Objects

3.4.1   Layer Thickness-Based Watermark

Delmotte et al. [48] propose a new blind watermarking algorithm for 3D printed objects based on fused deposition modeling (FDM) 3D printers, which is implemented by modifying the thickness of the printed layer on small pieces of the object surface. The scheme minimizes distortion by locally modifying the layers.

During the watermark embedding process, the local modification layer thickness is selected according to the watermark sequence, as shown in Fig. 3.24. To embed an N bit watermark, we first reshape the signal into an HW matrix, where $HW = N$, and add parity bit rows and columns for error detection to produce a $(H+1)(W+1)$ matrix.

For each bit, the 3D printing layer is divided into coding and separation regions of equal thickness. In the encoding region of each bit, the thickness of the bottom layer

Fig. 3.24 Schematic diagram
of the embedding process.
The red numbers are the
parity bits. The layer with
white background is the
coding layer, and the gray one
is the separation layer

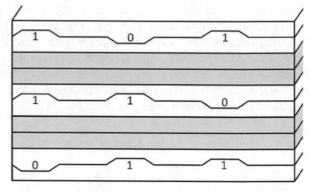

is multiplied by $(1+\alpha)$ or $(1-\alpha)$ to encode 1 or 0 bits, respectively. The thickness of the top layer of the encoding layer is then set to complementary to the bottom layer to keep the sum of the two thicknesses constant. And both the separation region and the separation layer are used to simplify detection and correlation during the extraction and to reduce distortion by performing smooth transitions. To embed a watermark patch, the number of layers required is $2(H + 1)$ encoding layers and HM separation layers, for a total of $H(M+2)+2$ layers. The width of the pattern is equal to the width per bit width multiplied by $(W + 1)$. In practice, they set H and W to even numbers to allow parity check to detect whether all bits have been inverted. This is because during extraction it is not possible to determine whether the watermark pattern has undergone 180° rotational distortion, and relying on the parity check can recover that distortion.

To embed the watermark message, they modified the 3D printed layer thickness by adjusting the amount of plastic extrusion while keeping the layer width constant. In the simplified model they used, the cross-sectional area of the layer is approximated as a rounded rectangle, and its volume can be calculated as

$$A_{layer} = h(w - h) + \pi \frac{h^2}{4}, \tag{3.103}$$

where w is the layer width and h is the layer height. They obtain the volume of the plastic by multiplying the cross-sectional area by the layer length and the filament length by dividing the volume of the plastic by the filament cross-sectional area as follows:

$$L_{filament} = \frac{A_{layer} L_{layer}}{\pi (\phi_{filament}/2)^2}, \tag{3.104}$$

where $L_{filament}$ is the filament length, $\phi_{filament}$ is the filament diameter, and L_{layer} is the length of the layer.

For these areas with modified layer thicknesses, high-speed printing produces more artifacts. Because of the nonlinearity in the liquefier, the plastic flow cannot be changed instantaneously. Therefore, they reduce the printing speed in these areas in the 3D printing process.

In the extraction process, they use a paper scanner to obtain a scanned image of the 3D model and then use the Fourier transform to align the image so that the layer edges become horizontal. Specifically, we detect the peak magnitude value of the Fourier transform, calculate the corresponding angle, and reposition the image. The edges of the separated layers can then be easily detected because they are horizontally straight and the regularity of the pattern makes the distance between successive separated layers constant. It is possible to distinguish the encoded layers from the separated layers because their encoded regions have a different thickness from their separated regions. After a robust estimation of each edge, we can calculate the value of each bit by measuring the average thickness of the layers in the encoding region to decode the watermark information.

In summary, the method proposes a physical watermark that protects the 3D printed model by adjusting the layer thickness with good invisibility and greater capacity. However, this method is currently only applicable to 3D models with flat surfaces.

3.4.2   Layer Color-Based Watermark

Maia et al. [49] proposed LayerCode as a tagging method that embeds elaborate barcode patterns into 3D printed objects. The embedding process uses an encoding algorithm that allows the 3D printed layer to carry information without changing the geometry of the object. The decoding algorithm could extract the LayerCode embedded in the 3D printed physical object by one captured picture.

The core idea of LayerCode is to interleave two "types" of layers in the 3D printing process to embed information on the 3D printed object and even to implement labels, hyperlinks, or watermarks. This "type difference" is mainly a difference in color, yet other "type differences" such as thickness could also be used to encode data. Their coding scheme is as follows. As shown in Fig. 3.25, if the thickness ratio of two consecutive layers is $1/M$ or M, then the bit "1" is encoded,

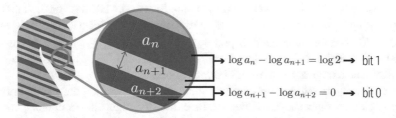

Fig. 3.25 The encoding scheme of LayerCode. Each pair of adjacent layers encodes one bits according to the ratio of layer thicknesses

where M is a constant greater than 1. And if that ratio is 1, then bit "0" is encoded. The first layer is the standard thickness h. Then, depending on the current bit b_{n+1} and the previous layer thickness a_n, the next layer thickness a_{n+1} is h or M_h, namely,

$$a_{n+1} = \begin{cases} a_n & \text{if } b_{n+1} = 0 \\ Mh & \text{if } b_{n+1} = 1 \text{ and } a_n = h \\ h & \text{if } b_{n+1} = 1 \text{ and } a_n = Mh. \end{cases} \quad (3.105)$$

The decoding process is the inverse of the encoding process:

$$b_{n+1} = \begin{cases} 1 & \text{if } \log a_n - \log a_{n+1} = \pm \log M, \\ 0 & \text{if } \log a_n - \log a_{n+1} = 0. \end{cases} \quad (3.106)$$

In order to extract LayerCode from the captured images, they also propose a graph-based algorithm to obtain the thickness sequence of encoded layers.

First, they construct a graph to represent the layer structure. Through a preprocessing step, all pixels in the captured LayerCode are marked as black or white pixel regions. Each region is represented as a graph node, and two nodes are connected if their regions are adjacent to each other. Next, each edge e will be associated with two quantities, a two-dimensional vector v in image space and a binary label r. Consider an edge e connecting nodes A and B. Its vector v represents the approximate direction in which it can be moved from image region A to region B. This direction will guide the order of layer traversal without getting stuck in a loop. To compute v, they first identify the boundary pixels in each region. At each boundary pixel, a boundary normal direction is estimated as the direction in which a different region can be accessed by moving the shortest distance. Then v is defined as the average normal direction of all boundary pixels between region A and region B.

The binary label r is associated with an undirected edge, which is denoted as $r_{A \leftrightarrow B}$ and could be calculated as follows. First, from each boundary pixel p between A and B, we estimate the layer thickness of region A by first finding the shortest image plane vector d_m between p and another region that is not A or B but is connected to A. Then $h_A(p)$ is set to the length of the d_m projected on the normal direction n_p for p. Similarly, they also estimate the layer thickness $h_B(p)$ of B using a similar procedure. Then, pixel p votes for $r_{A \leftrightarrow B}$. It votes for the label "0" if $|\log h_A(p) - \log h_B(p)| < \frac{1}{2} \log M$, indicating that the bit encoded between A and B is "0." On the other hand, if $|\log h_A(p) - \log h_B(p)| \geq \frac{1}{2} \log M$, it votes for the label "1," which indicates that A and B encode bit "1." The final label $r_{A \leftrightarrow B}$ is considered as a majority vote for all boundary pixels.

Overall, LayerCode presents a novel method for embedding data on 3D printed objects with complex shapes. However, its extraction algorithm contains a computationally complex search process. And the fabrication of LayerCode needs a dual extruder 3D printer or a better one.

3.4.3   Slicing Parameters-Based Watermark

Rather than modifying the digital 3D mesh or modifying the shape or internal structure of the 3D printed model, Dogan et al. [63] propose a method of embedding data using 3D model slicing parameters, called G-ID. It should be noted that G-ID does not add anything to the 3D printed object, but it rather uses patterns that appear as byproducts of the slicing, a necessary step in the FDM 3D printing process.

Considering common user-available slicing parameters, G-ID is designed based on the following modifiable parameters. On the bottom surface of the 3D printed object, the resolution and angle in the 3D printing setup are adopted to encode the data. Specifically, these two parameters mentioned above affect the path to infill the bottom surface. The width setting of a single line on the bottom surface determines the final resolution of the bottom layer, while the infilling angle setting of the bottom determines its infilling direction; see Fig. 3.26.

Similarly, for intermediate layers, the resolution and angle can be similarly adjusted by controlling the relevant parameters. The layer height setting can adjust the overall 3D print resolution. Moreover, the angle of layers could be modified by rotating the 3D printing orientation; see Fig. 3.27. Finally, for the internal infill, besides the resolution and angle settings, the infill pattern could be modified, such as a grid or a triangle. All of the above modifiable parameters can be used to embed G-IDs for 3D printed objects, reaching up to about 14 bits of data.

The authors designed a G-ID tagging interface to facilitate the fabrication of G-IDs. This interface can automatically adjust the slicing parameters based on the

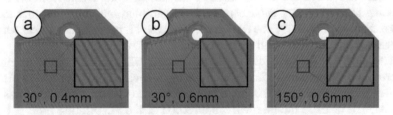

Fig. 3.26   Combination of different line widths and angles of infilling lines

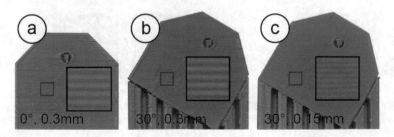

Fig. 3.27   Combination of different layer thicknesses and angles of 3D printing layers

input model and tagging information and use these parameters to slice the target 3D model to generate the G-code file required for 3D printing.

For the printed 3D model with G-ID, the authors first consider the alignment problem when the G-ID is embedded on the bottom surface of the 3D model. Since the user processes the 3D model in the G-ID fabrication interface, the base contour of the model is saved in the database as a binary image. When the user reads the G-ID of the corresponding model, the application displays the saved contours to the user to help them capture the object from the correct angle. Then, some image processing steps are applied to the captured G-ID, such as bilateral filters to smooth out the different color and shadow areas without blurring their borders. In addition, affine transformations are adopted to align the captured image exactly with the target contour; see Fig. 3.28b. Considering that the trajectory of the 3D printed surface has a periodic layout, the width and angle of the 3D printed infilling line can be detected by the Fourier spectrum of the 3D printed surface. Performing a 2D Fourier transform on the captured G-ID, the angle of the bottom infilling line θ can be determined by extracting the slope of the line where the periodic peak is located; see Fig. 3.28c. Then, the magnitude values on this line can then be converted to a one-dimensional array, and the average distance between peaks Δx can be calculated; see Fig. 3.28d. Since the line width d is inversely proportional to Δx, the line width d could also be calculated.

In order to detect the G-ID encoded by the infilling pattern inside the 3D printed object, the authors propose to add a small light source to illuminate the object so that its inside structure could be observed on the bottom surface. Then, for the captured bottom surface of the 3D printed object, the authors use a series of image processing operations to remove the noise caused by the surface bottom line from the image, including image contrast enhancement, Gaussian blur, and adaptive thresholding binarization; see Fig. 3.29. The final processing result is compared with known infill patterns to determine the infill pattern type.

In summary, G-ID provides a way to identify 3D printed objects by precise patterns on their bottom surface, which are byproducts of the 3D printing process. The detection process of G-ID could be implemented by commodity cameras. The advantage of G-ID is the minimal modification of the 3D printing process by the

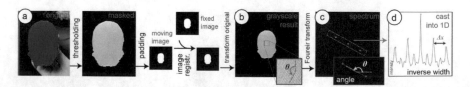

Fig. 3.28 The extraction process of the G-ID embedded in the bottom surface of the 3D printed object. (**a**) The captured outline is registered with the saved bottom surface outline. (**b**) The line angle θ could be calculated by the peak angle in its Fourier transform in (**c**). (**d**) The distance Δx between amplitude peaks is inversely proportional to the line width d

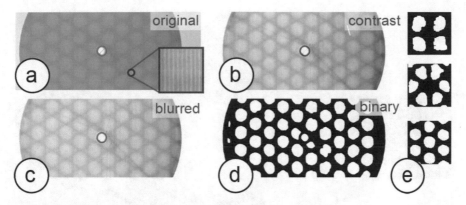

Fig. 3.29 Image processing operation to enhance the infilling pattern inside the 3D printed object. (**a**) The captured G-ID. (**b**) Image contrast enhancement. (**c**) Gaussian blur. (**d**) Adaptive thresholding binarization. (**e**) Compare it with the known infilling pattern templates, including grid, triangles, and trihexagon (from top to bottom)

embedding process, but it also has the disadvantage of a small information capacity. The slower contour matching method is also a limitation for G-ID applications.

3.4.4 Terahertz-Based Watermark

Willis et al. propose InfraStructs [64], an object structure-based tag that can embed information into objects generated through digital fabrication techniques, including 3D printing and computer numerical control (CNC) milling. Because terahertz (THz) imaging can safely penetrate many common materials, the use of terahertz imaging opens up new possibilities for encoding information into the object.

To date, the most common terahertz imaging method is TimeDomain Spectroscopy (TDS) [65], which performs active illumination and measures the signal reflected back from the scene. The TDS system not only measures the time of flight of the signal but also emits broadband pulses of THz radiation and measures the entire reflected signal as a waveform. Each "pixel" in the TDS image contains a time-domain signal whose peak value represents the reflected energy from the outer and inner surfaces of the object in the scene. The entire image forms a volumetric dataset that can be used to slice the object along the depth axis and display the 3D structure.

Figure 3.30 shows a conceptual overview of the encoding, fabrication, imaging, and decoding processes of InfraStructs. Notice that the ability of InfraStructs to encode information comes from the different reflective transmission properties to terahertz due to the different fabrication materials. Specifically, the authors model the material properties of the tags based on two factors: reflected radiation— the amount of radiation reflected at the interface between the two materials, and

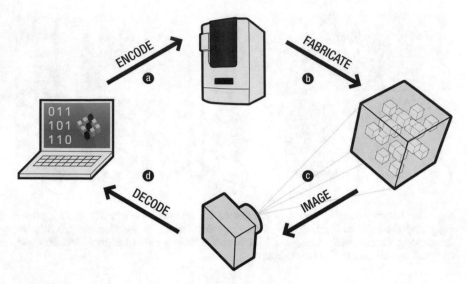

Fig. 3.30 InfraStructs are manufactured by (**a**) encoding information into a digital model and then (**b**) be fabricated to one physical object. The internal volume of this object is (**c**) imaged by the terahertz and (**d**) decoded into meaningful information

transmitted radiation—the amount of radiation transmitted after attenuation through the material. Assuming that the terahertz signal is incident vertically, the amount of reflected radiation r is calculated using the refractive index n_1 of the current material and the refractive index n_2 of the material into which the radiation will enter:

$$r = \left(\frac{n_1 - n_2}{n_1 + n_2} \right)^2 . \tag{3.107}$$

Then the unreflected radiation will continue to pass through the next material, where the amount of radiation t through the material is given by the following equation:

$$t = se^{-ab}, \tag{3.108}$$

where a is the material absorption coefficient, b is the thickness of the material, and s is the input radiation. The signal returned from the last layer encounters the most signal loss. For a structure with i layers, the end layer will experience $4i - 3$ signal losses due to reflections at the interface of each layer and $2i - 2$ signal losses due to attenuation through each layer.

The InfraStruct label design should aim to maximize t by selecting materials with low absorption coefficients and minimal thickness in the terahertz region. The choice of r value should be based on the number of layers. When fewer layers are used, the greater the refractive index difference between the materials, the stronger the signal can be produced. And when more layers are used, a smaller refractive

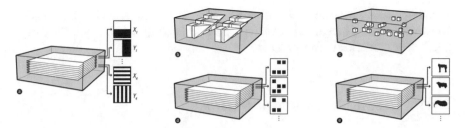

Fig. 3.31 Prototype designs for InfraStruct tags including (**a**) gray code, (**b**) geometric, (**c**) random void, (**d**) matrix, and (**e**) visual designs

index should be used so that most of the signal can reach the end layers of the InfraStruct.

InfraStructs tags can encode information in a variety of ways. The authors have designed five prototypes of InfraStructs that demonstrate different types of information and encoding methods; see Fig. 3.31. Each tag design is tailored to a specific terahertz imaging configuration and application scenario, with unique advantages and limitations. For either tag design, the overall process of detection and decoding is similar.

Following terahertz detection, the authors designed decoding algorithms to convert the THz time-domain data detected from InfraStructs into the spatial domain and decode the tag structure. This conversion process is mainly the transformation of time-domain data to "optical distance," which is defined as the product of the distance the radiation propagates and the refractive index of the medium it propagates through. The optical distance d can be converted to the actual distance by the following equation:

$$d = \frac{tnc}{2}, \tag{3.109}$$

where t is the time required for the radiation to travel a distance, n is the refractive index of the medium, and c is the constant speed of light in a vacuum. Considering that the time-domain data is based on terahertz reflection detection, the final value is divided by 2 to be the real-world distance.

When the terahertz signal propagates from the air to the shell, its reflection causes the first negative peak to appear. Then, as the signal leaves the shell, it generates a positive peak. This peak feature can be used as a starting point p to search for more peaks inside the InfraStructs tag. Depending on the optical thickness of the material used to make the InfraStructs, the negative peak is searched iteratively at a given offset from p. If a peak above a given threshold is found, it indicates that InfraStructs has a bit "1" at that location. This process is repeated until all layers are decoded as bit sequences representing the embedded signal.

In summary, InfraStructs provides a novel scheme for encoding and decoding information inside physical objects and yields possible applications for position encoding, pose estimation, object recognition, data storage, and authentication. However, terahertz imaging is not yet a popular technology, which limits the current application scenarios of InfraStructs.

3.4.5   Thermal Image-Based Watermark

Okada et al. [56] propose a far-infrared light technique to read information embedded in real objects non-destructively. With 3D printing technology, they can create fine structures inside objects as watermarks that cannot be observed from the outside, embedding copyright information into solid objects generated by 3D printers. The information is then read nondestructively from inside the solid object by using far-infrared light during the extraction process.

The fine structure of the information embedded inside the object could be used to form many different shapes. An effective way to protect security codes is to form fine structures, for example, by encoding watermark information into cavity patterns. Specifically, the watermark is first converted into a bit stream, and then "1" and "0" bits can be represented by the presence and absence of the cavity at the specified location; see Fig. 3.32.

In a similar work, non-destructive reading of information embedded in 3D printed objects can be done by techniques such as x-ray, ultrasound, far infrared, etc. However, the authors believe that techniques applicable to 3D printing, in general, should be safe, practical, easy to use, and reasonably priced. Therefore, as shown in Fig. 3.32, they propose a method for non-destructive reading of the internal messages of 3D printed objects using thermal imaging cameras. The surface of the object is heated by illumination, and then, heat flows from the surface of the object to the interior of the object from top to bottom. Since the thermal conductivity of

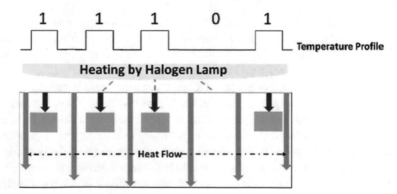

Fig. 3.32 Schematic diagram of heat conduction in a 3D printed object with cavities. The location where the cavity is located has lower heat, so the thermal image can be used to determine if there is a cavity at that location

the region with cavities is lower than that of the region without cavities, the heat is blocked by these small cavities, therefore. Therefore, the surface temperature above the area with cavities is slightly higher than the other areas, and the temperature distribution on the surface can accurately reflect the cavity distribution inside the 3D printed object.

The algorithm for embedded cavities for flat samples is very simple. For curved samples, the hole size needs to be changed according to the curvature of the surface and the cavity layout.

In the extraction, two halogen lamps are placed on the left and right sides of the sample for heating. The two lamps are positioned to irradiate the sample at the same angle and at the same distance. They then determined whether the embedded bits were "0" or "1" based on whether the temperature difference was greater than a threshold value.

In summary, the proposed method reads the message embedded inside the 3D printed object by analyzing the image of the temperature distribution on the surface of the object captured with thermal imaging. However, this method can only be applied to 3D printed objects with a specific shape.

3.4.6   Reflectance-Based Watermark

Suzuki et al. [57] propose that information can be embedded invisibly into a 3D printed object by creating patterns within the object's shell that have high reflectivity to near infrared light (NIR light). This information can then be read non-destructively from inside the real object by analyzing the NIR light and the reflected image of the object captured by the camera.

Figure 3.33 is a schematic representation of the structure inside the 3D printed object, with the modified fine structure represented as small protrusions inside. The binary information of the watermark is then represented by the presence or the absence of small protrusions at the specified locations. With a dual extrusion head 3D printer, the protrusions in the inner part of the 3D printed object are made of a highly reflective material, while in other areas they are filled with a resin material. Near-infrared light usually passes through the resin material; therefore, if a near-infrared light source and a camera are set up, as shown in Fig. 3.34, it is possible to obtain a projected image of the interior of the 3D printed object and read out the embedded information.

The experimental results show that the embedded information can be read out clearly when the size of the fine structure with high reflectivity is more than 2 mm. However, this solution has to use a dual extrusion head 3D printer and is affected by the color of the 3D printed object surface.

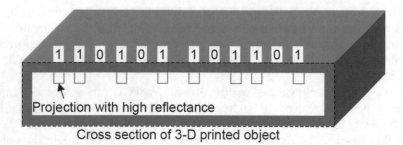

Fig. 3.33 Schematic diagram of the internal structure of a 3D printed object embedded with a watermark. Where the location representing the bit "1" is filled inside using a high reflectivity material

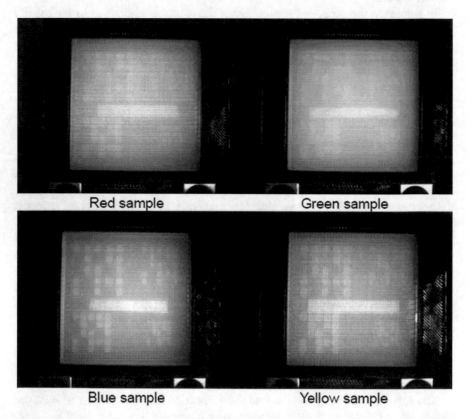

Fig. 3.34 Images of the interior of 3D printed objects taken with the NIR camera, where the blue and yellow objects have clearer images than the red and green ones

3.4.7 Printing Speed-Based Watermark

ElSayed et al. [60] proposed a watermark embedding scheme to embed messages into 3D printed objects by controlling the parameters of 3D printing, i.e., print speed parameters. Specifically, they first generate a binary bit sequence containing the desired message, and these bit strings are mapped to a region on the surface of the 3D model. The bit sequence consists of R rows and C columns, where $R \times C = n$. Figure 3.35 shows a one-dimensional alternating bit sequence, its original image of the encoded surface, and preprocessed height data. The values of R and C can be adjusted to achieve a higher information capacity. Then, in the G-code segment corresponding to this area, they modify the print speed therein so that the print speed for the "0" bits is different from the print speed for the "1" bits. In the implementation, the 3D printing speed for the "0" position was set to 60 mm/s and the speed for the "1" position was set to 7 mm/s.

After the model is 3D printed, an optical profile profilometer is used to obtain surface profile data (i.e., height data) from the 3D part and analyze it to decode the embedded information. First, the input surface height data is equalized using the Contrast-Limited Adaptive Histogram Equalization (CLAHE) algorithm [61] to better capture local variations in height. The image is then blurred using a Gaussian filter with a standard deviation of 7 pixels to remove high-frequency noise from the image. They assume that it is possible to know in advance which regions of the

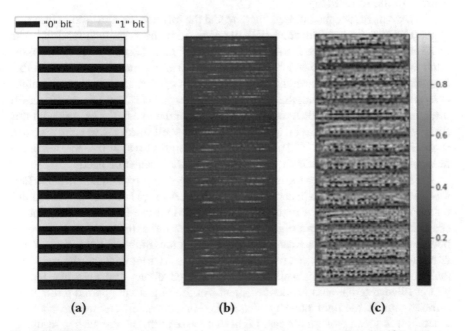

Fig. 3.35 Different representations of the coding regions used to train the classifier: (a) one-dimensional embedded bit strings, (b) original images, and (c) normalized height data

surface encode the bits and that the image can be further divided into regions for each bit embedding. In practice, this assumption can be justified by asserting that all embedding messages are applied to the same regions of the part surface and carry bit information in some regular pattern on the surface. The classifier is then trained based on this data and an 80% accuracy of watermark extraction is obtained.

In summary, this work is less demanding and easier to implement than similar 3D printing watermarking schemes in terms of printing equipment. However, it requires an optical profilometer to perform the extraction process. And the extraction accuracy needs to be improved.

3.4.8   Infrared-Based Watermark

Dogan et al. propose a simple, low-cost method for embedding inconspicuous tags into 3D objects, called InfraredTags [62], which are generally implemented as 2D tags or barcodes that are imperceptible to the naked eye and could be 3D printed as part of the object. And during the extraction, InfraredTags can be quickly detected by low-cost near-infrared cameras. The fabrication of InfraredTags requires 3D printing the object with the infrared transmitting filaments with air gaps for data embedding. When using a dual extruding head 3D printer for InfraredTags fabrication, the infrared opaque material could be used to further improve the contrast of the InfraredTags.

First, we introduce the infrared filament and the infrared camera used in Infrared-Tags. The authors used infrared (IR) filament from the manufacturer 3dk.berlin ($\sim$\$5.86/100g), which is made from polylactic acid (PLA), one of the most common fused deposition modeling (FDM) 3D printing materials. Although that filament is slightly translucent black, it would look opaque after 3D printing multi-layered objects. Considering that almost all commercial cameras have an IR cut-off filter, in order to capture IR light, the authors recommend using a camera with this filter removed or a separate image sensor. Off-the-shelf inexpensive cameras, such as the Raspberry Pi NoIR (\$20), can detect wavelengths up to $800 \sim 850$ nm in the near-infrared range, which is sufficient for the authors' detection needs.

As shown in Fig. 3.36, the authors propose two approaches for InfraredTags fabrication, one for single-material printing (IR PLA only) and the other for multi-material printing (IR PLA + regular PLA). Both options use IR PLA to 3D print the shape structure of the target object. For the former, the authors use the difference between air gaps and filled areas to embed information. Since IR light transmission is reduced by 45% per *mm* of IR filament, under IR illumination, the light first penetrates the IR filament wall of the 3D printed object and then hits the air gap or filled internal area inside the object. As the object is captured through the infrared camera, the light intensity of each pixel is reduced differently depending on whether it is located on an air gap. Light that passes through the air gap results in brighter pixels because they penetrate less material than other light. This difference

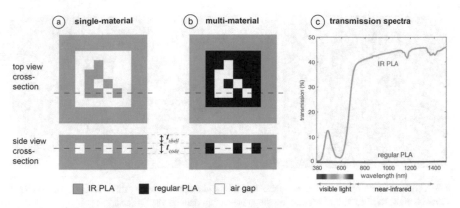

Fig. 3.36 Two methods of generating InfraredTags: (**a**) using a single IR PLA and (**b**) using IR PLA and regular PLA. (**c**) The transmission spectrum of the IR PLA and regular PLA

in intensity in the resulting image is sufficient to convert the detected air gap and filled areas into embedded information.

For the dual-material fabrication approach, the data is encoded by regular PLA and air gaps. Specifically, when the user captures an image, the air gaps would appear as brighter pixels because they transmit infrared light. In contrast, the regular PLA filament would appear as a darker pixel because it is almost completely opaque in the infrared region, which results in a higher contrast ratio than the single-material fabrication mentioned above. To facilitate the fabrication of InfraredTags, the authors also built a user interface that could integrate common tags (QR codes) with object geometries, making them available for 3D printing as InfraredTags.

To detect InfraredTags embedded on 3D printed objects, the authors built an additional imaging module, which can be easily attached to an existing cell phone. The module contains an infrared camera (Raspberry Pi NoIR) that can see infrared light because it removes the infrared cut-off filter that would normally block infrared light in a normal camera. In addition, a visible cutoff filter was added to the camera to remove the interference of visible light and 2 IR LEDs (940 nm) were adopted to illuminate objects in the dark environment. For the images captured by the imaging module, the authors further performed image processing steps to increase the contrast to be read robustly, including a contrast limited adaptive histogram equalization (CLAHE) filter, Gaussian blur, and adaptive threshold binarization. Finally, the final black-and-white binary image containing the embedding information is obtained; see Fig. 3.37.

The authors' evaluation shows that InfraredTags can be detected with almost no near-infrared illumination ($0.2\,lux$) at distances of up to 250 cm. And various applications can be designed based on InfraredTags for object tracking and embedding metadata for augmented reality and tangible interaction. However, this solution is constrained by the IR filament color and requires a flat surface on the 3D printed object. And for HCI applications, it is difficult to get inexperienced users to align the invisible embedding position to the camera.

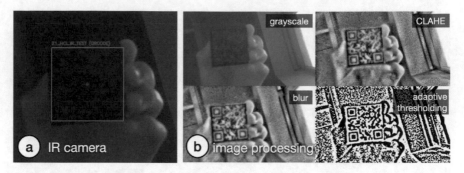

Fig. 3.37 Image processing to enhance the QR code embedded as InfraredTags. (**a**) Infrared camera view. (**b**) Individual processing steps needed to decode the QR code

References

1. Zhou, Hang and Chen, Kejiang and Zhang, Weiming and Yao, Yuanzhi and Yu, Nenghai, "Distortion design for secure adaptive 3-d mesh steganography", *IEEE Transactions on Multimedia*, vol. 21, no. 6, pp.1384–1398, 2018, IEEE.
2. Ohbuchi, Ryutarou and Masuda, Hiroshi and Aono, Masaki, "Watermaking three-dimensional polygonal models", *Proceedings of the fifth ACM international conference on Multimedia*, pp.261–272, 1997.
3. Wyvill, Brian and Guy, Andrew and Galin, Eric, "Extending the CSG tree. warping, blending and boolean operations in an implicit surface modeling system", *Computer Graphics Forum*, Online Library, vol. 18, no. 2, pp.149–158, 1999.
4. Benedens, Oliver, "Geometry-based watermarking of 3D models", 1999, *FRAUNHOFER INST FOR COMPUTER GRAPHICS DARMSTADT (GERMANY) VIRTUAL REALITY . . . .*
5. Wagner, Michael G, "Robust watermarking of polygonal meshes", *Proceedings Geometric Modeling and Processing* 2000. Theory and Applications, pp.201–208, 2000, IEEE.
6. Benedens, Oliver, "Robust watermarking and affine registration of 3d meshes", *International Workshop on Information Hiding*, pp.177–195, 2002, Springer.
7. Zafeiriou, Stefanos and Tefas, Anastasios and Pitas, Ioannis, "Blind robust watermarking schemes for copyright protection of 3D mesh objects", *IEEE Transactions on Visualization and Computer Graphics*, vol. 11, no. 5, pp. 596–607, 2005, IEEE.
8. Wang, Wei-Bo and Zheng, Guo-Qin and Yong, Jun-Hai and Gu, He-Jin, "A numerically stable fragile watermarking scheme for authenticating 3D models", *Computer-Aided Design*, vol. 40, no. 5, pp.634–645, 2008, Elsevier.
9. Ai, QS and Liu, Q and Zhou, ZD and Yang, La and Xie, SQ, "A new digital watermarking scheme for 3D triangular mesh models", *Signal Processing*, vol. 89, no. 11, pp. 2159–2170, 2009, Elsevier.
10. Wang, Kai and Lavoué, Guillaume and Denis, Florence and Baskurt, Atilla, "Robust and blind mesh watermarking based on volume moments", *Computers & Graphics*, vol. 35, no. 1, pp.1–19, 2011, Elsevier.
11. Luo, Ming and Bors, Adrian G, "Surface-preserving robust watermarking of 3-D shapes", *IEEE Transactions on Image Processing*, vol. 20, no. 10, pp.2813–2826, 2011, IEEE.
12. Singh, Law Kumar and Chaudhry, Deepak and Varshney, Gopalji, "A novel approach of 3d object watermarking algorithm using vertex normal", *International Journal of Computer Applications*, vol. 60, no. 5, 2012, Citeseer.
13. Wu, Hao-Tian and Cheung, Yiu-Ming, "A fragile watermarking scheme for 3D meshes", *Proceedings of the 7th workshop on Multimedia and security*, pp.117–124, 2005.

14. Molaei, Amir Masoud and Ebrahimnezhad, Hossein and Sedaaghi, Mohammad Hossein, "Robust and blind 3D mesh watermarking in spatial domain based on faces categorization and sorting", *3D Research*, vol. 7, no. 2, pp. 1–18, 2016, Springer.
15. Yang, Ying and Pintus, Ruggero and Rushmeier, Holly and Ivrissimtzis, Ioannis, "A 3D steganalytic algorithm and steganalysis-resistant watermarking", *IEEE transactions on visualization and computer graphics*, vol. 23, no. 2, pp.1002–1013, 2016, IEEE.
16. Bhattacharyya, Anil, "On a measure of divergence between two multinomial populations", *Sankhyā: the Indian journal of statistics*, pp. 401–406, 1946, JSTOR.
17. Cho, Jae-Won and Prost, Rmy and Jung, Ho-Youl, "An oblivious watermarking for 3-D polygonal meshes using distribution of vertex norms", *IEEE Transactions on Signal Processing*, vol. 55, no. 1, pp. 142–155, 2006, IEEE.
18. Bors, Adrian G and Luo, Ming, "Optimized 3D watermarking for minimal surface distortion", *IEEE Transactions on Image Processing*, vol. 22, no. 5, pp.1822–1835, 2012, IEEE.
19. Levenberg, Kenneth, "A method for the solution of certain non-linear problems in least squares", *Quarterly of applied mathematics*, vol. 2, no. 2, pp.164–168, 1944.
20. Marquardt, Donald W, "An algorithm for least-squares estimation of nonlinear parameters", *Journal of the society for Industrial and Applied Mathematics*, vol. 11, no. 2, pp.431–441, 1963, SIAM.
21. Rolland-Neviere, Xavier and Doërr, Gwenaël and Alliez, Pierre, "Triangle surface mesh watermarking based on a constrained optimization framework", *IEEE transactions on information forensics and security*, vol. 9, no. 9, pp.1491–1501, 2014, IEEE.
22. Cayre, François and Rondao-Alface, Patrice and Schmitt, Francis and Macq, Benoıt and Maitre, Henri, "Application of spectral decomposition to compression and watermarking of 3D triangle mesh geometry", *Signal Processing: Image Communication*, vol. 18, no. 4, pp.309–319, 2008, Elsevier.
23. Kai, Wang and Guillaume, Lavoue and Florence, Denis and Atilla, Baskurt, "Hierarchical watermarking of semiregular meshes based on wavelet transform", *IEEE Transactions on Information Forensics and Security*, vol. 3, no. 4, pp.620–634, 2008, IEEE.
24. Ryutarou, Ohbuchi and Hiroshi, Masuda, "Managing CAD data as a multimedia data type using digital watermarking", *Proc. IFIP TC5 WG5.2 Workshop Knowledge Intensive CAD to Knowledge Intensive Engineering*, pp.103–116, 2001, Springer.
25. Zaid, A Ouled and Hachani, Meha and Puech, William, "Wavelet-based high-capacity watermarking of 3-D irregular meshes", *Multimedia Tools and Applications*, vol. 74, no. 15, pp.5897–5915, 2015, Springer.
26. Hamidi, Mohamed and Haziti, El Mohamed and Cherifi, Hocine and Aboutajdine, Driss, "A robust blind 3-d mesh watermarking based on wavelet transform for copyright protection", *International Conference on Advanced Technologies for Signal and Image Processing*, pp.1–6, 2017, IEEE.
27. Liu, Yang and Prabhakaran, Balakrishnan and Guo, Xiaohu, "Spectral Watermarking for Parameterized Surfaces", *IEEE Transactions on Information Forensics and Security*, vol. 7, no. 5, pp.1459–1471, 2012, IEEE.
28. Liu, Yang and Prabhakaran, Balakrishnan and Guo, Xiaohu, "A robust spectral approach for blind watermarking of manifold surfaces," *ACM Workshop on Multimedia and Security*, pp.43–52, 2008, ACM.
29. Medimegh, Nassima and Belaid, Samir and Atri, Mohamed and Werghi, Naoufel, "3D mesh watermarking using salient points", *Multimedia Tools and Applications*, vol. 77, no. 24, pp.32287–32309, 2018, Springer.
30. Narendra, Modigari and Valarmathi, ML and Anbarasi, L Jani, "Optimization of 3D Triangular Mesh Watermarking Using ACO-Weber's Law", *KSII Transactions on Internet and Information Systems (TIIS)*, vol. 14, no. 10, pp.4042–4059, 2020, Korean Society for Internet Information.
31. Wang, F., Zhou, H., Fang, H., Zhang, W. & Yu, N. Deep 3D mesh watermarking with self-adaptive robustness. *Cybersecurity*. **5**, 1–14 (2022)

32. Feng, Wang and Hang, Zhou and Weiming, Zhang and Nenghai, Yu, "Neural Watermarking for 3D Morphable Models", *International Conference on Artificial Intelligence and Security (ICAIS)*, Communications in Computer and Information Science, Springer. vol. 1588, 2022.

33. Ranjan, Anurag and Bolkart, Timo and Sanyal, Soubhik and Black, Michael J, "Generating 3D faces using convolutional mesh autoencoders", *Proceedings of the European Conference on Computer Vision (ECCV)*, pp.704–720, 2018.

34. Szegedy, Christian and Zaremba, Wojciech and Sutskever, Ilya and Bruna, Joan and Erhan, Dumitru and Goodfellow, Ian and Fergus, Rob, "Intriguing properties of neural networks", *International Conference on Learning Representations (ICLR)*, 2014.

35. Goodfellow, Ian J and Shlens, Jonathon and Szegedy, Christian, "Explaining and harnessing adversarial examples", *International Conference on Learning Representations (ICLR)*, 2014.

36. Luo, Xiyang and Zhan, Ruohan and Chang, Huiwen and Yang, Feng and Milanfar, Peyman, "Distortion agnostic deep watermarking", *Proceedings of the IEEE/CVF Conference on Computer Vision and Pattern Recognition (CVPR)*, pp.13548–13557, 2020.

37. Feng, Wang and Hang, Zhou and Han, Fang and Weiming, Zhang and Nenghai, Yu, "Deep 3D Mesh Watermarking with Self-Adaptive Robustness", *arXiv*, 2021.

38. Romero, Javier and Tzionas, Dimitrios and Black, Michael J, "Embodied hands: modeling and capturing hands and bodies together", *ACM Transactions on Graphics (TOG)*, vol. 36, no. 6, pp.1–17, 2017, ACM New York, NY, USA.

39. Kaiming, He and Xiangyu, Zhang and Shaoqing, Ren and Jian, Sun, "Deep residual learning for image recognition", *Proceedings of the IEEE conference on computer vision and pattern recognition (CVPR)*, pp.770–778, 2016.

40. Taubin, Gabriel, "Geometric Signal Processing on Polygonal Meshes", *21st Annual Conference of the European Association for Computer Graphics, Eurographics*, 2000.

41. Mariani, Giorgio and Cosmo, Luca and Bronstein, Alexander M and Rodolà, Emanuele, "Generating Adversarial Surfaces via Band-Limited Perturbations", *Computer Graphics Forum*, vol. 39, no. 5, pp.253–264, 2020.

42. Fakhri, Torkhani and Kai, Wang and Jean-Marc, Chassery, "A Curvature Tensor Distance for Mesh Visual Quality Assessment", *Computer Vision and Graphics - International Conference*, vol. 7594, pp.253–263, 2012.

43. Nayar, S., Krishnan, G., Grossberg, M. & Raskar, R. Fast Separation of Direct and Global Components of a Scene Using High Frequency Illumination. *ACM Trans. Graph.*. **25**, 935-944 (2006,7), https://doi.org/10.1145/1141911.1141977

44. Li, D., Nair, A., Nayar, S. & Zheng, C. AirCode: Unobtrusive Physical Tags for Digital Fabrication. *Proceedings Of The 30th Annual ACM Symposium On User Interface Software And Technology*. pp. 449–460 (2017), https://doi.org/10.1145/3126594.3126635

45. Chen, Y., Ma, Z., Zhou, H. & Zhang, W. 3D Print-Scan Resilient Localized Mesh Watermarking. *2021 IEEE International Workshop On Information Forensics And Security (WIFS)*. pp. 1–6 (2021)

46. Mahdian, B. & Saic, S. Blind Authentication Using Periodic Properties of Interpolation. *IEEE Transactions On Information Forensics And Security*. **3**, 529–538 (2008)

47. Hou, J., Kim, D. & Lee, H. Blind 3D Mesh Watermarking for 3D Printed Model by Analyzing Layering Artifact. *IEEE Transactions On Information Forensics And Security*. **12**, 2712–2725 (2017)

48. Delmotte, A., Tanaka, K., Kubo, H., Funatomi, T. & Mukaigawa, Y. Blind Watermarking for 3-D Printed Objects by Locally Modifying Layer Thickness. *IEEE Transactions On Multimedia*. **22**, 2780–2791 (2020)

49. Maia, H., Li, D., Yang, Y. & Zheng, C. LayerCode: Optical Barcodes for 3D Printed Shapes. *ACM Trans. Graph.*. **38** (2019,7), https://doi.org/10.1145/3306346.3322960

50. Yamazaki, S., Kagami, S. & Mochimaru, M. Extracting Watermark from 3D Prints. *2014 22nd International Conference On Pattern Recognition*. pp. 4576–4581 (2014)

51. Ohbuchi, R., Takahashi, S., Miyazawa, T. & Mukaiyama, A. Watermarking 3D Polygonal Meshes in the Mesh Spectral Domain. *Proceedings Of Graphics Interface* 2001. pp. 9–17 (2001)

52. Praun, E., Hoppe, H. & Finkelstein, A. Robust Mesh Watermarking. *Proceedings Of The 26th Annual Conference On Computer Graphics And Interactive Techniques*. pp. 49–56 (1999), https://doi.org/10.1145/311535.311540

53. Levoy, M., Pulli, K., Curless, B., Rusinkiewicz, S., Koller, D., Pereira, L., Ginzton, M., Anderson, S., Davis, J., Ginsberg, J., Shade, J. & Fulk, D. The Digital Michelangelo Project: 3D Scanning of Large Statues. *Proceedings Of The 27th Annual Conference On Computer Graphics And Interactive Techniques*. pp. 131–144 (2000), https://doi.org/10.1145/344779.344849

54. Béla Bollobás, A. Modern Graph Theory. *Springer Science+Business Media New York* 1998. XIV, 394, https://doi.org/10.1007/978-1-4612-0619-4

55. Besl, P. & McKay, N. A method for registration of 3-D shapes. *IEEE Transactions On Pattern Analysis And Machine Intelligence*. **14**, 239–256 (1992)

56. Okada, A., Silapasuphakornwong, P., Suzuki, M., Torii, H., Takashima, Y. & Uehira, K. Non-destructively reading out information embedded inside real objects by using far-infrared light. *Applications Of Digital Image Processing XXXVIII*. 9599 pp. 849–855 (2015), https://doi.org/10.1117/12.2189486

57. Suzuki, M., Matumoto, T., Takashima, Y., Torii, H. & Uehira, K. Information Hiding Inside 3-D Printed Objects by Forming High Reflectance Projections. *Proceedings Of The International Conference On Video And Image Processing*. pp. 146–150 (2017), https://doi.org/10.1145/3177404.3177455

58. Delmotte, A., Tanaka, K., Kubo, H., Funatomi, T. & Mukaigawa, Y. Blind Watermarking for 3-D Printed Objects using Surface Norm Distribution. *2018 Joint 7th International Conference On Informatics, Electronics & Vision (ICIEV) And 2018 2nd International Conference On Imaging, Vision & Pattern Recognition (icIVPR)*. pp. 282–288 (2018)

59. Yamamoto, H. & Sano, K. A Watermarking Method for Embedding into the External Shapes of Objects. 2018 International Symposium On Information Theory And Its Applications (ISITA). pp. 321–325 (2018)

60. ElSayed, K., Dachowicz, A. & Panchal, J. Information Embedding in Additive Manufacturing through Printing Speed Control. *Proceedings Of The* 2021 Workshop On Additive Manufacturing (3D Printing) Security. pp. 31–37 (2021), https://doi.org/10.1145/3462223.3485623

61. Pizer, S., Amburn, E., Austin, J., Cromartie, R., Geselowitz, A., Greer, T., Ter Haar Romeny, B., Zimmerman, J. & Zuiderveld, K. Adaptive histogram equalization and its variations. *Computer Vision, Graphics, And Image Processing*. **39**, 355–368 (1987), https://www.sciencedirect.com/science/article/pii/S0734189X8780186X

62. Dogan, M., Taka, A., Lu, M., Zhu, Y., Kumar, A., Gupta, A. & Mueller, S. InfraredTags: Embedding Invisible AR Markers and Barcodes Using Low-Cost, Infrared-Based 3D Printing and Imaging Tools. *Proceedings Of The* 2022 CHI Conference On Human Factors In Computing Systems. (2022), https://doi.org/10.1145/3491102.3501951

63. Dogan, M., Faruqi, F., Churchill, A., Friedman, K., Cheng, L., Subramanian, S. & Mueller, S. G-ID: Identifying 3D Prints Using Slicing Parameters. *Proceedings Of The* 2020 CHI Conference On Human Factors In Computing Systems. pp. 1–13 (2020), https://doi.org/10.1145/3313831.3376202

64. Willis, K. & Wilson, A. InfraStructs: Fabricating Information inside Physical Objects for Imaging in the Terahertz Region. *ACM Trans. Graph.*. **32** (2013,7), https://doi.org/10.1145/2461912.2461936

65. Auston, D. & Cheung, K. Coherent time-domain far-infrared spectroscopy. *Journal Of The Optical Society Of America B-optical Physics*. **2** pp. 606–612 (1985)

Chapter 4
3D Mesh Steganography

Abstract In this chapter, we categorize the steganography techniques into four domains, i.e., two-state domain, LSB plane domain, permutation domain, and transform domain.

4.1 Two-State Steganography

In the early research on 3D mesh data hiding, steganography and watermarking were regarded as the same technique by researchers. A large number of steganography methods for meshes create multiple two-state domains and embed messages by aligning together the state information and message bit.

4.1.1 Macro Embedding Procedure Model

Cayre and Macq [1] are the first to propose a 3D mesh steganography method. The method requires two steps: first, build a list of mesh triangles that will contain the payload. The operation is driven by the secret key of the steganography process. Second, each so-called *admissible* triangle of the list is modified or unmodified according to the binary symbol it has to convey. The last operation is called the macro embedding procedure (MEP).

1. **Listing triangles to be processed.** The triangle list is built according to the scheme of Fig. 4.1. The starting triangle is determined based on the specific geometric features (see below). The next triangle in the list is either the first (its new entry edge is $\overline{v_i v_j}$) or the second (its new entry edge is $\overline{v_i v_k}$) in clockwise order, depending on the bit value of the key. The length of the key must be as long as the allowed triangle list required to deliver the payload. The key can also be the seed of the binary pseudo-noise sequence generator. A path to access a triangle is called a stencil.

H. Zhou et al., *Triangle Mesh Watermarking and Steganography*,
https://doi.org/10.1007/978-981-19-7720-6_4

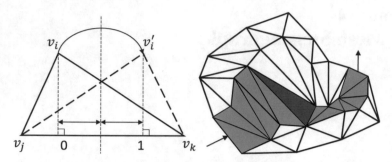

Fig. 4.1 (left) Diagram of the MEP. The triangle is viewed from the topology perspective, with the entry edge ($\overline{v_j v_k}$) related to the current message bit to be inserted and the two candidate exit edges ($\overline{v_i v_j}$ and $\overline{v_i v_k}$). The exit edges are ordered in a clockwise manner. (right) A polygonal mesh, shown with the TSPS path (gray). Each face represents a one-bit message, with the MEP shown in black. Figure from [1]

2. **MEP.** Each triangle is considered a two-state object. The state of the triangle is defined by the position of the orthogonal projection of the triangle vertex v_i on the entry edge $\overline{v_j v_k}$, and the position is denoted as $P(v_i)$. Then the $\overline{v_j v_k}$ interval is divided into two subsets $\mathbb{S}_0$ and $\mathbb{S}_1$. If $P(v_i) \in \mathbb{S}_0$, then the triangle is considered to be in the 0 state; otherwise, with $P(v_i) \in \mathbb{S}_1$, the triangle is in the 1 state. If the $\mathbb{S}_0$ and $\mathbb{S}_1$ subsets contain intervals defined as fractions of $\overline{v_j v_k}$, the state is invariant to the affine transformation of the mesh. To set a triangle to the $i (i = 0, 1)$ state, two cases are as follows:

$$P(v_i) \in \mathbb{S}_i : \text{No modification needs to be processed,}$$
$$P(v_i) \notin \mathbb{S}_i : v_i \text{ must move toward } v_i' \text{ so that } P(v_i') \text{ is in } \mathbb{S}_i. \tag{4.1}$$

With an affine transformation, the mapping of v_i to v_i' must be invertible and invariant. Furthermore, $|v_i - v_i'|$ must be small enough to avoid visual degradation of the mesh, but large enough to allow accurate payload detection. The steganography space is divided into subintervals and use the interval boundaries as symmetry axes. The v_i to v_i' mapping is symmetric on the nearest axis orthogonal to $\overline{v_j v_k}$ that intersects the boundary of the nearest subinterval to which it belongs.

A string containing bits indicating whether changes are required for each admissible triangle allows the data hider to retrieve an unmarked perfect copy of the original mesh, and this string is called the erasing key. It can be seen as a hash of a mesh parameterized by a key and payload. When the random selection of triangles results in an admissible triangle, it is easy to avoid it by inserting some hidden information into it. Depending on the difference in the bit values to be hidden and the initial state of the triangle, the triangle can be geometrically modified or not. If one wants to be able to restore the original state of the admissible triangle, one needs to store an erasing bit for each bit of the payload: if the state of the triangle

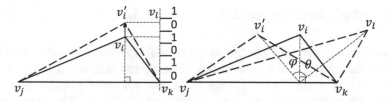

Fig. 4.2 Extending domain of MLEP (left). Rotating domain of MLEP (right). Figure from [3]

changes, the erasing bit is set to 1, otherwise it is set to 0. Therefore, the erasing key is constructed during embedding and is exactly the same size as the payload size.

To avoid peeling, first, determine the method used to move in the cell. In this case, the criteria for selecting the next cell to add to the stencil are not based on topology peeling. The rule is geometrical which uses the clockwise difference between the two exit edges, and one always leaves the cell using the exit chosen by the key. This way one does not need to peel off the stencil anymore and it is more secure. When choosing the next triangle, one uses a general rule that may be overridden by detailed exceptions. The rule is to always leave the current triangle with the exit edge corresponding to the current key bit. If the key bit is equal to 1, one uses the first edge, and if it equals 0, one uses the second edge. It is a geometric replacement (i.e., stay on the stencil) of the topological rules in the original TSPS [2] method. To solve problems caused by topological singularities of meshes (e.g., holes), the so-called steering edge is utilized to keep the stencil as long as possible. In fact, steering corresponds only to topological singularities of the cover mesh. In the classic TSPS algorithm, the template is strictly topologically separated from the mesh, and the stencil frontier is materialized by creating a list of already-used points. At each iteration, the vertex v_i used to hide a point that was either modified by or not by an MEP is added to this list of points. This list contains points corresponding to hidden embedding bits, which cannot be moved again during the embedding process. Triangles are not admissible if the paths generated during the embedding of the key later choose forbidden points in this list again. In this case, it is quite convenient to go through the mesh using the key without considering the triangles used for embedding or decoding. Since both sides of the algorithm are symmetric, this list is maintained on both the embedding and decoding sides.

Besides, a metric for measuring the perceptibility is designed by the signal-to-noise ratio (SNR), which is dedicated to regularly sampled signals, and Hausdorff distance, which is based on an infinite norm. In summary, the method is robust to affine transformations and vertex reordering. Its theoretical upper-bound capacity is 1 bit per vertex. However, the algorithm has neither a large enough capacity nor computational efficiency because it has visible embedding modifications and requires too much preprocessing time to create the stencil. Because of the large modifications, it cannot resist steganalysis.

4.1.2 Multi-level Embedding Procedure Model

The method proposed by Cayre and Macq demonstrates the possibility of 3D mesh steganography with the ability of tracing all available triangles, yet it suffers from two drawbacks: limited data capacity and heavy computational complexity. For capacity, the naive quantization index modulation (QIM) can only embed one bit per vertex. For complexity, generating the sequence table requires a lot of search and comparison operations to decide the next triangle. These operations are the main cause of the problem. The stencil generation is costly with exponential growth when the filling rate reaches 80%, which makes it impossible for embedding data in larger 3D mesh models.

To solve the above problem, Wang and Cheng [3] proposed an efficient steganography technique based on a substitutive blind procedure in the spatial domain, as well as the multi-level embed procedure (MLEP), which includes sliding, extending, and rotating domains to embed messages based on the geometric properties of the message vertices. To quickly obtain the processing order of vertices, a hierarchical data structure is created based on the hierarchical kd-tree [37], triangular neighbor lists, and advanced jump strategy. Every level of MLEP can be used singly or all simultaneously, since these approaches are independent. In MLEP, the information is embedded by modifying the message vertex based on geometrical properties; it guides the change of the position of the orthogonal projection of the message vertex on the bottom edge, height of the triangle, and angle of the triangle plane. Using these three methods together speeds up the whole process, and the faster steganography method means that larger models can be used to carry more information.

The details of the improvements are explained below. First, to offset the extra time cost involved in tracing triangles, a hierarchical kd-tree structure is created. Suppose there is a set of vertices $\mathbb{P}$ in 3D space, these vertices are preprocessed into a kd-tree structure, so that given any query vertex q, those vertices in $\mathbb{P}$ that are closest to q can be effectively reported. kd-tree only finds the closest vertex in 3D space, thus each triangle is treated as a vertex to efficiently find each triangle's candidate neighbors. For this, the center of gravity of the triangle is used instead of the triangle itself, which limits the number of candidate triangles. Second, a triangular neighbor table (TNT) is constructed. This table indicates the neighbors and connections of available triangles. However, TNT itself is still time-consuming when working with large models, because building the table requires complicated search and comparison operations. This is where kd-tree comes into play: it offsets the overhead of these operations by reducing the number of candidate triangles needed to make comparisons. Third, an advanced jumping strategy (AJS) is proposed to improve performance. Tracing a triangle over and over takes massive processing time; more time is required toward the end of the tracing process as the process is nearing the limit of its capabilities. Instead of backtracking the same triangle repeatedly, this problem can be entirely avoided by designing AJS that chooses a new starting triangle based on PCA [28] ordering. This ordering is based on the position of the

Fig. 4.3 An interval $\overline{x_i x_{i+2}}$ is divided into two subintervals for embedding data. Figure from [4]

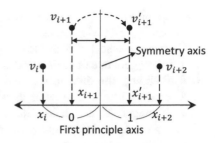

orthogonal projection of each triangle's center of gravity on the first principal axis. AJS then links this new ordering to the tail of the previous variable stencil and it does so automatically. The resulting triangle has never been tracked before, and it has only one vertex that has never been used before. In other words, this triangle has two vertices that have already been used. Thus, AJS effectively avoids backtracking already traced triangles. This greatly improves performance, especially near the capacity limits.

Figure 4.2 is a diagram of the extension domain. Let a vertex v_l and the line defined by v_l and v_k be orthogonal to the line $\overline{v_j v_k}$. The state of the triangle depends on the orthogonally projected location of the vertex v_i onto the virtual edge $\overline{v_l v_k}$. Depending on the message bits, v_i remains unchanged or moves to v_i'. Figure 4.2 (right) is a diagram of the rotation domain. The message is embedded in the angle between two triangular planes. v_l is the reference vertex obtained by the barycenter of the initial triangle. The message is embedded by adding or subtracting the angle ϕ.

In summary, this method is also robust to affine transformations and vertex reordering. It increases the capacity up to 6 bits per vertex and reduces the calculation time, but the embedding capacity is still very low. Moreover, it also cannot resist steganalysis. Despite this improvement, the algorithm is still sensitive to various attacks, and the embedding capacity is still very low.

4.1.3 Symmetrical Swap Model

Wang and Wang [4] proposed the first steganography method for point-sampled geometry. The proposed symmetric swap algorithm (SSA) is our proposed method for digital steganography for point-sampled geometries in the spatial domain. The SSA algorithm embeds the payload according to the following three steps.

1. **Constructing PCA axes.** PCA is used to generate three principal axes for the point sampling model to construct a new coordinate system. Then the coordinates of the original point are transformed to the new coordinate system. Obviously, this new coordinate system has a new origin, the center of gravity of the point

sampling model; it also has three basis vectors, or three principal axes, called x-axis, y-axis, and z-axis.

2. **Create three sorted lists.** Next, the point coordinates for each axis are sorted. This will generate three lists with sorted indices.

3. **Embedding the data into a list.** Each bit in each interval of the x-y-z axis determined by the key is embedded into the list for generating a random sequence with integer values. These values represent the indices used in our algorithm to embed secret bits at the corresponding intervals. This operation is called a symmetric swap process.

For simplicity, only the x-axis is used to illustrate the basic idea. Suppose $x_1, x_2, \ldots, x_m$ is the x coordinate value of the sorted point $v_1, v_2, \ldots, v_m$, where m is the number of points in the point sampling model, and each interval (composed of two values x_i and x_{i+2} ($1 \leq i \leq m-2$) on x axis) is considered a two-state object. The x-coordinate x_{i+1} of the vertex v_{i+1} is used to define the state of the interval and partitioned the line segment $\overline{x_i x_{i+2}}$ into two sets S_0 and S_1. If $x_{i+1} \in S_0$, the interval is considered to be in the 0 state; otherwise, it is $x_{i+1} \in S_1$, and the interval is in the 1 state. To embed data, if the embedded message is equal to the state, then no modification is required; otherwise, the subinterval boundary must be utilized as the symmetry axis to move v_{i+1} toward v'_{i+1}.

The $v_{i+1} \rightarrow v'_{i+1}$ mapping must remain unchanged by the similarity transformation. Furthermore, the mapping must be invertible for restoring the original state of the legitimate points. To avoid the visual degradation of the point sampling model, the interval $\overline{x_i x_{i+2}}$ is subdivided into $2k$ ($k \geq 1$) subintervals, so that the geometric distortion $|v_{i+1} - v'_{i+1}|$ becomes smaller as k increases. On the other hand, a larger k can lead to bit retrieval errors due to limited machine precision. The $v_{i+1} \rightarrow v'_{i+1}$ mapping is the symmetry of the nearest axis orthogonal to $\overline{x_i x_{i+2}}$, which intersects the boundary of the nearest subinterval belonging to S_0 or S_1. To restore the original state of the legal point well, an extra bit for each bit of the payload is needed to store into the carrier, and thus the size of the embedded data is exactly the size of the payload. The extra bit is set to 1 if the interval state has changed, and 0 otherwise. The extra bits are built during embedding. In this way, exact reversibility is only granted to the holder of the extra bits and secret keys.

With our SSA extraction algorithm, the secret key, the three main axes, and the center of gravity of the overlay model are together performed during extraction phase, as shown in Fig. 4.3. The detailed steps are:

1. Find an interval $\overline{x_i x_{i+2}}$ by interpreting the key.
2. Extract a data bit from the interval of the x coordinate value x_{i+1}.
3. Repeat step 1 and step 2 for all legal points v_{i+1} on a given covert model.

In addition, SSA located the list of macro embedding primitives and embedded up to 6 bits at each macro embedding primitive to increase the capacity. In summary, the upper-bound capacity of the method is $6/2 = 3$ bpv. Additionally, this method is robust to affine transformations and vertex reordering. The method is easy to attack by PCA transform-targeted steganalysis.

Fig. 4.4 Diagram of the state region q_i and its changed and unchanged regions. During the data-embedding period, vertices are moved into change regions while no vertices are moved into unchanged regions. Figure from [5]

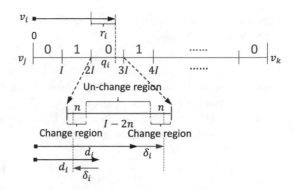

4.1.4 Multi-layer Embedding Model

In [4], Chao et al. [5] proposed a multi-layer embedding algorithm for high-capacity steganography on 3D meshes. The single-layer embedding scheme is first described and then the multi-layer version is detailed.

Single-Layer Embedding Algorithm First, select the three vertices of the cover model denoted v_i, v_j, and v_k, which are also referred to *end vertices*. The three end vertices are determined using PCA of the covering model. Given the first and second principal axes, all vertices are orthogonally projected onto these two axes. The vertices falling on both ends of the first principal axis are selected as the end vertices v_i and v_j. Select the vertex that falls on the farthest end of the second principal axis as the third end vertex v_k. If there are multiple candidates for an end vertex, the closest candidate (closest to the main axis) is chosen as the end vertex and move the others slightly so that an end vertex is uniquely defined. The next step is to transform the cover model to align vector $v_i v_j$ and $v_i v_j \times v_i v_k$ with x-axis and y-axis, respectively, and make the vertex v_i coincide with the origin of the Cartesian coordinate system. Next, the interval $\overline{v_j v_k}$ is evenly partitioned into two-state region sets in an interleaved manner (for example, 010101 . . .), expressed as S_0 and S_1, as shown in Fig. 4.4. The suffixes of S_0 and S_1 indicate binary feature states 0 and 1. The region, in which vertex v_i is located, can be calculated using the following equations:

$$d_i/I = q_i \ldots r_i,$$
$$q_i = \lceil d_i/I \rceil, \tag{4.2}$$
$$r_i = d_i \% I,$$

where . . . is the modulo operation, d_i is the projection distance between vertex v_i and end vertex v_j of the x component. I indicates the width of the interval in the state region. q_i represents the state region to which the vertex v_i belongs, and r_i

represents the position of the vertex in the state region q_i. There are two cases of embedded message bits:

Case 1. $q_i \in S_k$ and $bit(i) = k, k = 0$ or 1: No modification.

Case 2 $q_i \in S_k$ and $bit(i) \neq k, k = 0$ or 1: Move the vertex v_i to the adjacent change region in q_i. If $d_i \% I \leq I/2$, shift v_i to the range $[0, n]$; if not, shift v_i to the range $[I - n, I]$. The offset $\delta_i = \min(r_i, I - r_i)(1 - 2n/I)$, and the new position is acquired by

$$d_i' = \begin{cases} d_i - \delta_i, & \text{if } r_i \leq I/2 \\ d_i + \delta_i, & \text{if } r_i > I/2 \end{cases}. \tag{4.3}$$

The major disadvantage of the method is that the change area may be too small to precisely embed the payload. To solve this, the first approach is to optimize the number of $n_{intervals}$ in the state region. The goal of this optimization is to enlarge the region of change while reducing distortion. Another way is to enlarge the change area by simply reducing the unchanged area to the range $[I/4, 3I/4]$ and setting the change area to the area $[0, I/4]$ and $[3I/4, I]$. Thus, the above small offset δ_i can be redefined as $\delta_i = \min(r_i, I - r_i)/2$. Therefore, when a 1-bit data is embedded into a vertex v_i, the new position d_i' of that vertex can be computed as

$$d_i' = \begin{cases} d_i + (I/4 - r_i/2), & \text{if } q_i \in S_k, \text{ bit}(i) = k \\ d_i + \text{sign}(\delta_i), & \text{if } q_i \in S_k, \text{ bit}(i) = k \end{cases}, \tag{4.4}$$

where

$$\text{sign}(\delta_i) = \begin{cases} -1 & \text{if } x < 0, \\ 1 & \text{if } x \geq 0. \end{cases} \tag{4.5}$$

In general, the offset $d - d'$ must be small enough to avoid visual degradation of the cover model, but large enough to allow accurate payload detection.

Multi-Layer Embedding Algorithm It is easy to extend the single-layer embedding scheme to the multi-layer version by directly adding more layers, as follows: similar with the single-layer version, in our multi-layer embedding, the two-state region subsets of each layer are interleaved to arrange regions. Differently, a slight modification is made that the state regions in the even layers are shifted to the right by $I/2$. With this arrangement, the direction of movement of the vertices is bidirectional. When a payload is embedded on a vertex, the vertex oscillates back and forth within half the interval of the state area. In this way, more data on each vertex can be potentially embedded in the multi-layer and not enlarge the coverage model distortion. The lower bound distortion is limited to $I/2$. In the multi-layered embedding method, the variable r_i for vertex v_i can be rewritten as

$$r_i = \begin{cases} d_i \% I, & \text{if embedded in odd layers,} \\ (d_i + I/2)\% I, & \text{if embedded in even layers.} \end{cases} \tag{4.6}$$

For example, in the first layer, $n = \frac{1}{4}I$, and the change region is $[0, \frac{1}{4}I] \cup [\frac{3}{4}I, I]$. Iteratively, for the second layer, $n = \frac{3}{8}I$, and the change region is $[0, \frac{3}{8}I] \cup [\frac{5}{8}I, I]$. Thus, in the nth layer, the change region is $[0, \frac{2^n-1}{2^{n+1}}I] \cup [\frac{2^n+1}{2^{n+1}}I, I]$. Since the precision of a single floating point is 2^{-23}, the distance between the two boundaries has to be larger than the precision, i.e., $\frac{2^n+1}{2^{n+1}}I - \frac{2^n-1}{2^{n+1}}I \geq 2^{-23}$. Thus, $n \leq \log_2 I + 23$.

The overall multi-layer embedding algorithm is processed as follows:

1. Compute the variable d_i for each vertex v_i.
2. Compute the variable r_i of v_i.
3. Embed the data in v_i by moving its payload slightly position, i.e., the variable $d_i \to d_i'$ (i.e., v_i is moved to a new location).
4. Repeat steps 2 and 3 for the next layer of embedding until all payloads are fully embedded in vertices.

In this way, data can be embedded on three spatial components of the vertex coordinates, respectively. In each layer, each vertex can hide 3 bits of information, except for the end vertices v_i, v_j and v_k. These three vertices cannot embed any messages because they are the basis of the extraction process. Note that if the distortion of the steganography model is too large, the end vertices and initial triangles obtained from the cover model and the stego model, respectively may not be the same. Fortunately, this is very rare because the offset of the vertex position is very small.

Multi-Layer Extraction Algorithm In the multi-layer extraction process, the payloads are extracted in reverse embedding order, i.e., from the last layer to the first layer. First, the variables d_i, q_i, and r_i for each vertex v_i can be computed. Then it is easy to detect which region (change or unchange region) a vertex is in using the following decision equation:

$$\begin{cases} v_i \in \text{change region}, & \text{if } r_i < I/4 \text{ or } r_i > 3I/4, \\ v_i \in \text{unchange region}, & \text{if } r_i \geq I/4 \text{ or } r_i \leq 3I/4. \end{cases} \tag{4.7}$$

The bit value $\text{bit}(i)$ can be extracted by checking its corresponding state region:

$$\text{bit}(i) = \begin{cases} q_i \% 2, & \text{if } v_i \in \text{unchange region,} \\ 1 - q_i \% 2, & \text{if } v_i \in \text{change region.} \end{cases} \tag{4.8}$$

To restore the vertex positions of the previous layer, a small offset δ_i is subtracted from the variable d_i and then extend the state region from $[I/4, 3I/4]$ to $[0, I]$. The vertex positions of the previous layer, i.e., proportionally shifted back to the previous layer, can then be calculated using the following equation:

$$d_i' = \begin{cases} d_i - (I/2 - r_i), & \text{if } d_i \in \text{ embedded in odd layers,} \\ d_i + \text{sign}(I/2 - r_i)r_i, & \text{if } d_i \in \text{ embedded in odd layers.} \end{cases} \tag{4.9}$$

The overall multi-layer extraction algorithm is processed as follows:

1. Compute the variable d_i for each vertex v_i.
2. Use Eq. (4.6) to compute the variable r_i for each vertex.
3. Use Eq. (4.8) to extract a bit value from v_i.
4. Use Eq. (4.9) to restore the vertex positions of the previous layer.
5. Repeat steps 1–4 for the previous layer extraction until all payloads are fully extracted.

In summary, when $I = 1$, considering the x, y, z-coordinates, the method has a theoretical upper-bound capacity of 69 bpv, and it can resist vertex reordering and affine transform attacks. However, it can be easily attacked via PCA transform-targeted steganalysis.

4.1.5   Static Arithmetic Coding Model

Itier and Puech [6] designed a 3D steganography method based on constructing Hamiltonian paths on the entire vertex graph without using connectivity information. Figure 4.5 is a diagram of the embedding scheme. The method is based on

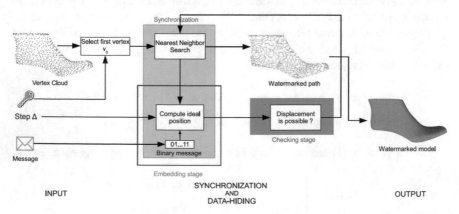

Fig. 4.5 Diagram of the static arithmetic coding model for 3D mesh steganography. Figure from [6]

the conjunction of synchronization and embedding. Since synchronization is very sensitive to vertex displacement, it is straightforward to jointly synchronize and embed data vertex by vertex in the building path order. The synchronization consists of finding the nearest neighbors of the current vertex. Then the ideal position of the new current vertex can be computed as a function of its parent, message and a displacement bound. The Hamiltonian path is a uniquely traversed path of all the vertices starting from the one selected by the secret key. For each stage, the nearest neighbor vertex v_{i+1} of the present vertex v_i is selected. As a matter of fact, the message is embedded with its synchronization with the message sequence guaranteed. Once the vertex v_{i+1} is added to the path, the message can be embedded by changing the relative location of the vertex v_{i+1} to its predecessor v_i. To achieve a high embedding capacity, the vertex moves along three coordinate components in the spherical coordinate system.

Hamiltonian Path and Synchronization A Hamiltonian path is a path that visits each vertex only once. To define a path along the data of the mesh and only deal with geometry and not connectivity, ordering vertices by their position and relationship in space can be efficient. To ensure synchronization, it is also required that the traversal of the point cloud from the starting vertex is unique in order to produce the same path between encoding and decoding stages. The main idea is to build an ordered structure on the vertex cloud using their spatial distribution. Amat et al. [30] proposed to build an Euclidean minimum spanning tree (EMST) to cover all vertices of the mesh. First, define the order of vertices in a mesh as the order of vertex selection in the Prim-Jarník algorithm starting from a given starting vertex. Yet this method has two main drawbacks, complexity and robustness, but it has some nice properties: it gives an implicit order, does not degrade mesh quality and does not depend on connectivity.

Compared to EMST, this method reduces the time complexity and the Hamiltonian path is more stable to geometric changes when constructed. In fact, finding nearest neighbors from a single vertex provides fewer choices than finding nearest neighbors from a set of vertices given by Prim's algorithm. Figure 4.6 compares the construction stages between the EMST (left) and the Hamiltonian path (right), given an input vertex. The construction of the Hamiltonian path is done by choosing the least weighted edge in the Euclidean distance. At step $t = i$, the red edges belong to the structure, and the green edges indicate the edges to be compared to find v_{i+1}. Note that in the case of EMST, the number of edge weights to be compared at each step is much larger.

For a mesh consisting of n vertices, the Hamiltonian path is built on the complete graph of vertices in order to keep interesting qualities outward. There are no necessary and sufficient conditions for finding a Hamiltonian path, but there are many sufficient conditions. For example, Dirac's theorem states that a simple graph with $n \geq 3$ vertices is a Hamiltonian graph if the valence of each vertex is greater than or equal to $n/2$. More generally, the Koenig-Redei theorem states that a complete graph is a Hamiltonian graph. A weighted graph is denoted as $G_n = (V_n, E_m, w)$, which is defined as the complete graph over all vertices of the

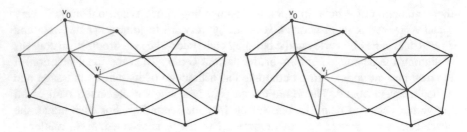

Fig. 4.6 The building path at step $t = i$, vertices and edges in red are covered, green edges are compared in order to find the next vertex, for: (left) EMST built with Prim's algorithm, (right) Hamiltonian path. Figure from [6]

Fig. 4.7 State of the sets at step i: v_i is the current vertex. Figure from [6]

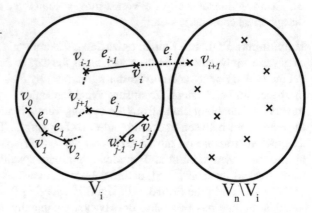

mesh, where $w : E \rightarrow \mathbb{R}^+$. E_m represents graph edges that are distinct from mesh connectivity, $m = n(n - 1)/2$. Each edge e_i has a weight, defined as its length in Euclidean distance. The path constructed at step i is in the set $V_i = \{v_0, v_1, \ldots, v_i\}$, by the selected edge $\{e_0, e_1, \ldots, e_{i-1}\}$. Any vertex is either in V_i or the set of unvisited vertices in $V_n \backslash V_i = \{v_{i+1}, v_{i+2}, \ldots, v_n\}$ as shown in Fig. 4.7.

The secret key directly selects the first vertex v_0 among n vertices to construct the Hamiltonian path. To construct it, the nearest neighbor v_{i+1} of the current vertex v_i is recursively chosen through the smallest edge $e_i \in E_m$, e.g., $w(e_i) = \min \|v_i, v_k\|_2, v_k \in V_n \backslash V_i$. Obviously, after the last step, $\mathbf{P}_n$ is a Hamiltonian path on G_n. The computational complexity of finding a Hamiltonian path in a complete graph depends on the nearest neighbor search step. Storing the nearest neighbors for each vertex is not enough because the Hamiltonian path only visits each vertex once. Therefore, a simple method is used to find all nearest neighbors in $O(n^2)$. By defining this order, a new relationship between the two vertices is also created, given by the edges of the path $\mathbf{P}_n$.

Embedding Given an arbitrary first vertex v_0, $0 \leq i \leq n$, vertex v_{i+1} relative to its predecessor v_i is moved for each iteration i of path construction. This method allows us to insert data on the $n - 1$ edges of the path $\mathbf{P}_n$. Furthermore, in order to have a larger embedding field, we propose to permute those vertices on the three components ρ, θ, ϕ after changing the Cartesian coordinates to spherical coordinates after transformation. The transformation is done relative to the previous vertex in the path. Then the vector between $v_i(x_i, y_i, z_i)$ and $v_{i+1}(x_{i+1}, y_{i+1}, z_{i+1})$ as well as the vector of the spherical coordinates is computed. In this way, the embedding space for message embedding is established.

Langdon [31] introduced an approach based on static arithmetic coding (SAC). The principle of SAC is to use a real number interval between 0 and 1 to represent a symbol sequence, and each value of this interval corresponds to a unique word to be encoded. SAC starts calculating probabilities and then associates each symbol with the corresponding subinterval. The proposed method considers the value distribution of the original message to fit interval slices in q subintervals. In this way, secret messages can be embedded into the cover meshes and extract the hidden data losslessly. The method can achieve a maximum capacity of 24 bits per vertex but cannot resist steganalysis attack.

4.1.6 Anti-steganalysis Static Arithmetic Coding Model

Li et al. [7] reconsidered the method of static arithmetic coding model to improve its resistance to steganalysis. The original steganography method [6] embeds data into all three coordinate components of the edge vector in the spherical coordinate system. However, changes in polar and azimuthal coordinates have a greater impact on steganalytic features (such as LFS76 [8]) than in the radial coordinate system. Therefore, the method is resistant against steganalysis through modification of only the radial component represented by the edge vector in the spherical coordinate system.

Motivation In the study of [6], the mesh distortion caused by embedding was analyzed by peak signal-to-noise ratio (PSNR) and mesh structure distortion measurement (MSDM2) [32], the latter having better correlation with human perception. However, the resistance of steganography to 3D steganalysis was not considered. Existing image steganalysis methods [33, 34] cannot be applied to 3D meshes, as unlike 3D objects, images are represented on regular lattices. The first 3D steganalysis algorithm was proposed in [35]. Li and Bors [36] then developed an improved method for 3D steganalysis using local feature sets. Both 3D steganalysis methods use statistics of local 3D features as input to the algorithms of machine learning methods that train steganalyzers to distinguish cover and stego 3D objects.

Information embedding in 3D objects only changes very slightly the mesh surface. According to the studies from [35, 36], statistics of localized 3D features can be successfully used for 3D steganalysis. A 52-dimensional feature vector was proposed for 3D steganalysis in [36]. Before extracting the features, Laplacian smoothing is applied to the meshes of both cover-objects and stego-objects. The features are then extracted from the original and smoothed meshes. Then, the

Fig. 4.8 Illustration of the embedding changes in SCS. (**a**) The edge vector from v_i to v_{i+1} represented in SCS as (r, ρ, ϕ). (**b**) The changes produced by HPQ in the radial coordinate of the edge vector in SCS

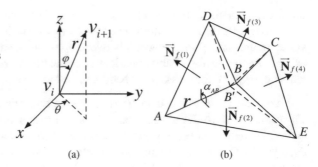

(a)   (b)

first four moments, representing the mean, variance, skewness and kurtosis, of the difference between the geometrical information of the original and smoothed meshes are used as inputs for the steganalyzer. The 3D steganalytic features include the following: the vertex position and norm in the Cartesian coordinate system; the vertex position and norm in the Laplacian coordinate system; the face normal; the dihedral angle of two neighboring faces; the vertex normal; the Gaussian curvature and curvature ratio.

Embedding The design of the embedding that can increase the resistance of 3D steganography [6] to steganalysis includes three aspects: the interval parameter Δ, a different selection of subintervals s and a different embedding styles in SCS. First the displacement of vertex v_i is analyzed in the context of increasing resistance to steganalysis. As embedding is applied in a spherical coordinate system (see Fig. 4.8a), the displacement of vertices along radial coordinates is considered for disguising steganalysis. Assuming that the subintervals have uniformly distributed features, the displacement of vertices in radial coordinates is defined as

$$
D_\rho = \sum_{j=1}^{s} \sum_{k=1}^{s} P_j Q_k |j - k| \frac{\Delta}{s}, \tag{4.10}
$$

where P_j is the probability that vertex v_i is in the jth subinterval, Q_k is the probability that the modified position of vertex v_i is in the kth subinterval, and $\frac{\Delta}{s}$ is the length interval of each subinterval. It is assumed that vertices v_i lie randomly in the interval such that $P_j = \frac{1}{s}, j = 1, 2, \ldots, s$. If the words in the message are uniformly distributed, the modified position of the vertex v_i is correspondingly located randomly within the interval, and $Q_k = \frac{1}{s}, k = 1, 2, \ldots, s$. Hence the above equation can be simplified to:

$$
D_\rho = \frac{\Delta}{3} \left(1 - \frac{1}{s^2} \right). \tag{4.11}
$$

Similarly, the equation for calculating the displacement of the vertex in the other two angular coordinates of the SCS is similar to Eq. (4.11). It can be inferred from the equation that if the interval parameter Δ is reduced, the displacement of the vertex will also decrease. At the same time, when the number of subintervals s increases, the embedding capacity increases and so does the displacement. Yet the number of subintervals has little effect on the displacement, as $dD_\rho/ds = 2\Delta/3s^3$ is very small when s is large. According to this analysis, it is worth keeping the interval parameter Δ as small as possible to limit the effect of distortions produced by information embedding on those features used for steganalysis.

Then the effect of the distortion produced by the information embedding on the features used for 3D steganalysis is analyzed. The original version of HPQ steganography [6] embeds all three coordinates of edge vectors in SCS. However, changes in the two angular coordinates θ and ϕ of the SCS may have a greater impact on steganalytic features than changes in the radial coordinate r. Figure 4.8b illustrates how the changes produced by the information embedding apply only to the radial coordinate of the edge vector $\overrightarrow{AB}$ between vertices A and B. The new position of vertex B is B', which is not moving from the direction of the edge $\overrightarrow{AB}$. The face normals of faces $\triangle ABD$ and $\triangle ABE$, $\overrightarrow{\mathbf{N}}_{f(1)}$ and $\overrightarrow{\mathbf{N}}_{f(2)}$, are not affected by the displacement of vertex B. The dihedral angles between the two faces are defined as:

$$\alpha_{AB} = \arccos \frac{\overrightarrow{\mathbf{N}}_{f(1)} \cdot \overrightarrow{\mathbf{N}}_{f(2)}}{\|\overrightarrow{\mathbf{N}}_{f(1)}\|\|\overrightarrow{\mathbf{N}}_{f(2)}\|}. \tag{4.12}$$

The dihedral angle α_{AB} is also unaffected by the modification of vertex B. However, the displacement of vertex B changes the direction of the face normals $\overrightarrow{\mathbf{N}}_{f(3)}$ and $\overrightarrow{\mathbf{N}}_{f(4)}$, unless all faces are in the same plane. In fact, many plane surfaces exist in CAD 3D objects. Smooth regions appear locally flat in high-resolution 3D objects. Therefore, subsequent edge vectors are only slightly affected by the displacement of their preceding edges. It can be observed that in either of the two angle coordinates of the SCS, any modification to the edge vector $\overrightarrow{AB}$ results in a change in the face normal $\overrightarrow{\mathbf{N}}_{f(1)}$, $\overrightarrow{\mathbf{N}}_{f(2)}$ and Dihedral angle α_{AB}. These features are used for steganalysis, and their modifications will be recognized by the steganalyzer.

Based on the above analysis, the resistance of 3D embeddings to steganalysis is improved when only the radial components represented by edge vectors in SCS are modified. However, the edges used by steganography are generated during the construction of the Hamiltonian path, and some of these edges may not actually exist in the original mesh. Nevertheless, the overlap between the edges of the original mesh and the edges in the Hamiltonian path is very high, so ultimately this problem does not significantly affect the steganalysis results. In other words, the upper-bound embedding capacity is only 8 bits per vertex.

4.2 LSB Plane Steganography

4.2.1 Gaussian Curvature Model

Yang et al. [9] designed an adaptive data hiding algorithm that balances a high embedding capacity and low embedding distortion, where vertices with larger Gaussian curvature are kept unchanged. The obtained relationship between spatial noise and normal noise describes the trade-off between embedding capacity (in the form of unused bits in vertex coordinates) and visual distortion (in the form of normal degradation). Therefore, they can be used directly to inform the least significant bit data hiding algorithm about the carrier embedding capacity for a given distortion tolerance.

A simplified Gaussian curvature κ_i, as the smoothness of the mesh at vertex v_i, is defined as:

$$\kappa_G(v_i) = 2\pi - \sum_{v_j \in \mathcal{N}_1(v_i)} \theta_j, \tag{4.13}$$

where $\mathcal{N}_1(v_i)$ is the one-ring neighbor of vertex v_i and θ_j represents the angles of the incident triangles at vertex v_i. $|\kappa_G(v_i)|$ could reflect the smoothness of the local region of the ith vertex. Based on $\kappa_G(v_i)$, the normal degradation tolerance ϵ_j at the jth triangle is given by:

$$\epsilon_j = \min_n \{\alpha - \phi(\kappa_G(v_i); \alpha, \mu, \sigma) + \epsilon_0\}, \tag{4.14}$$

where $\phi(\kappa_G(v_i); \alpha, \mu, \sigma)$ is the Gaussian function with peak value α, mean μ, standard deviation σ and ϵ_0 is the threshold of normal degradation being acceptably considered. As there exist linear correlations between the expected normal change with the noise magnitude when the noise is added to all the three vertices of the triangle, the quantization level i of each triangle can be computed by comparing its optimal level of quantization with its normal degradation tolerance ϵ_j.

Since visual distortion is closely related to normal degradation, the least significant bit (LSB) replacement is used [10] (which embeds data by replacing the lowest bit with the message bit) to inform the capacity under a given distortion tolerance.

To make the data hiding algorithm blind and robust against vertex permutation, two orderings of vertex sets, $\pi_1(\cdot)$ and $\pi_2(\cdot)$, obtained from the projections of the sets from unlabeled $\mathbb{V}$ and labeled $\mathbb{V}_0$ quantized vertices onto their respective *first principal axes* are utilized. These two orderings will help the extraction process to find the embedding order of the message bits, avoiding potential synchronization problems. The details of the embedding and extraction algorithms are as follows:

Embedding Given a vector triangle mesh with a set of vertices $\mathbf{v} = (v_1, v_2, \ldots, v_N)$ represented in 32 bits, and a normal degenerate tolerance, the vectors $\mathbf{i} = (i_1, i_2, \ldots, i_N)$ of quantization levels are computed. All unused vertex coordinate bits are set to zeros and the message bits are embedded by a bit-replacement operation. More specifically, to label the jth vertex, the i_j most significant and the c least significant bits of its coordinates are kept unchanged, and the other $32 - i_j - c$ bits with message bits are sequentially replaced by embedded data. The embedding utilizes vertex ordering $\pi_1(\mathbf{v})$. The resulting set of vertices is denoted by $\mathbf{v}' = (v'_1, v'_2, \ldots, v'_N)$. The c least significant bits of the vertex coordinates of $\mathbf{v}'$ will carry side information, recording the change in quantization level between the vertices of the marked and unmarked meshes. In particular, a vector of quantization levels $\mathbf{i}' = (i'_1, i'_2, \ldots, i'_N)$ of $\mathbf{v}'$ and the original quantization levels i the correction vector are computed:

$$\mathbf{e} = (i_1 - i'_1, i_2 - i'_2, \ldots, i_N - i'_N). \tag{4.15}$$

The components of $\mathbf{e}$ according to the order $\pi_2(\cdot)$ are sorted and $\pi_2(\mathbf{v})$ is compressed and embedded into the least significant bits of c in $\mathbf{v}'$'s vertex coordinates, which can be compressed very efficiently.

Extraction Given a stego mesh and a normal degradation tolerance ϵ, the key for extracting the message bits is to recover the orderings $\pi_1(\cdot)$ and $\pi_2(\cdot)$. To compute $\pi_2(\cdot)$, the c least significant bits of the stego mesh are set to zeros and then the resulting vertex set is quantized, which is a permutation of $\mathbf{v}'$. The quantized vertices are projected onto their first principal axis. Note that because the first principal axis is invariant under vertex displacement, the ordering obtained from the projection is $\pi_2(\cdot)$. After recovering $\pi_2(\cdot)$, the c least significant bits of the input stego mesh are extracted and decompressed in the order of $\pi_2(\cdot)$ to obtain the correction vector $\pi_2(\mathbf{v})$. To recover $\pi_1(\cdot)$, the displacement quantization level of the original mesh is first obtained by

$$\pi_2(\mathbf{i}) = \pi_2(\mathbf{e}) + \pi_2(\mathbf{i}'). \tag{4.16}$$

Next, the vertices of $\pi_2(\mathbf{v}')$ are quantized to the original level $\pi_2(\mathbf{i})$, resulting in a $\pi_2(\cdot)$ ordering of unlabeled quantized vertices. Again exploiting the invariance of the first principal axis under vertex permutation, the projection of unlabeled quantized vertices on their first principal axis gives $\pi_1(\cdot)$. After restoring $\pi_1(\cdot)$, the message can be extracted from the quantization level $\pi_1(\mathbf{i})$ of the marked vertices $\pi_1(\mathbf{v}')$ and the unmarked vertices. To extract information from the jth vertex, simply remove the i_j most significant and c least significant bits of its coordinates, and treat the remaining $32 - i_j - c$ bits as the embedded message. It is worth noting that the capacity increases monotonically with ϵ, and the extra capacity comes at the cost of increased embedding distortion.

The main advantage of the algorithm is the high capacity capable of embedding at least 10 bits per vertex for $\epsilon = 1°$, which is 10 bits more than the multi-layer embedding model [5]. As each vertex coordinate is in the 32-bit IEEE 754 single precision standard format. Apart from the top bit, which indicates whether the coordinate is positive or negative, the remaining 31 bits can be embedded with the messages. Considering the x, y, z coordinates altogether, each vertex has a maximum 93-bit capacity. In summary, this method can achieve high capacity and low distortion, but when the amount of embedded noise becomes larger, the error will greatly increase. This method is robust to the vertex reordering attack but is fragile against PCA transform-targeted steganalysis.

4.2.2   Truncated Space Steganography Model

Li et al. [11] proposed a steganography method that constructs a truncated data space instead of directly using connectivity information. First, as in [4, 5], the method transforms the coordinate system through PCA. Second, the truncated region is constructed by decomposing the real number region into the truncated region and the remaining region. Specifically, an x-coordinate x (v_i) can be represented by

$$x\,(v_i) = F_s \times (x_t\,(v_i) + x_r(v_i)), \tag{4.17}$$

where F_s is a sign function that has either a positive or negative sign, x_t is the unsigned truncation data in the truncated region, and x_r is the unsigned residual data in the residual region. Third, the truncated region is divided into several isometric intervals in ascending order. The message is embedded into the truncated region by shifting the vertices in one interval to the corresponding positions in other intervals controlled by the key.

In summary, the truncated region limits the deformation degree of each component of the stego mesh within the region, which implies that the embedding distortion can be designed under control. The upper-bound capacity in this method is 93 bpv. This method is robust against the vertex reordering attack but is fragile to PCA transform-targeted steganalysis.

4.2.3   Adaptive Steganography Model

Zhou et al. [12] proposed an adaptive steganography technique to resist steganalysis. Unlike previous methods (belonging to the nonadaptive mode) that shift the vertex coordinates to embed messages without considering steganalysis, this technique provides vertices with various costs for determining the probability of modification.

Considering the storage form of the uncompressed mesh, each vertex coordinate is usually specified as a 32-bit single precision pattern, where the significant precision number is 23 bits [5]. These coordinates are converted into multiple binary bitplanes [13]. Considering that steganography in a low-level bitplane causes fewer artifacts in the overall coordinates, the data are first embedded into the low-level bitplane and then iteratively embedded into the high-level bitplane. These bitplanes are embedded by LSB replacement, except for the highest bitplane determined by the message.

The Buckets effect reveals that the capacity of a bucket depends on the shortest board. Similarly, the security performance of steganography mainly depends on the most effective steganalytic features. As we do not know which submodel of the steganalytic features is significant for designing steganography, the association of costs ρ_i to the features is generally very tough. By paying equal attention to each elements during steganography, we obtain cover-stego pair that can be utilized to analyze which steganalytic features dominate in the discrimination of covers and stegos. The constant distortion (CD) based matrix embedding proposed in [25] is used for paying equal attention to each elements on the operated bitplane for steganography, in which the goal is to solve the problem of minimizing the number of changed elements (the constant distortion profile) [14]. Afterwards, we evaluate the individual submodel of the steganalytic feature vector independently of each other and set the costs ρ_i to reflect this ranking, meaning the optimality of submodel of features.

The approach is as follows. First, create a set of stego meshes embedded with CD method under certain payload. Then, we use fisher linear discriminants (FLDs) criteria to evaluate how good are individual features for detecting given embedding changes. The values of FLD criteria of individual elements may be either utilized directly to set the costs of embedding changes ρ_i or used to obtain insight into the problem and set the costs heuristically. We use FLDs as base learners due to their simple and fast training. Denoting the cover and stego features from the training set as $\mathbf{x}^{(m)}$ and $\overline{\mathbf{x}}^{(m)}$, $m = 1, \ldots, N^{trn}$, respectively. The training makes use of the so-called *out-of-bag* (OOB) error estimate [26]:

$$E_{OOB}^{(L)} = \frac{1}{2N^{trn}} \sum_{m=1}^{N^{trn}} \left(B^{(L)}(\mathbf{x}^{(m)}) + 1 - B^{(L)}(\overline{\mathbf{x}}^{(m)}) \right). \tag{4.18}$$

We start by computing the OOB estimates for each submodel, including its different embedding payloads (0.1 bpv under varying layers), for CD method. The intention is to investigate how the submodel ranking is affected by the payload on difference layers. Note that the ensemble classifier is built using random structures (randomness enters the selection of subspaces for base learners and the bootstrap sample formation), which is why we repeated each run five times and report the average values of OOB estimates. To investigate the nature of submodels, in Fig. 4.9 we plot for each submodel its OOB error estimate averaged over matrix embedding algorithm and two payloads, 0.1 bpv under 7 and 10 layers. The fact that submodels from "f37–f40" consistently provide lower OOBs than other submodels allows us to grasp the vulnerability of steganography to contend against "f37–f40," which is the absolute value of angles between face normals. Figure 4.9 also nicely demonstrates that steganography on higher bitplane results in better detection rates, which should

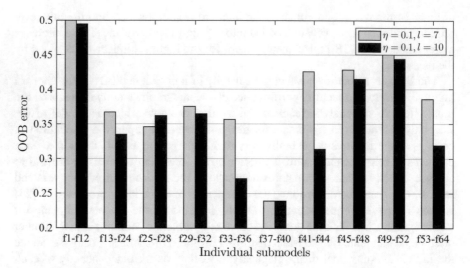

Fig. 4.9 OOB error estimates averaged over matrix embedding method and two payloads (0.1 bpv under 7 and 10 layers)

be attributed to deeper artifacts caused by modification. In summary, vertex normal features contributes to the design of steganography, which motivate us to design distortion function in the following subsection. As was already mentioned above, we consider this analysis as a good guide to derive heuristics to build the embedding costs ρ_i. In the following, we introduce two distortion models: vertex normal based distortion function and discrete Gaussian curvature based distortion function.

Vertex Normal Distortion Model (VND)   Following previous work, we use vertex normal of polygonal approximation which is defined by Nelson [27], the weighted sum of the normals of the faces that contain that vertex, to guide distortion definition, and it is formulated by

$$\overrightarrow{N}_{\mathbf{v}_i} = \sum_{F_j \in F_{\mathbf{v}_i}} \frac{S_j^{(i)} \cdot \overrightarrow{N}_{F_j'}}{||e_{(\mathbf{v}_i, \mathbf{v}_{F_j}')}|| \cdot ||e_{(\mathbf{v}_i, \mathbf{v}_{F_j}'')}||}, \tag{4.19}$$

where $F_{\mathbf{v}_i}$ is the set of faces that contains the vertex $\mathbf{v}_i$, $\mathbf{v}_{F_j}'$ and $\mathbf{v}_{F_j}''$ are the two vertices adjacent to vertex $\mathbf{v}_i$ in the face F_j, $e_{(\mathbf{v}_1, \mathbf{v}_2)}$ represents the edge connecting vertices $\mathbf{v}_1$ and $\mathbf{v}_2$, and areas of an adjacent triangle $S_j^{(i)}$ are obtained by

$$S_j^{(i)} = \sqrt{q_j^{(i)} \left(q_j^{(i)} - e_j^{(i)}\right) \left(q_j^{(i)} - e_{j+1}^{(i)}\right) \left(q_j^{(i)} - p_j^{(i)}\right)}, \tag{4.20}$$

and semi perimeter $q_j^{(i)} = \left(e_j^{(i)} + e_{j+1}^{(i)} + p_j^{(i)} \right)/2$, as shown in Fig. 4.10. Therefore, the distortion design against targeted steganalytic features is considerately regarded as a major contribution to the distortion function. We quantify the distortion using outputs of a vertex normal to construct the distortion function in this manner. The cost value is obtained by the reciprocal of absolute value of the ℓ_2 norm of vertex normal between cover mesh and Laplacian-smoothed mesh,

$$\rho_i = \frac{1}{g(||\overrightarrow{N}_{\mathbf{v}_i} - \overrightarrow{N}_{\mathbf{v}_i'}||_2) + \sigma}, \qquad i = 1, 2, \ldots, N, \qquad (4.21)$$

where $g(x)$ is a typically monotonous mapping function utilized for promoting steganography performance and $\sigma > 0$ is a constant stabilizing the numerical calculations.

Gaussian Curvature Distortion Model (GCD) Likewise, we employ an inferior feature as distortion so as to have a comparative trial. Discrete Gaussian curvature of a vertex is related to angles and faces that are connected to that surface. As shown in Fig. 4.10, the sharpness of the spherical polygon is approximated by the angle deficit of the polyhedron $\Delta(\mathbf{v}_i)$,

$$\Delta(\mathbf{v}_i) = 2\pi - \sum_{j=1}^{E} \theta_j^{(i)}, \qquad (4.22)$$

where E is the number of adjacent triangles of the inspected point, and $\theta_j^{(i)}$ is the angle between two successive edges $e_j^{(i)}$ and $e_{j+1}^{(i)}$ of the ith vertex, which is acquired by

$$\theta_j^{(i)} = \arccos \left[\frac{\left(e_j^{(i)} \right)^2 + \left(e_{j+1}^{(i)} \right)^2 - \left(p_j^{(l)} \right)^2}{2 e_j^{(i)} e_{j+1}^{(i)}} \right], \qquad j = 1, 2, \ldots, E, \qquad (4.23)$$

where p_i is the side which is opposite of the angle and $e_1^{(i)} = e_{E+1}^{(i)}, i = 1, 2, \ldots, N$. The area of each triangular face of the polyhedron can be partitioned into three equal parts, one corresponding to each of its vertices, so that the total area related to point $\mathbf{v}_i$ on the polyhedron is $\sum_{j=1}^{E} S_j^{(i)}/3$. Assume that the curvatures are uniformly distributed around the vertex, discrete Gaussian curvature is determined as

$$K(\mathbf{v}_i) = \frac{\Delta(\mathbf{v}_i)}{\sum_{j=1}^{E} S_j^{(i)}/3}. \qquad (4.24)$$

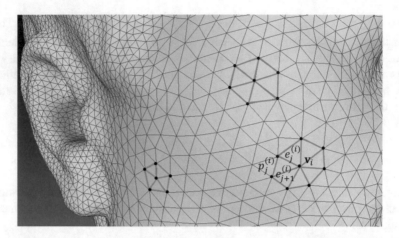

Fig. 4.10 Example of 1-ring neighbors of triangulation in Cartesian coordinate system, selected from zoomed region from a ShapeNet model. $\mathbf{v}_i$ is the selected vertices, which is surrounded by 7 triangles. Another two local regions each has 6 and 5 adjacent triangles (Refer to [13] for more investigation of distributions of quantity of adjacent triangles)

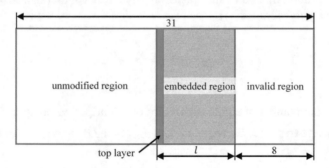

Fig. 4.11 Illustration of the operation zone on a regular mesh consisting of unmodified region, embedded region, and invalid region. In the embedded region, the top layer is adaptive embedded and other layers are embedded with LSBR

If a local region v_i is smooth, then $K(\mathbf{v}_i)$ tends to be a small value converging to zero. Intuitively, a fine embedding algorithm embeds data into noisy areas with sharpness and irregularity that are not easily modellable or predictable, and these areas should be paid low costs. Hence, we introduce the following distortion function based on discrete Gaussian curvature as follows:

$$\rho_i' = \frac{1}{|K(\mathbf{v}_i)|^\alpha + \sigma}, \qquad i = 1, 2, \ldots, N, \tag{4.25}$$

where α is a scalar element.

As shown in Fig. 4.11, the operation zone on a regular mesh consists of unmodified region, embedded region, and invalid region. The invalid regions include

8 bitplanes that are all zeros. Generally speaking, in consideration of the fact that LSBs make the least effects on the original mesh than Most Significant Bits (MSBs), there exists favorable distribution with several LSBs carrying full bits while upper bitplanes maintain distribution form with the best performance against steganalysis. To simplify the model of mesh steganography, in the embedded region, we determine to adaptively embed messages on the top layer and embed messages with LSBR on the remaining lower layers. Because each element of any bitplane has two modes of modification, the maximum length of message that a bitplane carries is $N \cdot \log_2 2 = N$ bits. The remaining message is adaptively embedded with STCs on the top bitplane with the above designed distortion function.

Embedding Strategy As mentioned before, in additive distortion model, the modifications on elements are assumed to be independent and thus minimizing the overall costs is equivalent to minimizing the sum of costs of individual changed elements. The simplest way to implement payload distribution in additive distortion rule is to serve each dimension of triple unit as the same cost and thus the previous cost value is evenly paid to x, y, and z axes by

$$\rho^{(i)}(x) = \rho_i,$$

$$\rho^{(i)}(y) = \rho_i, \tag{4.26}$$

$$\rho^{(i)}(z) = \rho_i.$$

Note that each channel is individually embedded with syndrome-trellis codes (STCs) [14] or steganographic polar codes (SPCs) [15] without affecting the distortions of other channels.

In summary, the method has a maximum capacity of 69 bpv, but it is fragile against the existing attacks, including affine transform, vertex reordering, noise addition, smoothing, and simplification. However, it is strong enough to contend against existing steganalysis when the embedding payload is low.

4.2.4 Gaussian Model

Zhu et al. [24] proposed an additive Gaussian noise model for 3D mesh steganography. The pursue is an alternative approach based on a locally estimated multivariate Gaussian cover 3D mesh model that is sufficiently simple to derive a closed-form expression for the power of the most powerful detector of content-adaptive LSB replacement but, at the same time, complex enough to capture the non-stationary character of natural images. Following MG [29], the cover model and the embedding algorithm used by Alice are described and the statistical model for stego meshes is derived based on the quantized Gaussians and minimization of the total KL divergence. To obtain vertex-changing probabilities, a payload-limited sender (PLS) problem is constructed aimed at minimizing the Kullback–Leibler divergence between the cover and stego mesh distributions for a given payload. The vertex coordinates are quantified so that the PLS problem can be solved in practice. Then a ternary embedding method is taken as a typical steganography case.

Cover Model   As the inter-component correlation of x-, y- and z-axis is low, the embedding operation is decomposed into three independent tasks and perform steganography individually. For simplicity, only the x-axis embedding is considered and the embedding space $\mathbf{v} = \{v_1, v_2, \ldots, v_N\}$ is modeled of independent realizations of N Gaussian random variables $V_n \sim \mathcal{N}(\mu_n, \omega_n^2)$, $n = 1, 2, \ldots, N$, quantized to discrete points k, $k \in \mathbb{Z}$. Here, μ_n is the noise-free content and ω_n^2 is the variance of the Gaussian acquisition noise. Let $\hat{\mu}_n \in \mathbb{Z}$ be an estimate of the 1-ring neighborhood of the nth vertex. The differences $w_n = v_n - \hat{\mu}_n$ will thus contain both the acquisition noise as well as the modeling error. w_n is modeled as independent Gaussian random variables $W_n \sim \mathcal{N}(0, \sigma_n^2)$, where $\sigma_n^2 \geq \omega_n^2$ because of the inclusion of the modeling error. Assuming the fine quantization limit, the probability mass function (PMF) of the nth element is given by $\mathcal{P}_{\sigma_n^2} = (p_{\sigma_n^2}(k))_{k \in \mathbb{Z}}$ with

$$p_{\sigma_n^2}(k) = \mathbb{P}(w_n = k) \propto \frac{1}{\sigma_n \sqrt{2\pi}} \exp\left(-\frac{k^2}{2\sigma_n^2}\right). \tag{4.27}$$

Note that the vertices are assumed to be quantized utilizing an unlimited number of levels (bits). This assumption is adopted to simplify the following theoretical exposition. For the actual embedding scheme, the limited dynamic range of vertices must be considered account, e.g., by disabling embedded changes. This will result in overwriting values other than dynamic scope. The fine quantization limit does not apply to saturated (overexposed) vertex areas, but it does not cause problems as any content-adaptive embedding should avoid them. This can be arranged in practice by assigning very small embedding change probabilities to vertex from these regions.

Stego Model   A widely adopted and well-studied model for data hiding is mutual independence embedding, where Alice makes embedding changes at each element independently of each other. In particular, one of the simplest settings is adopted when element values are changed by at most ± 1 (so-called LSB matching or LSBM). Given a cover mesh represented with $\mathbf{w} = \{w_1, w_2, \ldots, w_N\}$, the stego mesh $\mathbf{w}' = \{w_1', w_2', \ldots, w_N'\}$ is obtained by independently applying the following probabilistic rules:

$$\mathbb{P}(w_n' = w_n + 1) = \beta_n,$$
$$\mathbb{P}(w_n' = w_n - 1) = \beta_n, \qquad (4.28)$$
$$\mathbb{P}(w_n' = w_n) = 1 - 2\beta_n,$$

with change rates $0 \le \beta_n \le 1/3$. For simplicity, denote $\delta_n = w_n' - w_n$.

Statistic Model Since the distributions of w_n and its stego version $\hat{w}_n$ have been obtained, it is easy to enhance the security of steganography by reducing the Kullback–Leibler divergence of the two distributions. Based on the assumption that the embedding changes of all vertices are mutually independent, when the payload α is determined for one coordinate component:

$$\alpha N = \sum_{n=1}^{N} h\,(\delta_n) = -\sum_{n=1}^{N} \int_I g(\delta_n) \ln(g\,(\delta_n)) \mathbf{d}\delta_n, \qquad (4.29)$$

and the following optimization problem can be easily formulated for each component:

$$\min \sum_{n=1}^{N} \mathrm{KL}(\mathbb{P}(w_n)||\mathbb{P}(\hat{w}_n)),$$

$$\text{s.t.} \quad \sum_{n=1}^{N} h\,(\delta_n) = \alpha N, \qquad (4.30)$$

where

$$\mathrm{KL}\left(\mathbb{P}\,(w_n)\,\|\mathbb{P}\,(\hat{w}_n)\right) = \int \mathbb{P}\,(w_n = k) \ln \frac{\mathbb{P}\left(\hat{w}_n = k\right)}{\mathbb{P}\,(w_n = k)} \mathbf{d}k. \qquad (4.31)$$

The first step is the construction of embedding domain. For an uncompressed mesh model, its vertex coordinates are commonly represented as single precision floating point numbers [13], each of which takes up 4 bytes and has up to 7 decimal significant digits. In this case, the decimal coordinates can be transformed to integer coordinates first before steganography and construct the embedding domain I. The optimization problem of Eq. (4.30) can be solved in a discretization manner. By adding or subtracting an integer, the stego version given the secret message can be obtained. Therefore, the problem can be rewritten in the following discrete form:

$$\min \sum_{n=1}^{N} \sum_{k \in \mathcal{K}} \mathbb{P}(w_n = k) \ln \frac{\mathbb{P}(\hat{w}_n = k)}{\mathbb{P}(w_n = k)},$$

$$\text{s.t.} \ - \sum_{n=1}^{N} \sum_{\delta_{i,j} \in I} g(w_n) \ln(g(w_n)) = \alpha N, \tag{4.32}$$

where $\mathcal{K}$ is the layer set and

$$\mathbb{P}(\hat{w}_n = k) = \sum_{w_n \in I} g(w_n) \mathbb{P}(w_n = k + \delta_n). \tag{4.33}$$

Following MG [29], calculate Fisher information first and then establish an optimization problem for change rate β_n. After that, the distortion ρ_i can be obtained by:

$$\rho_n = \ln(1/\beta_n - 1). \tag{4.34}$$

In summary, the method is the first model based 3D mesh steganography method and has competitive anti-steganalytic performance than previous methods.

4.3   Permutation-Based Steganography

Permutation steganography [16] hides data in the order of the set elements. Each permutation of the set can be mapped to an integer and encode the message into the cover object by altering the element order in the set. The 3D mesh contains a group of rearrangeable vertices and triangles, which provides space for permutation-based steganography without changing the geometry of the mesh.

Given n elements, assuming that they are rearrangeable, the embedded data can be encoded by arranging elements related to the known reference order. With $n!$ possible orders, the standard permutation steganography is able to encode no more than $\log_2(n!) = O(n \log n)$ bits of the optimal message capacity at the cost of a computational complexity of $\Omega(n^2 \log^2 n \log \log n)$.

The specific implementation of the optimal permutation steganography algorithm is described below. Let $\mathbf{m}$ represent the secret data. $\mathbf{m}$ comprises multiple consecutive 0s and 1s and can be regarded as a long integer m. The core purpose is to obtain the replacement π related to the value of m on $\mathcal{V}$ recursively. For the ith iteration step, the ith element of the permutation is determined as the m/b_ith residual element of a reference ordering of $\mathcal{P}$, in which $b_i = (i - 1)!$ is regarded as the factorial

Fig. 4.12 Schematic diagram of steganography and message extraction of vertex index embedding by rearranging vertex indexes

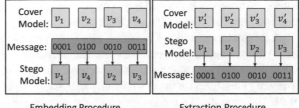

Embedding Procedure   Extraction Procedure

basis; in addition, m is updated using $m\%b_i$. Through this processing, the message is embedded by arranging π. To accurately recover m from π on the receiver side, some methods for the canonical traversal of meshes are usually utilized to determine the unique reference order of $\mathcal{P}$ [17]. This simple method is illustrated in Fig. 4.12.

In summary, owning to the fact that the reference ordering is obtained by traversing via the mesh compression algorithm called *Edgebreaker* [17] based on the mesh connectivity only, permutation steganography is robust and resistant to geometric affine transformation attacks. However, due to the integer algorithm, this algorithm has a very large runtime complexity, which makes it difficult to use the standard permutation steganography method for a large number of elements. Therefore, various variants of the method are put forward to find a feasible trade-off between embedding capacity and computational complexity. Because the adjacent correlation is broken, this method is fragile to permutation-targeted steganalysis.

4.3.1 Order Encoding Model

Bogomjakov et al. [18] proposed a permutation steganography algorithm, which can be efficiently implemented. The idea is to maximize the length of the bitstream while encoding each embedded message with the larger index of an embedding value in the reference ordering as much as possible. The encoding and the decoding algorithm consists of two stages. In the first stage a reference ordering of the mesh vertices and faces is computed. In the second stage the message is encoded as a permutation of the mesh vertices and faces relative to their reference order, or decoded by comparing the ordering present in the dataset to the reference one. One part of the message can be embedded by rearranging the vertices and the other part by rearranging the faces. The vertex and face reorderings are independent of each other and use the same encoding and decoding procedure.

Reference Ordering To apply our data hiding method to 3D mesh datasets, a *canonical* ordering of the mesh elements is needed which can be easily computed by both the encoder and decoder. One possibility is to compute such an ordering based on the mesh geometry using some kind of spatial sorting, e.g., by sorting the vertices along one coordinate axis and breaking ties using the other two axes. This requires access to vertex geometry and is sensitive to geometric distortion. Instead a reference ordering is defined based on the mesh connectivity alone. This makes our method immune to any kind of attack on the geometry.

A reference ordering of the mesh faces and vertices is simultaneously computed using the traversal performed by the Edgebreaker mesh compression algorithm. Once the initial vertex and edge are specified, the entire traversal is uniquely defined. The only condition on the connectivity is that the mesh is manifold and orientable. Both the encoder and decoder compute this ordering without any information beyond the identity of the initial vertex and edge and the mesh connectivity. One possible way to ensure consistent selection of the initial vertex and edge during encoding and decoding is to exclude the first face from encoding. Then start with the first edge of the first face when constructing the reference ordering for decoding.

Embedding Instead of dividing the two long integers, this method utilizes the next $k = \lfloor \log_2 i \rfloor$-bit data to select the $(n-i)$th element in the permutation π. To enlarge the capacity, Bogomjakov et al. used a special trick to encode one more bit of data: when the next $k + 1$-bit data point is selected, if the decimal integer is smaller than i but greater than or equal to 2^k, the element is able to encode $k + 1$ bits. Otherwise, the element can encode only a k-bit message and use the decimal integer to choose the correct element. Obviously, all the bitstreams of maximum length have the most significant bit "1." The expected capacity (in bits) is calculated by

$$E_1(C_i) = (k_i + 1)\frac{i - 2^{k_i}}{2^{k_i}} + (k_i)\frac{2^{k_i} - i}{2^{k_i}}. \tag{4.35}$$

In summary, the encoder and decoder have a computational complexity of $O(n)$, being more efficient than the optimal permutation steganography method. The upper bound of the embedding capacity is $\frac{1}{V}\sum_{i=1}^{V} \lfloor \log_2 i \rfloor$ bpv. The compact and simple computation of the method is efficient in implementation and loses only one bit per vertex compared with the optimal one regarding capacity. In addition, this method is fragile against permutation-targeted steganalysis.

4.3.2   Enhanced Order Encoding Model

Huang et al. [19] proposed a permutation steganography algorithm with high efficiency, which can increase the capacity to an amount closer to the optimal case while maintaining the same time complexity. Specifically, given different n elements, in Bogomjakov et al.'s algorithm, the first 2^k elements ($k = \lfloor \log_2 n \rfloor$) are encoded by a k-bit word of message. When n is not equal to an exponent of 2, the remaining $n - 2^k$ elements are encoded by a $(k + 1)$-bit word of message when applicable. In contrast, our algorithm virtually subdivides the n elements into three parts. The elements in the first part (m elements) and those in the third part (m elements) are encoded by the $(k + 1)$-bit word, where $m = n - 2^k$. Elements in the second part ($2^{k+1} - n$ elements) are encoded by k-bit words. This scheme allows our algorithm to offer a greater capacity than that can be achieved by Bogomjakov et al.'s algorithm. In short, the next k-bit data are chosen, and if their decimal integer is less than $i - 2^k$, then the element can encode the $k + 1$-bit message; otherwise, only the k-bit message can be encoded. The expected capacity (in bits) is calculated as

$$E_2(C_i) = (k_i + 1) \frac{i - 2^{k_i}}{2^{k_i+1}} + (k_i) \frac{2^{k_i+1} - (i - 2^{k_i})}{2^{k_i+1}}. \tag{4.36}$$

Because $E_2(C) = \sum E_2(C_i) > E_1(C) = \sum E_1(C_i)$, the expected capacity of the algorithm is closer to the optimum capacity than [18], i.e., the lower bound is $\frac{1}{V} \sum_{i=1}^{V} \lfloor \log_2 i \rfloor$ bpv. When n increases, our algorithm is nearer and faster to the optimal capacity than Bogomjakov et al.'s algorithm. As an example, 99.14% of optimal capacity is achieved when employing $n = 2^8$ elements. This result is in contrast to Bogomjakov et al.'s algorithm, which achieves only 95.47% of optimal capacity when employing the same element numbers. Our algorithm has a capacity very close to optimal (99.69%) when employing $n = 2^{20}$ elements and is only 60,088.43 bits fewer than optimal. In contrast, Bogomjakov et al.'s algorithm achieves 98.34% of optimal capacity, which is 322,227.18 bits fewer than optimal capacity. In addition, the same runtime complexity of $O(n)$ is achieved. Moreover, the method is fragile to permutation-targeted steganalysis.

4.3.3   Binary Tree Model

Tu et al. [20] improved the method of Bogomjakov et al. [18] by adopting a complete binary tree to embed and extract data, which doubles the probability of encoding the additional bit-length message. Bogomjakov et al. use a trick to encode one additional bit by peeking at the next $k + 1$ bits of the input message. If their value b is smaller than $n - i$ but also larger than or equal to $2k$ (i.e., if the first bit is one), the element at position b can encode $k + 1$ bits. Otherwise only k bits can be encoded and their value b for picking the element. The fact that Bogomjakov et al.'s mapping encodes interior nodes as well as their leaf nodes means that the prefixes of the corresponding bitstreams are represented twice. This is overcame inefficiency by changing the mapping such that only leaf nodes are encoded.

The number e of different $k + 1$ bits codes that can be encoded is twice the difference between n and highest $2k$ number smaller than n (i.e., $e = ((n - i) - 2k) \times 2$). We peek at the value b of the next $k + 1$ bits. If their value b is less than e, then b is directly used as the index of the next primitive in the reference ordering. Otherwise only k bits can be encoded and the offset $e/2$ is added to the value of these b bits before interpreting it as the index.

In summary, compared with the algorithm of [18], this method doubles the chance of encoding additional bits and increases the average capacity by 0.63 bits per vertex. In short, this scheme has the same minimum and maximum capacity, and the average embedding rate is still one bit per vertex less than the optimum. In addition, the method has the same embedding capacity (the upper bound is $\frac{1}{V}\sum_{i=1}^{V}\lfloor\log_2 i\rfloor$ bpv) and computational complexity $O(n)$ as those of [19] and is fragile against permutation-targeted steganalysis.

4.3.4 Coding Tree Model

Tu and Tai [21] established a left-biased binary coding tree for embedding bitstrings into primitives. The core operation of the method constitutes two parts: the left-skewed subtree, which extends the bitstring, and the right subtree, which is a complete binary tree. This method does not directly interpret the primitive indexes in the reference order as encoding/decoding bits but makes some modifications to the mapping. The number of different $k + 1$ bits is twice the difference between n and the highest 2^k less than n (i.e., $(i - 2^k) \times 2$). If the primitive is less than $2(i - 2^k)$, the method will peek at the next $k + 1$-bit data. Otherwise, only the k-bit data can be encoded, and the offset $i - 2^k$ is added to the value of these original bits, which is then interpreted as an index.

Coding Tree A binary tree could be treated as a coding tree. Each bit in a bitstream is used to branch (traverse) the coding tree, and the bitstream is encoded in the reached leaf node. The number of the encoded bits is the length of the path from the root to a leaf node. The coding tree containing n leaf nodes is recursively defined as

$$T(n) = T(l) + T(r), \tag{4.37}$$

where $T(n)$ represents the tree T having n leaf nodes, and $T(l)$ and $T(r)$ represent the left subtree having l leaf nodes and the right subtree having r leaf nodes respectively. $T(l)$ and $T(r)$ are of course coding trees. Also the number of leaf nodes in the tree is constrained as follows:

$$n = l + r, r = 2^{\lfloor\log_2 n\rfloor - 1}, n \geq 2. \tag{4.38}$$

The coding tree defined in this way is meant to have the following properties:

- The left subtree with respect to its parent is a sort of skewed tree that helps lengthen the bitstream, namely increasing the maximal capacity as far as possible.
- The right subtree with respect to its parent is a full binary tree that keeps the minimal capacity of embedding message the same as the complete binary tree.
- The shortest path length of the left subtree is not less than the longest path length of the corresponding right subtree.
- The number of the leaf nodes in the left subtree is not less than that of the nodes in the corresponding right subtree.
- The left and right subtrees have at least one leaf node.

Embedding The embedding message is divided into two parts. Our embedding procedures hide one part of message in the vertex primitive by rearranging the vertices and another part of message in the polygon primitive by rearranging the polygons. The same embedding procedures apply to both of the vertex and face primitives. Specifically, a primitive at position p in the reference ordering is selected to embed the next h bits in the embedding message if p, non-negative integer, is equal to the integer value of the h bits and the extended binary traversal stops at the leaf node p according to the next h bitstream. The encoder and recursive encoder procedures are applied in the embedding message stage. The encoder procedure is to rearrange (output) primitive according to the position (leaf node) visited by the recursive traversal of the recursive encoder procedure.

Assume that there are n primitives in the initial reference ordering. At each step i in the Encoder procedure, a primitive at position p, which is the returned value of the recursive encoder procedure, is chosen from the remaining $n-i$ primitives of the reference ordering and the output is regarded the next primitive of the permutation. The output primitive is removed by replacing it with the current last primitive in the reference order so that the remaining $n - i - 1$ primitives are sequentially stored in the array. The position p is the index of the leaf node which is determined by the result of our coding tree traversal according to the next h bits where h is the external path length from root to a leaf node. From left to right each bit of the next h bits is used to branch the traversal. If the message bit is zero, the left child will be traversed, otherwise the right child will be traversed. The traversal continues until the number of the leaf nodes is only one left. After stopping the recurrence, the position of the visited leaf node is computed level-by-level all the way back to the root. If the visited node is the right child with respect to its parent, then its local position must plus the number of the leaf nodes in left subtree to obtain the local position in each level. Therefore, position p is the index of the leaf node in the tree with respect to the next h bits in the embedding message.

Extraction Assume that there are n primitives in the initial permutation in the stego polygonal mesh. At each step i, the next primitive is chosen from the permutation to extract the embedded message bits. The position p from the remaining $n-i$ primitives of the reference ordering that has the same primitive with the primitive from the permutation is the value of being output bitstream. Inspired by Bogomjakov et al., to efficiently speedup the position computation, the primitive record with a ref field is extended that keeps the current position of the primitive in the reference ordering.

The embedded bits with respect to the remaining primitives at position p are extracted level-by-level from root to the leaf node p, and one level extracts one message bit. If the number (position) p is less than the number of the leaf nodes in the left subtree, position p is a leaf node in the left subtree. Hence output message bit 0 and traverse the left child, otherwise position p is a leaf node in the right subtree and output message bit 1. Then, update the number p by subtracting the number of the leaf nodes in the corresponding left subtree from it to have the local relative position of p in the right subtree. The extraction process recursively traverses the tree until the number of the leaf nodes is only one node left.

There are at least $\lfloor \log_2 (n - i) \rfloor$ bits embedded at each step i of the embedding procedure. Hence, given n embedding primitives, our method has the same minimal capacity $C(n)$ with Bogomjakov et al., $C(n) \geq \log_2 n! - n + 1$. Namely, our method is one bit per primitive less than the theoretical optimum, $\log_2 n!$, of the standard permutation steganography.

In summary, the minimum capacity of the method remains the same as that of the complete binary tree. The scheme has a computational complexity of $O(n \log (n))$. In addition, this method increases the embedding capacity of each vertex by 0.63 bits compared with [18], i.e., the upper bound is $\frac{1}{V} \sum_{i=1}^{V} \lfloor \log_2 i \rfloor + 0.63$ bpv. Moreover, the method is fragile to permutation-targeted steganalysis.

4.3.5 Maximum Expected Level Tree Model

When embedding and extracting a certain vertex, Tu et al. [22] established a maximum expected level tree for the remaining vertices in the reference order. At each level, the number of leaf vertices in the subtree is determined by the probability of the next message to be embedded. In this way, the distance between the root node and the leaf vertex can be as long as possible. Messages are represented by traversed paths. Given the message to be embedded, the message probability model of the 0-bit and 1-bit run-length histograms needs to be updated after each embedding or extraction. In the message extraction process, one needs to extract the message histogram from the stego model first and then extract the message from the histogram.

Message Probability Model A message probability model is proposed to represent a random phenomenon of the occurrence of 0-bits and 1-bits in a given embedding message. A run of bits indicates that the same bit value occurs in several consecutive bits, the run-length is the bit count in a run, and a run-length sequence is a sequence of run-lengths. The run-length histogram $Hist_x$ is constructed for the run-length sequence of x-bit with respect to a given message, and $Hist_x(k)$ gives the number of runs (frequency) with the same count k in $Hist_x$. Note that the bin of the histogram indicates the count of a run-length.

To accurately estimate the probability of the occurrence of a message bit, two events for the message probability model are required. The event $B_x(k)$ indicates that there are already k consecutive x-bits in the embedding/extracting message, and event $A_x(next)$ indicates that the next bit in the message will be x-bit. Based on the events $B_x(k)$ and $A_x(next)$, the probability of event $A_x(next)$, given the occurrence of event $B_{\hat{x}}$, namely the conditional probability of $P(A_x(next)|B_{\hat{x}})$, could be calculated as the probability of the occurrence of the next message bit. Please refer to the original paper for more details.

Coding Tree Based on the proposed message probability model, a maximum expected level (MEL) tree $T(n)$ is constructed level-by-level to maximize the hiding capacity as much as possible for the embedding primitive. $T(n)$ is actually a binary tree with n leaf nodes and is recursively defined as follows:

$$T(n) = T_L(nl) + T_R(nr),$$ (4.39)

where $T_L(nl)$ is the left subtree with nl leaf nodes and $T_R(nr)$ is the right subtree with nr leaf nodes. $T_L(nl)$ and $T_R(nr)$ are also MEL trees. The tree is a binary search structure that branches left for the next 0-bit and right for the next 1-bit in the embedding message. The traversal path from the root to a leaf node embeds a bitstring of the embedding message into the primitive in the node. Note that n leaf nodes in the MEL tree are indexed sequentially from left to right.

Embedding The same embedding procedure embeds a message in both embedding primitives, the vertex and face primitives. Given n embedding primitives, the Edgebreaker algorithm [17] computes a reference ordering of the embedding primitives, and the proposed approach stores it as a reference array. $Hist_x$ is obtained from the embedding message and is presented as a histogram array. The MEL tree $T(n)$ is constructed level-by-level based on $P(A_0(next)|B_x(k))$ to embed a bitstring of the embedding message into an embedding primitive. An embedding primitive, embedded with a bitstring, means that the tree traversal by the bitstring will reach that primitive.

Extraction Given a stego model with n primitives, the Edgebreaker algorithm computes the reference ordering. $Hist_x$ and the first message bit, the message header used in the embedding procedure, are extracted first. Based on the extracted $Hist_x$, the embedded message is then extracted by comparing the ordering of the primitive present in the stego model to that of the primitive in the reference ordering.

In summary, the capacity of this method is related to the run-length histograms of the embedded data, and it has a lower bound capacity of $\frac{1}{V}\sum_{i=1}^{V}\lfloor \log_2 i \rfloor + 0.63$ bpv. The computational complexity of the method varies from $O(n^2)$ to $O(n \log n)$ since it is directly correlative to the height of the constructed maximum expected level tree. Therefore, this method is analytically slower. In addition, this method is fragile against permutation-targeted steganalysis.

4.3.6 One-Ring Neighborhood Model

Previous permutation-based methods utilize the encoding capabilities of vertex and face lists to embed data. Although the vertex ordering is initially configured regularly and the order of the vertices is directly related to the surface normals, the permutation operation will destroy the correlation of the adjacent vertices and obfuscate the triangle normals.

To avoid bringing about global changes, Wang et al. [23] proposed to embed secret messages into the local neighbors of each vertex. In each embedding round, the 1-ring neighbor of the current vertex is utilized to carry the next few bits. In some cases, the vertices of the neighbor have already been utilized; thus, among all unused vertices, the method selects the vertex that appears first in the reference order and assigns an alias to it. Then, all the vertices not picked by i are cascaded in clockwise order. According to the next $\lfloor \log_2 i \rfloor$ bit value, the corresponding vertex is selected.

In summary, the embedding capacity of the method is much smaller than $\frac{1}{V} \sum_{i=1}^{V} \lfloor \log_2 i \rfloor$ bpv, but its security level is high since it can withstand permutation-targeted steganalysis and universal steganalysis.

References

1. F. Cayre and B. Macq, "Data hiding on 3-D triangle meshes," *IEEE Transactions on Signal Processing*, vol. 51, no. 4, pp. 939–949, 2003.
2. Ohbuchi, R., Masuda, H. & Aono, M. Watermaking three-dimensional polygonal models. *Proceedings Of The Fifth ACM International Conference On Multimedia*. pp. 261–272 (1997)
3. C.-M. Wang and Y.-M. Cheng, "An efficient information hiding algorithm for polygon models," in *Computer Graphics Forum*, vol. 24, no. 3. Wiley Online Library, 2005, pp. 591–600.
4. C.-M. Wang and P.-C. Wang, "Steganography on point-sampled geometry," *Computers & Graphics*, vol. 30, no. 2, pp. 244–254, 2006.
5. M.-W. Chao, C.-h. Lin, C.-W. Yu, and T.-Y. Lee, "A high capacity 3d steganography algorithm," *IEEE Transactions on Visualization and Computer Graphics*, vol. 15, no. 2, pp. 274–284, 2009.
6. V. Itier and W. Puech, "High capacity data hiding for 3d point clouds based on static arithmetic coding," *Multimedia Tools and Applications*, vol. 76, no. 24, pp. 26 421–26 445, 2017.
7. Z. Li, S. Beugnon, W. Puech, and A. G. Bors, "Rethinking the high capacity 3d steganography: Increasing its resistance to steganalysis," in *IEEE International Conference on Image Processing*. IEEE, 2017, pp. 510–514.
8. Z. Li and A. G. Bors, "Steganalysis of 3d objects using statistics of local feature sets," *Information Sciences*, vol. 415, pp. 85–99, 2017.
9. Y. Yang, N. Peyerimhoff, and I. Ivrissimtzis, "Linear correlations between spatial and normal noise in triangle meshes," *IEEE Transactions on Visualization and Computer Graphics*, vol. 19, no. 1, pp. 45–55, 2013.
10. J. Mielikäinen, "LSB matching revisited," *IEEE Signal Processing Letters*, vol. 13, no. 5, pp. 285–287, 2006.
11. N. Li, J. Hu, R. Sun, S. Wang, and Z. Luo, "A high-capacity 3d steganography algorithm with adjustable distortion," *IEEE Access*, vol. 5, pp. 24 457–24 466, 2017.
12. H. Zhou, K. Chen, W. Zhang, Y. Yao, and N. Yu, "Distortion design for secure adaptive 3-D mesh steganography," *IEEE Transactions on Multimedia*, vol. 21, no. 6, pp. 1384–1398, 2018.
13. R. Jiang, H. Zhou, W. Zhang, and N. Yu, "Reversible data hiding in encrypted three-dimensional mesh models," *IEEE Transactions on Multimedia*, vol. 20, no. 1, pp. 55–67, 2017.
14. T. Filler, J. Judas, and J. Fridrich, "Minimizing additive distortion in steganography using syndrome-trellis codes," *IEEE Transactions on Information Forensics and Security*, vol. 6, no. 3, pp. 920–935, 2011.
15. W. Li, W. Zhang, L. Li, H. Zhou, and N. Yu, "Designing near-optimal steganographic codes in practice based on polar codes," *IEEE Transactions on Communications*, 2020, https://doi.org/10.1109/TCOMM.2020.2982624.

16. D. Artz, "Digital steganography: Hiding data within data," *IEEE Internet Computing*, vol. 5, no. 3, pp. 75–80, 2001.
17. J. Rossignac, "Edgebreaker: Connectivity compression for triangle meshes," *IEEE Transactions on Visualization and Computer Graphics*, vol. 5, no. 1, pp. 47–61, 1999.
18. A. Bogomjakov, C. Gotsman, and M. Isenburg, "Distortion-free steganography for polygonal meshes," in *Computer Graphics Forum*, vol. 27, no. 2. Wiley Online Library, 2008, pp. 637–642.
19. N.-C. Huang, M.-T. Li, and C.-M. Wang, "Toward optimal embedding capacity for permutation steganography," *IEEE Signal Processing Letters*, vol. 16, no. 9, pp. 802–805, 2009.
20. S.-C. Tu, W.-K. Tai, M. Isenburg, and C.-C. Chang, "An improved data hiding approach for polygon meshes," *The Visual Computer*, vol. 26, no. 9, pp. 1177–1181, 2010.
21. S. Tu, H. Hsu, and W. Tai, "Permutation steganography for polygonal meshes based on coding tree," *International Journal of Virtual Reality*, vol. 9, no. 4, pp. 55–60, 2010.
22. S.-C. Tu and W.-K. Tai, "A high-capacity data-hiding approach for polygonal meshes using maximum expected level tree," *Computers & Graphics*, vol. 36, no. 6, pp. 767–775, 2012.
23. Y. Wang, L. Kong, Z. Qian, G. Feng, X. Zhang, and J. Zheng, "Breaking permutation-based mesh steganography and security improvement," *IEEE Access*, vol. 7, pp. 183 300–183 310, 2019.
24. Zhu, J., Zhang, Y., Zhang, X. & Cao, X. Gaussian Model for 3D Mesh Steganography. *IEEE Signal Processing Letters*. **28** pp. 1729–1733 (2021)
25. Fridrich, J. & Soukal, D. Matrix embedding for large payloads. *IEEE Transactions on Information Forensics and Security*. **1**, 390–395 (2006)
26. Fridrich, J. & Kodovsky, J. Rich models for steganalysis of digital images. *IEEE Transactions on Information Forensics and Security*. **7**, 868–882 (2012)
27. Max, N. Weights for computing vertex normals from facet normals. *Journal Of Graphics Tools*. **4**, 1–6 (1999)
28. Rencher, A. A review of "Methods of Multivariate Analysis,". (Taylor & Francis,2005)
29. Fridrich, J. & Kodovsky, J. Multivariate Gaussian model for designing additive distortion for steganography. *2013 IEEE International Conference On Acoustics, Speech And Signal Processing*. pp. 2949–2953 (2013)
30. Amat, P., Puech, W., Druon, S. & Pedeboy, J. Lossless 3D steganography based on MST and connectivity modification. *Signal Processing: Image Communication*. **25**, 400–412 (2010)
31. Rissanen, J. & Langdon, G. Arithmetic coding. *IBM Journal Of Research And Development*. **23**, 149–162 (1979)
32. Lavoué, G. A multiscale metric for 3D mesh visual quality assessment. *Computer Graphics Forum*. **30**, 1427–1437 (2011)
33. Li, Z., Hu, Z., Luo, X. & Lu, B. Embedding change rate estimation based on ensemble learning. *Proceedings Of The First ACM Workshop On Information Hiding And Multimedia Security*. pp. 77–84 (2013)
34. Abdulrahman, H., Chaumont, M., Montesinos, P. & Magnier, B. Color image steganalysis based on steerable gaussian filters bank. *Proceedings Of The 4th ACM Workshop On Information Hiding And Multimedia Security*. pp. 109–114 (2016)
35. Y. Yang and I. Ivrissimtzis, "Mesh discriminative features for 3D steganalysis," *ACM Transactions on Multimedia Computing, Communications, and Applications*, vol. 10, no. 3, p. 27, 2014.
36. Z. Li and A. G. Bors, "3D mesh steganalysis using local shape features," in *IEEE International Conference on Acoustics, Speech and Signal Processing*. IEEE, 2016, pp. 2144–2148.
37. Bentley, J. Multidimensional binary search trees used for associative searching. *Communications of the ACM*. **18**, 509–517 (1975)

Chapter 5
3D Mesh Steganalysis

Abstract In this chapter, we introduce triangle mesh steganalysis and its two categories: universal steganalysis and specific steganalysis. Universal steganalysis can detect embedded messages independent of steganographic algorithms, while specific steganalysis is designed for a specified type of steganographic method.

5.1 Universal Steganalysis

Universal steganalysis aims to detect steganographic artifacts by designing features based on the differences between the mesh object and its smoothed object. The performance of steganalysis is evaluated by machine learning classifiers [1, 2]. In the following, we first provide a framework for 3D mesh steganalysis and then introduce the existing 3D mesh steganalysis algorithms according to the date of publication. In addition, the notations of elements (vertex, edge, face, normal, etc.) are illustrated in Fig. 5.1.

5.1.1 Universal Steganalysis Framework

Figure 5.2 is a flowchart of the universal 3D mesh steganalysis. The framework is essentially based on the learning of residual feature statistics and classification, which includes calibrating the original mesh to a canonical version, Laplacian smoothing, extracting features, mapping features, and classification. Before feature extraction, the vertices are preprocessed into a canonical version by rotating the object and aligning its coordinates with the three principal directions collected by PCA. The object is then scaled to fit inside a unit cube.

Given a target watermarking/steganographic algorithm, the steganalytic algorithm extracts N-dimensional feature vectors $\mathbf{F}_i$ from a training set of cover and stego models:

$$\mathbf{F}_i = (f_{i,1}, f_{i,2}, \ldots, f_{i,N}), \tag{5.1}$$

Fig. 5.1 Notations of
elements in a local region,
which include vertices (v_i,
v_{i+1}, v_{i+2}), edges (e_k), faces
(f_j), normal vectors ($\mathbf{n}(v_i)$,
$\mathbf{n}(f_j)$, $\mathbf{n}(e_k)$), and dihedral
angles ($\theta(e_k)$)

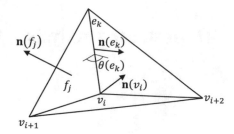

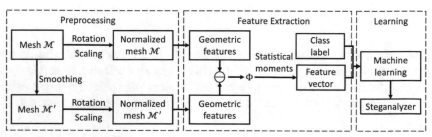

Fig. 5.2 The 3D mesh steganalysis framework based on learning from statistics of residual
features and classification. Figure from [12]

where i is the index of the model in the training set. These feature vectors are the
input of a supervised learning algorithm that produces a classifier associated with
the target watermarking/steganographic algorithm.

Normalization In a preprocessing step, the model is normalized by a coordinate
system change before feature extraction. We apply PCA to the vertex coordinates
and align the xyz axes of the coordinate system with the three principal directions
$\mathbf{q}_1$, $\mathbf{q}_2$, and $\mathbf{q}_3$, respectively, assuming that $\lambda_1 \geq \lambda_2 \geq \lambda_3$ for the corresponding
eigenvalues. After this coordinate system transformation, we uniformly scale the
model into the unit cube centered at $(0.5, 0.5, 0.5)$. The normalization ensures
that the feature vector $\mathbf{F}_i$ of each model is invariant under affine transformations.
Furthermore, normalization restricts the values of each component $f_{i,j}$ of $\mathbf{F}_i$ to
a limited range and thus prevents the large feature values from dominating the
smaller values. Notice that because of the use of PCA, we are not able to specify the
orientation of the axes of the new coordinate system. That means that all extracted
features should be invariant under an orientation change of any of the axes.

Calibration The reference mesh $\mathcal{M}'$ we use for calibration is produced by applying
one iteration of Laplacian smoothing on the original mesh $\mathcal{M}$. We utilize a standard
Laplacian operator corresponding to the Kirchhoff matrix [16] with entries

$$\mathbf{R}_{i,j} = \begin{cases} \mathrm{val}(v_i) & \text{if } i = j \\ -1 & \text{if } v_j \in \mathcal{N}(i) \quad 1 \leq i, j \leq V , \\ 0 & \text{otherwise,} \end{cases} \tag{5.2}$$

where v_i is the vertex indexed by i, val(v_i) and $\mathcal{N}(i)$ denote the valence and the 1-ring neighborhood of v_i, and V is the number of mesh vertices. We have found that this simple calibration process works well against all watermarking algorithms we have tested. Moreover, its simplicity gives a reasonable expectation that the experimental results will generalize well against other steganographic/watermarking algorithms that have been proposed or will be proposed in the future.

Feature Extraction The computation of the feature vector $\mathbf{F}_i$ is a two-step process: extracting features and computing components of $\mathbf{F}_i$. More specifically, we first compare the original and reference models and compute vectors with components corresponding to mesh vertices, edges, or faces. Next, these vectors are processed to produce the components of the feature vector $\mathbf{F}_i$. The motivation of such operation is from digital image steganalysis, and the difference between the stego image and its smoothed image is more significant than the difference between the cover and its smoothed image [13, 14]; similarly, it is expected that the differences related to 3D steganalysis comply with the same rules. By applying a unified Laplacian smoothing process to the original mesh $\mathcal{M}$ for one iteration, we can obtain a smoothed mesh $\mathcal{M}'$, which moves the current vertex $\mathbf{p}_i$ to its one-ring average as follows [15]:

$$\mathbf{p}_i \leftarrow \mathbf{p}_i + \frac{\tau}{\sum_{v_j \in \mathcal{N}_1(v_i)} w_{ij}} \sum_{v_j \in \mathcal{N}_1(v_i)} w_{ij}(\mathbf{p}_j - \mathbf{p}_i), \tag{5.3}$$

where τ is a scalar term and w_{ij} is a weighting term. Li et al. [12] analyze the influence of the 3D object smoothing with various levels of high-pass filtering by adjusting the value of τ. They vary the scale factor $\tau \in \{0.1, 0.2, 0.3, 0.4, 0.5\}$. When the scale factor $\tau = 0.3$, the steganalysis results for the 3D objects embedded by the multi-layer embedding model proposed by Chao et al. [21] are slightly better than the results obtained from the other hyperparameters.

Dimensionality Reduction Dimensionality reduction, or dimension reduction, is the transformation of data from a high-dimensional space into a low-dimensional space so that the low-dimensional representation retains some meaningful properties of the original data, ideally close to its intrinsic dimension. Working in high-dimensional spaces can be undesirable for many reasons: raw data are often sparse as a consequence of the curse of dimensionality, and analyzing the data is usually computationally intractable. Dimensionality reduction is common in fields that deal with large numbers of observations and/or large numbers of variables, such as signal processing, speech recognition, neuroinformatics, and bioinformatics. Methods are commonly divided into linear and nonlinear approaches. The approaches can also be divided into feature selection and feature extraction. In 3D steganalysis, Yang and Ivrissimtzis [4] proposed using 4 statistical moments, namely, mean, variance, skewness, and kurtosis as well as 4 approaches based on the histogram of the features. Let $\mathbf{f}$ be one of these extracted features. The purpose of the log transform on the features $(\log(\mathbf{f}))$ is to reduce the range of the values and also to increase the weight of small positive values. Specifically:

$$\text{Mean}(\mathbf{f}) = \frac{1}{N} \sum_{i=1}^{N} f_i, \tag{5.4}$$

$$\text{Variance}(\mathbf{f}) = \frac{1}{N} \sum_{i=1}^{N} (f_i - \text{Mean}(\mathbf{f}))^2, \tag{5.5}$$

$$\text{Skewmess}(\mathbf{f}) = \frac{1}{N} \sum_{i=1}^{N} \left(\frac{f_i - \text{Mean}(\mathbf{f})}{\sqrt{\text{Variance}(\mathbf{f})}} \right)^3, \tag{5.6}$$

$$\text{Kurt}(\mathbf{f}) = \frac{1}{N} \sum_{i=1}^{N} \left(\frac{f_i - \text{Mean}(\mathbf{f})}{\sqrt{\text{Variance}(\mathbf{f})}} \right)^4, \tag{5.7}$$

where N is the feature dimension.

For the other four components, we first build the histogram of $\mathbf{f}$ with

$$H = \left\lceil \frac{\max(\mathbf{f}) - \min(\mathbf{f})}{h} \right\rceil \tag{5.8}$$

bins, where the size of the bin is given by the Freedman–Diaconis rule

$$h = 2 \frac{\text{IQR}(\mathbf{f})}{n^{1/3}}, \tag{5.9}$$

where IQR denotes the interquartile range and n is the number of components in $\mathbf{f}$. By counting the number of elements in each bin, we obtain the frequency vector $\mathbf{n} = n_1, n_2, \ldots, n_H$ and its difference vector $\mathbf{n}' = (n_2 - n_1, n_3 - n_2, \ldots, n_H - n_{H-1})$. Then, the four remaining components of $\mathbf{F}_i$ obtained from $\mathbf{f}$ are the mean, variance, skewness, and kurtosis of $\log(\mathbf{n}')$.

Usually, ensemble classifiers [3] are trained for steganalysis. The core task for effective steganalysis is feature design; hence, we introduce different features below.

5.1.2 YANG208 Features

Yang and Ivrissimtzis [4] proposed the first 208-D steganalysis features of 3D meshes. The absolute values of the 3D coordinate difference between $\mathcal{M}$ and $\mathcal{M}'$ are calculated, and then the vector length of each for each vertex vector is determined. The features of the x,y,z-component are

$$\phi_1(i) = \left| x(v_i) - x(v_i') \right|. \tag{5.10}$$

$$\phi_2(i) = \left| y(v_i) - y(v_i') \right|. \tag{5.11}$$

$$\phi_3(i) = \left| z(v_i) - z(v_i') \right|. \tag{5.12}$$

$$\phi_4(i) = \left| \mathbf{p}(v_i) - \mathbf{p}(v_i') \right|. \tag{5.13}$$

The Laplacian coordinates of $\mathcal{M}$ and $\mathcal{M}'$ are calculated as $\bar{\mathbf{p}}_i = [\bar{x}(v_i), \bar{y}(v_i), \bar{z}(v_i)]^T$ and $\bar{\mathbf{p}}_i' = [\bar{x}(v_i'), \bar{y}(v_i'), \bar{z}(v_i')]^T$, where they are the outcome of the Cartesian coordinates multiplied by the Kirchhoff matrix [16] of the 3D mesh. The other four vectors, including the three absolute values of the difference between each of the three coordinate components of $\mathcal{M}$ and $\mathcal{M}'$ and the ℓ_2 norm of the coordinates, are calculated by the same absolute differences under Laplacian coordinates:

$$\phi_5(i) = \left| \bar{x}(v_i) - \bar{x}(v_i') \right|. \tag{5.14}$$

$$\phi_6(i) = \left| \bar{y}(v_i) - \bar{y}(v_i') \right|. \tag{5.15}$$

$$\phi_7(i) = \left| \bar{z}(v_i) - \bar{z}(v_i') \right|. \tag{5.16}$$

$$\phi_8(i) = \left| \bar{\mathbf{p}}(v_i) - \bar{\mathbf{p}}(v_i') \right|. \tag{5.17}$$

The above computations are made separately on vertices whose valences are less than, equal to, or greater than 6, excluding all boundary vertices, which make up 24 features.

Then, the absolute difference between the dihedral angles $\theta(e_i)$ of the adjacent faces in the vertical plane connected by the common edge e_i is calculated:

$$\phi_9(i) = \left| \theta(e_i) - \theta(e_i') \right|. \tag{5.18}$$

For mesh faces, the change in local surface direction is acquired by measuring the angle between the surface normal $\mathbf{n}(f_i)$ of the original object and the corresponding $\mathbf{n}(f_i)'$ of the smoothed 3D mesh:

$$\phi_{10}(i) = \arccos \frac{\mathbf{n}(f_i) \cdot \mathbf{n}\left(f_i'\right)}{\|\mathbf{n}(f_i)\| \cdot \left\|\mathbf{n}\left(f_i'\right)\right\|}. \tag{5.19}$$

Based on each of the above 26 vectors, the components of the eight feature vectors are calculated, thus acquiring a vector of 208 dimensions expressed as Φ_{208}. Suppose ϕ is one of these 26 vectors, and the first four components are constructed from the differences between the adjacent histogram bins of ϕ. The remaining four components are the mean, variance, skewness, and kurtosis of the logarithm $\log(|\phi| + \epsilon)$.

In summary, though the computational cost of YANG208 is not large, the feature number is relatively large, and its discriminability is weaker than that of other features (see below), which implies that a few features of YANG208 are not effective. In addition, the classification accuracy for different payloads is inconsistent, which indicates that YANG208 is not robust enough.

5.1.3   YANG40 Features

Li and Bors [5] proposed YANG40, which consists of 40-D features, including the most effective features in YANG208. The first 6 features are the absolute distance calculated along the 3D axis between the vertex positions of $\mathcal{M}$ and $\mathcal{M}'$, considered in both the Cartesian and Laplacian coordinate systems.

Moreover, the two variations measured by the ℓ_2 norm of the vertex vectors (from the mesh center to the vertex position) are calculated in the Cartesian and Laplacian coordinate systems, respectively. ϕ_9 and ϕ_{10} from YANG208 are regarded as two additional feature vectors. From each of the above 10 vectors, 4 components (mean, variance, skewness, and kurtosis) are calculated. These components form a vector of dimension 40, which is represented as Φ_{40}.

In summary, compared to YANG208, YANG40 does not calculate the feature vectors separately based on vertex groups with different valences, thus reducing the overall feature dimension, while still maintaining good steganalysis performance.

5.1.4   LFS52 Features

Li and Bors [5] proposed features based on the 52-D local feature set (LFS), including YANG40 and 12 local shape features.

Vertex Normal Features The first designed feature is calculated as the angle between the normal vectors of two specified vertices, in which the normal vector of the vertex is calculated as the weighted sum of the normal vectors of the triangles related to the vertex:

$$\mathbf{n}(v_i) = \frac{\sum_{f_j \in \mathcal{N}_1(\mathbf{v}_i)} A(f_j)\mathbf{n}(f_j)}{\left\| \sum_{f_j \in \mathcal{N}_1(v_i)} A(f_j)\mathbf{n}(f_j) \right\|}, \tag{5.20}$$

where $\mathcal{N}_1(v_i)$ is the one-ring neighboring face of v_i and $A(f_j)$ is the area of triangle f_j. Therefore, the absolute value of the angle between the two vertex normals $\mathbf{n}(v_i)$

and $\mathbf{n}(v_i')$ is regarded as the designed feature:

$$\phi_{11}(i) = \arccos \frac{\mathbf{n}(v_i) \cdot \mathbf{n}(v_i')}{||\mathbf{n}(v_i)|| \cdot ||\mathbf{n}(v_i')||}.$$ (5.21)

Curvature Features The surface curvature was utilized to characterize 3D shapes for recognition and object retrieval, which can be designed for 3D steganalysis. The Gaussian curvature and curvature ratio are known to model well surface variation [28]. In differential geometry, the two principal curvatures at a given point of a surface measure how the surface bends by different amounts in different directions and are given by the eigenvalues of the shape operator at that point. The method from [29] is used to obtain the two principal curvatures at the location of each vertex. The local shape curvature measures the surface smoothness of the 3D mesh, where the principal curvatures $\kappa_1(v_i)$ and $\kappa_2(v_i)$ reflect the bending degree of the local surface in the orthogonal direction at vertex v_i, and the Gaussian curvature [28] is calculated as the product of the minimum and maximum principal curvatures:

$$\kappa_G(v_i) = \kappa_1(v_i) \cdot \kappa_2(v_i).$$ (5.22)

The second feature is calculated as the absolute difference between the two Gaussian curvatures $\kappa_G(v_i)$ and $\kappa_G(v_i')$:

$$\phi_{12}(i) = |\kappa_G(v_i) - \kappa_G(v_i')|.$$ (5.23)

The curvature ratio [29] is obtained by taking the ratio of the minimum to the maximum principal curvature:

$$\kappa_r(v_i) = \frac{\min(|\kappa_1(v_i)|, |\kappa_2(v_i)|)}{\max(|\kappa_1(v_i)|, |\kappa_2(v_i)|)},$$ (5.24)

and the corresponding feature is obtained by taking the absolute differences of the two curvature ratios $\kappa_r(v_i)$ and $\kappa_r(v_i')$:

$$\phi_{13}(i) = |\kappa_r(v_i) - \kappa_r(v_i')|.$$ (5.25)

These two properties, the Gaussian curvature and the curvature ratio, can describe locally well the shape of 3D meshes while being sensitive to any small changes. In summary, compared with the features based on coordinates and face normals, the features containing vertex normals and curvatures own better discriminability.

5.1.5   LFS64 Features

Kim et al. [6] extended LFS52 and considered the edge normal vector, mean curvature, and total curvature together, forming a 64-D feature vector. In the 3D steganalysis approach, in addition, the homogeneous kernel map is applied to the local feature set, making it possible to bring much more discrimination via nonlinear mapping. The proposed feature set and its combination with the homogeneous feature map have shown good performance on steganalysis.

The edge normal vector $\mathbf{n}(e_i)$ is defined as the weighted sum of the triangle normal vectors connected by a common edge:

$$\mathbf{n}(e_i) = \frac{\sum_{f_j \in \mathcal{N}_1(e_i)} A(f_j)\mathbf{n}(f_j)}{\left\| \sum_{f_j \in \mathcal{N}_1(e_i)} A(f_j)\mathbf{n}(f_j) \right\|}, \tag{5.26}$$

and the absolute value of the angles between the two edge normal vectors $\mathbf{n}(e_i)$ and $\mathbf{n}(e_i')$ is calculated, which is regarded as the feature:

$$\phi_9(i) = |\mathbf{n}(e_i) - \mathbf{n}\left(e_i'\right)|. \tag{5.27}$$

The mean curvature $\kappa_m(v_i)$,

$$\kappa_m(v_i) = \frac{\kappa_1(v_i) + \kappa_2(v_i)}{2} \tag{5.28}$$

and the total curvature $\kappa_t(v_i)$,

$$\kappa_t(v_i) = |\kappa_1(v_i)| + |\kappa_2(v_i)| \tag{5.29}$$

contribute two additional features. The difference between $\kappa_m(v_i)$ and $\kappa_m(v_i')$ and that between $\kappa_t(v_i)$ and $\kappa_t(v_i')$ are regarded as new features:

$$\phi_{14}(i) = |\kappa_m(v_i) - \kappa_m\left(v_i'\right)|. \tag{5.30}$$

$$\phi_{15}(i) = |\kappa_t(v_i) - \kappa_t\left(v_i'\right)|. \tag{5.31}$$

Homogeneous Kernel Map The above features may not be linearly separable as they are not directly related to the embedding domain of watermarking or steganography, which deteriorates steganalytic classifiers. Although the FLD ensemble [2], which has been widely used in recent years, has nonlinearity, it is known to have almost the same performance as linear classifiers [1]. Therefore, before training a detector, apply explicit maps to the features instead of using a kernelized classifier considered as an implicit approach. There is an alternative way called Nyström's approximation [30, 31] that has shown superior performance in image steganalysis recently but did not employ it due to its following disadvantages. First, it is data-dependent. Second, it requires additional learning separately. In addition, [30] pointed out that it may not be effective if the features are low dimensional and dense. In 3D mesh steganalysis, it is appropriate to use the homogeneous kernel map that is data-independent and approximated without any additional learning since the number of data to be acquired is relatively small and the extracted features are low dimensional.

Given a cover and stego feature $\mathbf{x}, \mathbf{y} \in \mathbb{R}_+^D$, it is important to find the feature map $\Psi(\cdot)$ called the homogeneous kernel map such that $K(\mathbf{x}, \mathbf{y}) = \langle (\mathbf{x}), (\mathbf{x}) \rangle_N$, where N stands for a Hilbert space. The kernel satisfies additivity and homogeneity, i.e., $K(\mathbf{x}, \mathbf{y}) = \sum_{j=1}^{D} k(x_j, y_j)$, and x_j and y_j are jth components of $\mathbf{x}$ and $\mathbf{y}$, respectively. Again, $k(x_j, y_j)$ can be expressed using the so-called kernel signature $\mathcal{K}(\lambda)$ as follows:

$$k(x_j, y_j) = \sqrt{x_j y_j} \mathcal{K}(\log y_j - \log x_j). \tag{5.32}$$

According to Bochner's theorem, any positive-definite function $\mathcal{K}(\lambda)$ can be expressed as

$$\mathcal{K}(\lambda) = \int_{\mathbb{R}} e^{-i\omega\lambda} d\mu(\omega), \quad \lambda \in \mathbb{R}, \tag{5.33}$$

where $\mu(\omega)$ denotes a non-negative symmetric measure, and it is assumed that $\mu(\omega) = \kappa(\omega)d\omega$, i.e., $\kappa(\omega)$ is the spectrum of the kernel signature in the frequency domain. The following expression can be obtained by replacing the kernel signature $\mathcal{K}(\cdot)$ of Eq. (5.32) with (5.33).

$$k(x_j, y_j) = \int_{\mathbb{R}} \left[e^{-i\omega \log x_j} \sqrt{x_j \kappa(\omega)} \right]^* \left[e^{-i\omega \log y_j} \sqrt{y_j \kappa(\omega)} \right] d\omega$$

$$= \int_{\mathbb{R}} \left[\Psi(x_j) \right]_\omega^* \left[\Psi(y_j) \right]_\omega d\omega, \left[\Psi(x_j) \right]_\omega = e^{-i\omega \log x_j} \sqrt{x_j \kappa(\omega)}, \tag{5.34}$$

where $\Psi(x_j)$ is a continuous and infinite dimensional vector. Thus, the discrete and finite one $\hat{\Psi}(x_j)$ can be approximated by sampling and scaling it:

$$\left[\hat{\Psi}(x_j) \right]_k = \sqrt{\omega_0} \left[\Psi(x_j) \right]_{k\omega_0}, \quad k = -N, \ldots, N, \tag{5.35}$$

where ω_0 is the so-called fundamental frequency. Meanwhile, the multi-dimensional feature map $\hat{\Psi}(\mathbf{x})$ is generated by stacking the scalar ones as

$$\hat{\Psi}(\mathbf{x}) = \bigoplus_{j=1}^{D} \hat{\Psi}(x_j). \tag{5.36}$$

Note that the final feature map $\hat{\Psi}(\mathbf{x})$ is a $D(2N+1)$-dimensional vector because the dimensionality of $\hat{\Psi}(x_j)$ for x_j is $(2N+1)$ by Eq. (5.35). Now, the nonlinear feature sets of $64 \times (2N+1)$ dimensions are obtained for the cover and stego meshes.

In summary, this method outperforms LFS52 greatly because of its three features: edge normal vector, mean curvature, and total curvature.

5.1.6 LFS76 Features

Li and Bors [17] extended LFS52 and proposed features based on the spherical coordinates (R, θ, φ), thus forming a 76-D feature vector. Spherical coordinates provide a straightforward representation for most graphical objects in characterizing the distance from the center and the location of each vertex on a sphere. Certain 3D watermarking methods, such as those from [32, 33], specifically embed changes into spherical coordinates. The 3D objects are converted from the Cartesian coordinate system into the spherical coordinate system, considering the center of the object as its reference. The spherical coordinate system specifies a point in the 3D space by a radius and two angles, and the link to the Cartesian coordinate system is given by

$$v_i(x) = R\cos(\varphi)\cos(\theta),$$
$$v_i(y) = R\cos(\varphi)\sin(\theta), \tag{5.37}$$
$$v_i(z) = R\sin(\varphi),$$

where $v(x) = (v_x, v_y, v_z)$ represents the Cartesian coordinates of the vertex, and (R, θ, φ) is its spherical coordinates, representing R, the Euclidean norm from a fixed origin, θ, the azimuth angle, while φ is the elevation angle. The center of the spherical coordinate system is O, representing the center of the 3D object calculated by averaging all the vertices in the object, as shown in Fig. 5.3.

Fig. 5.3 The spherical coordinate system, where R is the radial distance of vertex v_i, and θ and φ are its azimuth angle and elevation angle, respectively

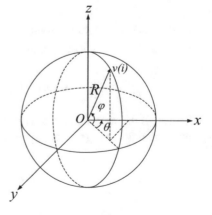

The absolute difference between each coordinate and its corresponding smoothed coordinate is taken as the new feature:

$$\phi_{16}(i) = |\theta(i) - \theta'(i)|,$$
$$\phi_{17}(i) = |\varphi(i) - \varphi'(i)|, \tag{5.38}$$
$$\phi_{18}(i) = |R(i) - R'(i)|.$$

The edge length in spherical coordinates is considered as the feature extraction element. e_i is the edge that connects v_j and v_k, and the edge vector $\mathbf{e}(e_i) = [\mathbf{p}_j, \mathbf{p}_k]$. The features extracted from the statistics of the edges are acquired by

$$\phi_{19}(i) = \left| |\theta(v_j) - \theta(v_k)| - |\theta'(v_j) - \theta'(v_k)| \right|,$$
$$\phi_{20}(i) = \left| |\varphi(v_j) - \varphi(v_k)| - |\varphi'(v_j) - \varphi'(v_k)| \right|, \tag{5.39}$$
$$\phi_{21}(i) = \left| |R(v_j) - R(v_k)| - |R'(v_j) - R'(v_k)| \right|.$$

A subset of the proposed feature set, LFS52 [5], did not include the 24-dimensional feature vector extracted from the spherical coordinate system of 3D objects. A higher dimensional feature set [4] is represented by the 208-dimensional vector defined as YANG208. This feature set considers separately the statistics of the first eight features described above, distinctly on vertex sets with valences less than, equal to, or greater than 6. The features described in this section are mainly local and centered on either the vertices or the edges or the faces forming the 3D meshes of the objects. During experimental studies, they have tested other features, either local or global, representing larger regions of 3D objects, but the results have not been satisfactory. In summary, in terms of steganalytic discriminability, the 6 new features do not improve the steganalysis performance.

5.1.7 LFS124 Features

Li et al. [7] extended LFS76, proposed an extended local feature set using edge vectors for steganalysis, and finally formed a 124-D feature vector. First, in the Cartesian coordinate system, the absolute difference of the edge length of the 3D component of the vector is calculated:

$$\phi_{22}(i) = \left| |x(v_j) - x(v_k)| - \left| x\left(v_j'\right) - x\left(v_k'\right) \right| \right|,$$
$$\phi_{23}(i) = \left| |y(v_j) - y(v_k)| - \left| y\left(v_j'\right) - y\left(v_k'\right) \right| \right|, \tag{5.40}$$
$$\phi_{24}(i) = \left| |z(v_j) - z(v_k)| - \left| z\left(v_j'\right) - z\left(v_k'\right) \right| \right|.$$

Second, the difference norm between the two vectors $\mathbf{e}(e_i)$ and $\mathbf{e}(e_i)$ in the Laplacian coordinate system is calculated. And another two features made up of the absolute differences between them and the angle between them are obtained.

The Laplacian coordinates of the ith vertex $[v_x(i), v_y(i), v_z(i)]$ are the ith row of matrix $\mathbf{L}$, given by

$$\mathbf{L} = \mathbf{M} \begin{bmatrix} v_x(1) & v_y(1) & v_z(1) \\ v_x(2) & v_y(2) & v_z(2) \\ \vdots & \vdots & \vdots \\ v_x(N) & v_y(N) & v_z(N) \end{bmatrix}, \tag{5.41}$$

where $v_x(i)$ is the x-coordinate of the ith vertex in the Cartesian coordinate system and $\mathbf{M}$ is the Kirchhoff matrix. Based on the Laplacian coordinate system, another six features are calculated in the same manner, all of which constitute 12 features.

In summary, LFS124 is efficient in implementation and performs better than the previous steganalytic features, including LFS52 and LFS76, indicating that the edge vector plays a vital role in steganalysis.

5.1.8 Normal Voting Tensor Model

In this section, Zhou et al. [8] proposed high-level 100-D steganalytic features using a tensor voting model, which gathers the local shape context. Conventional steganalytic features consist of low-level mesh features (points, edges, triangle faces, etc.), and it is difficult to extract the available features from the intrinsic shapes collected from the original meshes. Compared with the features extracted from the stego versions of the meshes, the differences are not significant. The normal voting tensor represents the local shape [25] and can therefore measure the local smoothness and neighborhood correlation. Because steganographic modification breaks the neighborhood correlations of the vertices, the normal voting tensor can be used to extract steganalytic features. Motivated by this fact, we first introduce the definition of the second-order symmetric tensor; then, we present several neighborhood descriptions of meshes, propose a few normal voting tensors that reflect the local surface shapes, and finally design new steganalytic features.

Second-Order Symmetric Tensor A first-order local description of a surface patch is given by the point coordinates and its associated normal. A second-order description would also include the principal curvatures and their directions. To capture the information of the first-order differential geometry and its singularities, a second-order symmetric tensor is used. This tensor captures both orientation information and its confidence [26].

Intuitively, the shape of the tensor defines the type of information captured (points, curves, or surface elements). To express a second-order symmetric tensor

T, which is graphically depicted by an ellipsoid in 3D, we take the associated quadratic form and diagonalize it. This process leads to a representation based on the eigenvalues $\lambda_1, \lambda_2, \lambda_3$ and the eigenvectors $\mathbf{e}_1, \mathbf{e}_2, \mathbf{e}_3$. In a more compact form,

$$\mathbf{T} = \sum_{k=1}^{3} \lambda_k \mathbf{e}_k \mathbf{e}_k^T = \lambda_1 \mathbf{e}_1 \mathbf{e}_1^T + \lambda_2 \mathbf{e}_2 \mathbf{e}_2^T + \lambda_3 \mathbf{e}_3 \mathbf{e}_3^T, \tag{5.42}$$

where $\lambda_1 \geq \lambda_2 \geq \lambda_3 \geq 0$. Note that because **T** is a second-order symmetric tensor, the eigenvalues are real and non-negative and the eigenvectors form an orthonormal basis. The above formula can be decomposed into

$$\begin{aligned}\mathbf{T} = (\lambda_1 - \lambda_2)\mathbf{e}_1 \mathbf{e}_1^T + (\lambda_2 - \lambda_3) \left(\mathbf{e}_1 \mathbf{e}_1^T + \mathbf{e}_2 \mathbf{e}_2^T\right) \\ + \lambda_3 \left(\mathbf{e}_1 \mathbf{e}_1^T + \mathbf{e}_2 \mathbf{e}_2^T + \mathbf{e}_3 \mathbf{e}_3^T\right),\end{aligned} \tag{5.43}$$

where $\mathbf{e}_1 \mathbf{e}_1^T$ describes a stick, $\mathbf{e}_1 \mathbf{e}_1^T + \mathbf{e}_2 \mathbf{e}_2^T$ describes a plate, and $\mathbf{e}_1 \mathbf{e}_1^T + \mathbf{e}_2 \mathbf{e}_2^T + \mathbf{e}_3 \mathbf{e}_3^T$ describes a ball [26].

Neighborhood Steganographic modification breaks the neighborhood correlation of vertices; hence, by analyzing the local smoothness and neighborhood correlations, we can better discriminate stego meshes from cover meshes. Let us consider combinatorial neighborhoods of vertices and faces. There are four possible *neighbors*: neighborhood vertices of a vertex; neighborhood faces of a vertex; neighborhood faces of a face connected by mutual edges; and neighborhood faces of a face connected by mutual vertices:

1. The neighborhood (also referred to as a ring) of a vertex $\mathbf{v}_i$ is the set $\mathbf{v}_i^\star = \{\mathbf{v}_j \in \mathcal{V} : \mathbf{v}_i \sim \mathbf{v}_j\}$, as shown in Fig. 5.4a. The degree of a vertex $\mathbf{v}_i$ is defined as the cardinality of $\mathbf{v}_i^\star$, which is denoted by $\left|\mathbf{v}_i^\star\right|$.
2. We denote by $\mathcal{F}(\mathbf{v}_i^\star)$ the set of triangles of the ring $\mathbf{v}_i^\star$, as shown in Fig. 5.4b.
3. We denote by $f_i^\star$ the set of all triangles that share an edge with triangle $f_i \in \mathcal{F}$ of a mesh; see Fig. 5.4c. For a closed mesh, the number of adjacent triangles of any triangle in the set $f_i^\star$ is 3, while for a non-closed mesh, the triangles on the boundaries are partially defective. Thus, the number of adjacent triangles of each triangle is 1 or 2.
4. We denote by $f_i^\star$ the set of all triangles that share a vertex with a triangle $\overline{f}_i \in \mathcal{F}$ of a mesh, as shown in Fig. 5.4d.

Normal Voting Tensor Based on the above definition of a tensor and the description of the neighborhood, we propose three normal voting-based tensors with different neighbors.

(a) Face normal of a vertex neighbor. Sun et al. [24] define the normal voting tensor of a vertex on a triangular mesh by using the unit normal vectors of the neighbor

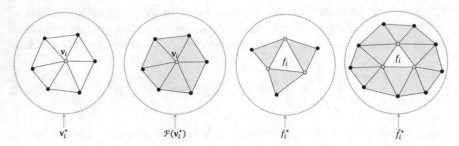

Fig. 5.4 Illustration of diverse neighbors. (**a**) Vertex neighborhood $\mathbf{v}_i^\star$; (**b**) Triangles of ring $\mathbf{v}_i^\star$ denoted by $\mathcal{F}(\mathbf{v}_i^\star)$; (**c**) Triangle neighborhood $f_i^\star$ is the set of all triangles sharing an edge with a triangle $f_i \in \mathcal{F}$; (**d**) Triangle neighborhood $\bar{f}_i^\star$ is the set of all triangles sharing a vertex with a triangle $f_i \in \mathcal{F}$

triangles. If we consider the covariance matrix $\mathbf{C}_{f_j}$ of each triangle $f_j \in \mathcal{F}(\mathbf{v}_i^\star)$ in Fig. 5.4b, $\mathbf{C}_{f_j}$ can be written by the unit normal of the triangle as

$$\mathbf{C}_{f_j} = \mathbf{n}_{f_j} \cdot \mathbf{n}_{f_j}^T. \tag{5.44}$$

Then, the normal voting tensor $\mathbf{T}_i$ of a vertex $\mathbf{v}_i \in \mathcal{V}$ can be generated by accumulating the weighted covariance matrices of its neighbor triangles:

$$\mathbf{T}_i = \sum_{f_j \in \mathcal{F}(\mathbf{v}_i^\star)} \mu_{ij} \mathbf{n}_{f_j} \cdot \mathbf{n}_{f_j}^T = \sum_{f_j \in \mathcal{F}(\mathbf{v}_i^\star)} \mu_{ij} \mathbf{C}_{f_j}, \quad i = 1, \ldots, N, \tag{5.45}$$

where the weight μ_{ij} is a vote decided by the area ratio among neighbor triangles and the distance between the vertex and barycenter $\mathbf{c}_{f_j}$ of each triangle following [24]:

$$\mu_{ij} = \frac{A(f_j)}{\max\left(A(\mathcal{F}(\mathbf{v}_i^\star))\right)} \exp\left(-\frac{\|\mathbf{c}_{f_j} - \mathbf{v}_i\|}{1/3}\right). \tag{5.46}$$

In a word, we denote by ξ_1 the first tensor model, and the eigenvalues are computed from it. The eigenvalues are taken as the first part of the proposed features.

(b) Face normals of a face neighbor. The normal voting tensor for a mesh face f_i is formulated as the sum of the weighted covariance matrices from its 1-ring or 2-ring neighboring faces [27]. One case is the neighborhood faces of one face conjoined by the shared edges, as shown in Fig. 5.4c:

$$\mathbf{T}_i = \frac{1}{\sum_{f_j \in f_i^\star} w_{ij} A(f_j)} \sum_{f_j \in f_i^\star} w_{ij} A(f_j) \mathbf{n}_j \cdot \mathbf{n}_j^T, \tag{5.47}$$

where w_{ij} is the weighting function. Here, we simply set all w_{ij} equal to 1. Furthermore, we denote the second tensor model by ξ_2.

Another case is based on the neighborhood faces of one face conjoined by shared vertices, as shown in Fig. 5.4d:

$$\mathbf{T}_i = \frac{1}{\sum_{f_j \in \vec{f_i^*}} w_{ij} A(f_j)} \sum_{f_j \in \vec{f_i^*}} w_{ij} A(f_j) \mathbf{n}_j \cdot \mathbf{n}_j^T. \tag{5.48}$$

Similarly, we denote the third tensor model by ξ_3.

Because the obtained tensor is a symmetric and positive semidefinite matrix, we can represent $\mathbf{T}_i$ using an orthonormal basis of the eigenvectors $\mathbf{e}_k$ and real eigenvalues λ_k by Eq. (5.42). Our geometrical interpretations are given below. By a 3D decomposition of the tensor $\mathbf{T}_i$ with Eq. (5.43), we can classify a vertex on the mesh as a corner, a sharp edge, or a face by the eigenvalues of the tensor $\mathbf{T}_i$. In Fig. 5.5, the characteristics of the eigenvalues of the normal voting tensor are depicted. On a noise-free triangulated mesh, a planar area has only one dominant eigenvalue in the surface normal direction. Two dominant eigenvalues indicate edge features where the weakest eigenvector will be in the edge direction. At a corner, all three of the eigenvalues are dominant. For example, consider a cube model where the eigenvalues of the tensor are sorted in decreasing order $\lambda_1 \geq \lambda_2 \geq \lambda_3 \geq 0$ and normalized. Then, for the orthogonal features, we can write $\{\lambda_1 = 1, \lambda_2 = \lambda_3 = 0\}$ (face), $\{\lambda_1 = \lambda_2 = \frac{\sqrt{2}}{2}, \lambda_3 = 0\}$ (edge), and $\{\lambda_1 = \lambda_2 = \lambda_3 = \frac{\sqrt{3}}{3}\}$ (corner) [27].

Feature Design As explained above, the eigenvalues can reflect the shape of the normal voting tensor. Thus, the eigenvalues are effective features for representing the shape of a local surface patch, as shown in Fig. 5.5. Formally, the absolute values of the differences between the eigenvalues of the two tensors (from the original face and the smoothed face) are regarded as features. The well-designed three-tensor models (ξ_1, ξ_2, ξ_3) are such that each extracts three eigenvalue differences to form a total of 9 features, which are denoted by $\phi_{23} - \phi_{31}$. Following the former convention, for each eigenvalue λ_k from each tensor voting model ξ_j,

$$\phi_k(i) = |\lambda_k(f_i) - \lambda_k(f_i')|, \quad i = 1, \ldots, |\mathcal{F}|, \quad k = 1, 2, 3, \tag{5.49}$$

where f' is the triangle face from the smoothed mesh $\mathcal{M}'$. After extracting the statistical moments, the proposed features form $9 \times 4 = 36$ features. We combine the proposed NVT features and LFS64 to form a new feature set NVT+, and the dimension of NVT+ reaches 100.

NVT constitutes a total of $9 \times 4 = 36$ features. By combining the NVT features and LFS64 features, the dimension of NVT+ can be as high as 100. In summary, NVT+ offers an obvious improvement in classification accuracy, which indicates that the distribution of a local region's face normals is an effective indicator for

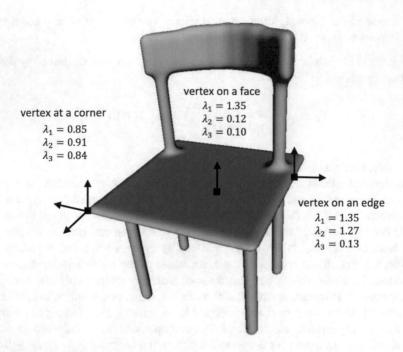

vertex at a corner
$\lambda_1 = 0.85$
$\lambda_2 = 0.91$
$\lambda_3 = 0.84$

vertex on a face
$\lambda_1 = 1.35$
$\lambda_2 = 0.12$
$\lambda_3 = 0.10$

vertex on an edge
$\lambda_1 = 1.35$
$\lambda_2 = 1.27$
$\lambda_3 = 0.13$

Fig. 5.5 Eigenvalues of the normal voting tensor for different features (a corner, an edge, and a face)

detecting stego meshes. However, the calculation cost of this method is very high because it is very time-consuming to calculate each feature of the adjacent face.

5.1.9 WFS228 Features

Li and Bors [9] proposed using multiresolution 3D wavelet analysis as a new set of 228-D steganalysis features. The features are originally designed to detect messages embedded in watermarks based on the 3D wavelet algorithm, and for most steganographic methods, they are effective for boosting steganalysis.

3D wavelet decompositions provide a transformation between the scales of meshes for a 3D object. Wavelet coefficient vectors (WCVs), which are produced following the 3D wavelet decomposition, encode essential information about the 3D shape of the object. An outline of the 3D wavelet analysis methodology is first provided and how this can be applied to extract features that are useful for steganalysis. Figure 5.6 illustrates how, by using 3D wavelet analysis, the original object M is decomposed into a lower resolution mesh M^l and WCVs, shown to the left, by using the 3D lazy wavelet decomposition [18]. The same mesh is subdivided, as shown on the right side of Fig. 5.6, into a higher resolution mesh M^h and the

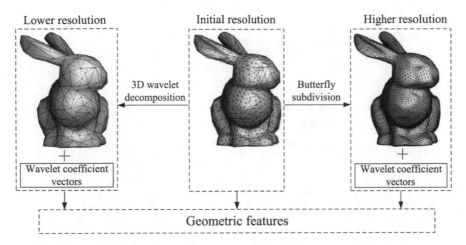

Fig. 5.6 Generating multiresolution meshes using the 3D wavelet decomposition and Butterfly subdivision

corresponding WCVs, using the Butterfly scheme [19]. Geometric features, which are then used for steganalysis, are generated using the initial resolution mesh, the lower resolution, the higher resolution, and the corresponding WCVs, resulting from the processes of down-scaling or up-scaling the 3D object. Most of the 3D wavelet-based watermarking approaches modify the WCVs and their corresponding edges from the lower resolution of the mesh to hide information into the 3D mesh. This motivates us to find characteristic features from the lower resolution meshes and their corresponding WCVs and use them for steganalysis. Meanwhile, the vertices from the higher resolution mesh are obtained from the corresponding larger neighborhood of vertices from the original mesh. This indicates that the geometric features from the higher resolution mesh are likely to be more sensitive to the changes than that of the lower resolution mesh.

Because most of the wavelet-related embedding methods embed messages by modifying both the WCVs and edges obtained from the low-resolution version of the 3D mesh, it is helpful to find and use these features in 3D mesh steganalysis. In addition, the vertices of the high-resolution 3D mesh are acquired by analyzing the larger vertex neighbors of the original 3D mesh, which shows that the geometric features of the high-resolution 3D mesh are more sensitive to changes in the original mesh. The features for steganalysis are extracted based on the transformations of both up-scaling and down-scaling the given mesh and the corresponding WCVs.

Initial Mesh Feature Extraction The first two geometric features are extracted from the initial mesh and represent the edge vector and its corresponding flipped edge vector. The edge vectors $\mathbf{e}(e_i) = [\mathbf{p}_j, \mathbf{p}_k]$ represent the vectors from the vertex v_j to the vertex v_k, where v_j and v_k are adjacent in the initial resolution mesh. An example of edge vector is illustrated in Fig. 5.7 as $\mathbf{e}_{(2,3)}$. Each flipped edge vector $\{\mathbf{e}_{(i,j)*}\}$ connects the opposite vertices, from the triangles that share the associated

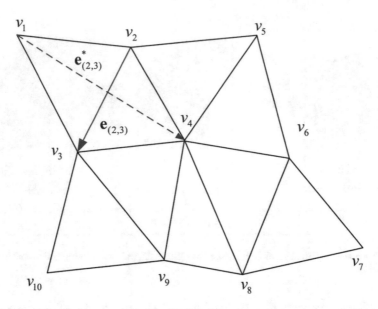

Fig. 5.7 Extracting edge vectors and their flipped counterparts from the mesh of initial resolution

edge vector $\{\mathbf{e}_{(i,j)}\}$. For example, the vector $\{\mathbf{e}_{(2,3)*}\}$ from Fig. 5.7, connecting two vertices v_1 and v_4, is the flipped edge vector of the edge vector $\{\mathbf{e}_{(2,3)}\}$. The direction of the flipped edge vector is oriented from the vertex with a lower index to the one with a higher index, as shown in Fig. 5.7.

Low-Resolution Mesh Feature Extraction The lower resolution mesh is obtained after one iteration of the 3D lazy wavelet decomposition, which is illustrated in Fig. 5.8. In this figure, four triangles $\triangle v_4 v_5 v_6$, $\triangle v_4 v_6 v_8$, $\triangle v_6 v_7 v_8$, and $\triangle v_4 v_8 v_9$ from the initial resolution mesh are merged into a single larger triangle $\triangle v_5 v_7 v_9$ as part of a coarser mesh at a lower resolution of surface representation. The vertices, v_4, v_6, and v_8 in Fig. 5.8 corresponding to the terminal points for the three WCVs, $\mathbf{w}^l_{(5,9)}$, $\mathbf{w}^l_{(5,7)}$, and $\mathbf{w}^l_{(7,9)}$, are removed while down-scaling the mesh. The subscripts of $\mathbf{w}^l_{(i,j)}$ represent the two vertices v_i and v_j of the WCV's support edge $\mathbf{e}^l_{(i,j)}$ from the lower resolution mesh. Meanwhile, the initial point of the WCV, $\mathbf{w}^l_{(5,9)}$, is the midpoint of its support edge $\mathbf{e}^l_{(5,9)}$ in the lower resolution mesh. Consequently, each edge vector from the lower resolution mesh is associated with one WCV. $\mathbf{w}^l_{(i,j)}$ and the edge vector, $\mathbf{e}^l_{(i,j)}$, from the lower resolution mesh representation are considered as components of the proposed 3D wavelet feature vector used for steganalysis. The reason for choosing these WCVs and their support edge vectors as steganalytic features is because these are changed when information is hidden by the steganographic algorithms. Two other features are considered from the lower resolution mesh. The first is represented by the angle between the WCV and its

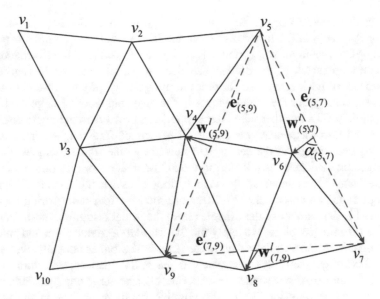

Fig. 5.8 Illustration of the 3D wavelet decomposition for a mesh down-scaling from its original resolution to a lower resolution

support edge vector in the lower resolution mesh, defined as

$$\alpha_{(i,j)} = \arccos \left(\frac{\mathbf{w}^l_{(i,j)} \cdot \mathbf{e}^l_{(i,j)}}{\left\| \mathbf{w}^l_{(i,j)} \right\| \cdot \left\| \mathbf{e}^l_{(i,j)} \right\|} \right), \tag{5.50}$$

where i and j are the indices of two adjacent vertices in the lower resolution mesh. For example, as illustrated in Fig. 5.8, $\alpha_{(5,7)}$ is the angle between $\mathbf{w}^l_{(5,7)}$ and its support edge vector, $\mathbf{e}^l_{(5,7)}$. The other one is the ratio between the Euclidean norm of the WCV and that of its support edge vector in the lower resolution mesh, defined as

$$\rho^l_{(i,j)} = \frac{\left\| \mathbf{w}^l_{(i,j)} \right\|}{\left\| \mathbf{e}^l_{(i,j)} \right\|}. \tag{5.51}$$

These two geometric features are used to carry information payloads in various 3D wavelet watermarking methods such as those proposed in [34, 35], and this is the reason why they are also considered in our 3D steganalytic method. One important aspect when considering the 3D wavelet decomposition is that the steganalyst may not be able to know what set of triangle faces had been grouped when the information was embedded into the 3D shape. In fact, the grouping of the triangle faces determines how the WCVs are produced. For instance, in Fig. 5.8, if the four triangles $\triangle v_2 v_3 v_4$, $\triangle v_4 v_4 v_9$, $\triangle v_4 v_8 v_9$, and $\triangle v_3 v_9 v_{10}$ would merge into a larger triangle $\triangle v_2 v_8 v_{10}$ in the lower resolution mesh, we would not be able to retrieve certain WCVs, such as $\mathbf{w}^l_{(5,9)}$ and $\mathbf{w}^l_{(7,9)}$. By not knowing this information, we can have a mismatch of the 3D wavelet decompositions that would degrade the performance of the steganalysis. In order to mitigate this problem, we consider all possible groupings for the triangle faces in the given neighborhood, generating all the possible WCVs together with their support edge vectors in the lower resolution meshes. As a consequence, we define all groups of four neighboring triangles including one triangle in the center, surrounded by other three triangles, that can be merged into a larger triangle during the 3D wavelet decomposition. Since each triangle from a fully connected mesh can be the central triangle used in 3D wavelet decomposition, we can obtain $|F|$ different groups of four neighboring triangles, where $|F|$ is the number of the triangles from the initial resolution mesh. For each of these triangle groupings, we apply the 3D wavelet decomposition and calculate the geometric features as described before in this section. Meanwhile, we remove the duplicated geometric features, such as the WCVs and edge vectors that are generated more than once when considering all triangle groupings. Finally, the resulting features, considering all the possible grouping options in the wavelet decomposition, form the geometric features from the lower resolution mesh.

High-Resolution Mesh Feature Extraction When transforming the given mesh into a higher resolution mesh, each triangle from the original resolution mesh is subdivided into four smaller triangles by inserting three new vertices, each located on one of the edges from the initial resolution triangle. In the higher resolution mesh, each newly inserted vertex is adjacent to the two ends of the support edge of the initial resolution triangle, while it is also adjacent to the other newly inserted vertices. As illustrated in Fig. 5.9, the vertices v_{11}, v_{12}, v_{13}, v_{14}, and v_{15} are added to the local mesh in order to produce the higher resolution mesh following the 3D wavelet transformation. Since the subdivision is based on the Butterfly scheme [19], the position of each newly added vertex is computed from eight vertices that define a neighborhood resembling the shape of a butterfly. One iteration subdivision is applied using the Butterfly scheme with the tension parameter $\omega = 1/16$, as in [19]. When $\omega \to 0$, the surface of the 3D object becomes more like that of a piecewise linear polyhedron. The tension parameter characterizes the smoothness, and for $\omega = 1/16$, the resulting surface has globally $\mathbf{C}_1$ continuity. For example, the position of the vertex v_{13} associated to edge vector $\mathbf{e}_{(3,4)}$ in Fig. 5.9 is given by

$$v_{13} = \frac{1}{2}(v_3 + v_4) + \frac{1}{8}(v_2 + v_9) - \frac{1}{16}(v_1 + v_5 + v_8 + v_{10}). \tag{5.52}$$

The WCV from the higher resolution mesh, denoted as $\mathbf{w}^h_{(i,j)}$, is the vector from the midpoint of the support edge $\mathbf{e}_{(i,j)}$ in the initial resolution mesh to the newly added vertex. For example, as shown in Fig. 5.9, the WCVs $\mathbf{w}^h_{(2,3)}$, $\mathbf{w}^h_{(2,4)}$, and $\mathbf{w}^h_{(3,4)}$ are associated to the support edge vectors, $\mathbf{e}_{(2,3)}$, $\mathbf{e}_{(2,4)}$, and $\mathbf{e}_{(3,4)}$, from the initial

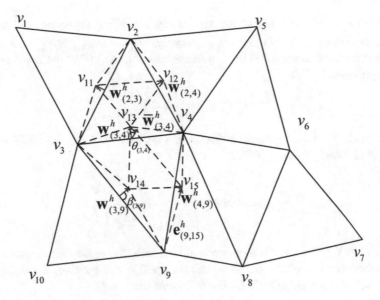

Fig. 5.9 Illustration of the 3D wavelet subdivision when the mesh is transformed from the original resolution to a higher resolution

resolution mesh. The WCVs from the higher resolution mesh as one of the geometric features are used for 3D steganalysis.

The edge vector in the higher resolution mesh, $\mathbf{e}^h_{(i,j)}$, is also considered as a geometric feature. An example of edge vector in the higher resolution mesh is $\mathbf{e}^h_{(9,15)}$ in Fig. 5.9. Two geometric features, $\beta_{(i,j)}$ and $\rho^h_{(i,j)}$, which are analogue to $\alpha_{(i,j)}$ and $\rho^h_{(i,j)}$ from the lower resolution mesh, are obtained from the higher resolution mesh. $\beta_{(i,j)}$ is the angle between $\mathbf{w}^h_{(i,j)}$ and its support edge vector $\mathbf{e}_{(i,j)}$ from the initial resolution mesh, which is calculated in a similar way to Eq. (5.50). For instance, $\beta_{(3,9)}$ shown in Fig. 5.9 is the angle between $\mathbf{w}^h_{(3,9)}$ and $\mathbf{e}_{(3,9)}$. Meanwhile, $\rho^h_{(i,j)}$ represents the ratio between the Euclidean norm of the WCV, $\mathbf{w}^h_{(i,j)}$, and that of its support edge vector, $\mathbf{e}_{(i,j)}$, from the initial resolution mesh. In order to capture the relationship between each WCV and its neighboring WCVs, the average of the neighboring WCVs for each given WCV from the higher resolution mesh is considered. We define that two WCVs are neighbors only when their terminal points are adjacent in the higher resolution mesh. The set of neighboring WCVs of a given WCV $\mathbf{w}^h_{(i,j)}$ is denoted as $\mathcal{N}(\mathbf{w}^h_{(i,j)})$. Then the average neighboring WCVs of $\mathbf{w}^h_{(i,j)}$ is calculated as

$$\overline{\mathbf{w}}^h_{(i,j)} = \frac{1}{\left|\mathcal{N}\left(\mathbf{w}^h_{(i,j)}\right)\right|} \sum_{\mathbf{w}^h_{(k,l)} \in \mathcal{N}\left(\mathbf{w}^h_{(i,j)}\right)} \mathbf{w}^h_{(k,l)}, \tag{5.53}$$

where $\cdot$ represents the size of the set. In Fig. 5.9, $\overline{\mathbf{w}}^h_{(i,j)}$ represents the average of the neighboring WCVs for $\mathbf{w}^h_{(3,4)}$, namely, $\mathbf{w}^h_{(2,4)}$, $\mathbf{w}^h_{(2,3)}$, $\mathbf{w}^h_{(3,9)}$, and $\mathbf{w}^h_{(4,9)}$. Another feature considered is the difference between the WCV and the average of its neighboring WCVs:

$$\mathbf{w}^h_{(i,j)} = \mathbf{w}^h_{(i,j)} - \overline{\mathbf{w}}^h_{(i,j)}. \tag{5.54}$$

Meanwhile, another geometric feature is the angle between the WCV and the average of its neighboring WCVs:

$$\theta_{(i,j)} = \arccos\left(\frac{\mathbf{w}^h_{(i,j)} \cdot \overline{\mathbf{w}}^h_{(i,j)}}{\left\|\mathbf{w}^h_{(i,j)}\right\| \cdot \left\|\overline{\mathbf{w}}^h_{(i,j)}\right\|}\right). \tag{5.55}$$

For each WCV from the higher resolution mesh, the mean and variance of the angles between the WCV and its neighboring WCVs are considered as geometric features. These are given by the following formulae:

$$\mu^M_{(i,j)} = \frac{1}{\left|\mathcal{N}\left(\mathbf{w}^h_{(i,j)}\right)\right|} \sum_{\mathbf{w}^h_{(k,l)} \in \mathcal{N}\left(\mathbf{w}^h_{(i,j)}\right)} \delta_{(k,l)},$$
$$\mu^V_{(i,j)} = \frac{1}{\left|\mathcal{N}\left(\mathbf{w}^h_{(i,j)}\right)\right|} \sum_{\mathbf{w}^h_{(k,l)} \in \mathcal{N}\left(\mathbf{w}^h_{(i,j)}\right)} \left(\delta_{(k,l)} - \mu^M_{(i,j)}\right)^2, \tag{5.56}$$

where $\delta_{(k,l)}$ is the angle between $\mathbf{w}^h_{(i,j)}$ and its neighboring WCV, $\mathbf{w}^h_{(i,j)} \in \mathcal{N}\left(\mathbf{w}^h_{(i,j)}\right)$:

$$\delta_{(k,l)} = \arccos\left(\frac{\mathbf{w}^h_{(i,j)} \cdot \mathbf{w}^h_{(k,l)}}{\left\|\mathbf{w}^h_{(i,j)\|} \right\| \cdot \left\|\mathbf{w}^h_{(k,l)}\right\|}\right). \tag{5.57}$$

The mean and variance of the absolute differences between the Euclidean norms of each WCV and its neighboring WCVs are also considered, namely:

$$\kappa^M_{(i,j)} = \frac{1}{\left|\mathcal{N}\left(\mathbf{w}^h_{(i,j)}\right)\right|} \sum_{\mathbf{w}^h_{(k,l)} \in \mathcal{N}\left(\mathbf{w}^h_{(i,j)}\right)} \left\|\left\|\mathbf{w}^h_{(i,j)}\right\| - \left\|\mathbf{w}^h_{(k,l)}\right\|\right\|,$$
$$\kappa^V_{(i,j)} = \frac{1}{\left|\mathcal{N}\left(\mathbf{w}^h_{(i,j)}\right)\right|} \sum_{\mathbf{w}^h_{(k,l)} \in \mathcal{N}\left(\mathbf{w}^h_{(i,j)}\right)} \left(\left\|\mathbf{w}^h_{(k,l)}\right\| - \kappa^M_{(i,j)}\right)^2. \tag{5.58}$$

Feature Design   For the scalar geometric features, the absolute differences between the geometric feature from the original mesh, denoted as $\mathbf{g}_t$, and that from the smoothed mesh $\mathbf{g}'_t$ are considered:

$$\phi_t = \left| \mathbf{g}_t - \mathbf{g}'_t \right|, \tag{5.59}$$

where t is the index of the geometric feature.

The difference between $\mathbf{g}_t$ and $\mathbf{g}'_t$ is calculated in four different ways. First, the absolute differences are calculated for features defined in the Cartesian coordinate system, such as

$$
\begin{aligned}
\phi_{t_1} &= \left| \mathbf{g}_{t,x} - \mathbf{g}'_{t,x} \right|, \\
\phi_{t_2} &= \left| \mathbf{g}_{t,y} - \mathbf{g}'_{t,y} \right|, \\
\phi_{t_3} &= \left| \mathbf{g}_{t,z} - \mathbf{g}'_{t,z} \right|,
\end{aligned}
\tag{5.60}
$$

where $\mathbf{g}_{t,x}$ represents the x-component of the vector $\mathbf{g}_t$ in the Cartesian coordinate system. Second, the norm of the difference between vectors $\mathbf{g}_t$ and $\mathbf{g}'_t$ is calculated as

$$\phi_{t_4} = \left\| \mathbf{g}_t - \mathbf{g}'_t \right\|, \tag{5.61}$$

and the absolute differences between the norms of the two vectors are also considered, namely,

$$\phi_{t_5} = \left| \left\| \mathbf{g}_t \right\| - \left\| \mathbf{g}'_t \right\| \right|. \tag{5.62}$$

Eventually, the angle between the two vectors, $\mathbf{g}_t$ and $\mathbf{g}'_t$, is considered as well,

$$\phi_{t_6} = \arccos \left(\frac{\mathbf{g}_t \cdot \mathbf{g}'_t}{\left\| \mathbf{g}_t \right\| \cdot \left\| \mathbf{g}'_t \right\|} \right). \tag{5.63}$$

The differences between the geometric features from the original mesh and those of the smoothed one are summarized into a set of $8 \times 6 + 9 = 57$ elements, $\Phi = \{ \phi_t | t = 1, 2, \ldots, 57 \}$. In order to introduce evenness in the feature distribution representation, the logarithm for each entry of Φ is calculated. Finally, the first four statistical moments, representing the mean, variance, skewness, and kurtosis, of $\{ \lg(\phi_t) | \phi_t \in \Phi \}$ result into a $57 \times 4 = 228$ dimensional feature vector $\mathbf{X}$. The feature vector $\mathbf{X} = [\chi_1, \chi_2, \ldots, \chi_{228}]$ and the class label y, corresponding to a training set of meshes, are used as inputs to a machine learning algorithm in order to train the 3D steganalyzer. The proposed 228-dimensional 3D wavelet feature set is labeled as WFS228.

It can be observed that there are more features extracted from the higher resolution mesh than from the lower resolution mesh. This is due to the uncertainty arising when grouping the triangles forming mesh neighborhoods, during the 3D wavelet decomposition, due to the difficulty to predict which WCVs are the neighbors for a certain WCV from a lower resolution mesh. The geometric features that would represent the information of the neighboring WCVs cannot be extracted from the lower resolution mesh. Moreover, the features extracted from the higher resolution mesh may have linear dependencies to some extent because the location of the vertex in the higher resolution mesh relies on a linear combination of the vertices in the Butterfly neighborhood from the original resolution mesh.

In summary, based on these analyses, the authors proposed features based on the edge vector, WCVs, and their variants at three resolutions for 3D mesh steganalysis. Their method outperforms LFS76 by a large margin, yet its computational complexity is also very high because of the search for local vertices.

5.1.10   Feature Selection Model

In real scenarios, the training and testing sets are not from the same distributions. This is a challenging task for the existing steganalyzers, called the cover source mismatch (CSM) problem, which is caused by the limited generalizability of steganalyzers. Li and Bors [10, 11] assess the robustness of 3D steganalyzers in the context of the CSM problem. This problem is represented by the realistic scenario that the objects used for training a steganalyzer may be originating from a cover source that is different from the one used in the training stage [36]. A known example of CSM in the area of image steganalysis was addressed during the "Break Our Steganographic System" (BOSS) contest [37]. The mismatch of the training set and testing set caused many difficulties to the participants in this contest [36, 38, 39]. In general, the CSM problem in the image domain was addressed by considering the following aspects: the training sets, the feature sets, and the machine learning methods used for steganalysis.

In the case of digital images, the cover source mismatch problem is analyzed by testing the steganalyzers on images that are taken by cameras with different characteristics from those used during the training. Differences considered in those studies include different ISO levels of noise, characterizing various cameras, as well as different JPEG quality factors [40, 41]. Gul and Kurugollu [39] proposed a feature selection algorithm, for their participation in the BOSS contest, which calculates the correlation between a feature and the embedding rate as the criterion for its selection. Pasquet et al. [42] proposed to use the ensemble classifier with feature selection [43] for the CSM problem. The feature selection is performed by evaluating the importance of each feature in the learning process [43]. A feature condensing method, called calibrated least squares (CLS), is proposed in [44] to make the high-dimensional feature sets compatible with the anomaly detector employed for steganalysis. A method to mitigate the CSM due to changes in the cover feature is presented in [45]. This approach shifts all the centers of the cover features from different steganographers toward the origin by subtracting the centroid of each steganographer's cover feature distribution. Other research studies addressing the CSM problem in images aim to find a classifier that would be robust to the variation between the training and testing data. In [46], it was shown that simple classifiers, such as FLD ensemble and the online ensemble average perceptron (OEAP), have better performances, when faced with the cover source mismatch problem than more complex classifiers. To mitigate the mismatch due to various changes in stego features, Ker and Pevný [45] used an ensemble of classifiers that gives more weight to those classifiers that are robust to changes in the stego features. A similar weighting strategy for improving the FLD ensemble's performance in CSM paradigm is presented in [41]. The robustness and relevance based feature selection (RRFS) algorithm is proposed for addressing the CSM problem in 3D steganalysis. In order to increase the supposed diversity of 3D objects, during the testing, certain transformations are applied on the cover objects before hiding information in the 3D objects. The Pearson correlation coefficient (PCC) is utilized to evaluate the relevance of each feature with respect to the class label. PCC is then used for estimating the robustness of the 3D features to the variation of the cover source. The variation is ensured by considering certain transformations, such as mesh simplification and additive noise, applied on the cover objects. The features used in the training and testing stages will be selected from an existing feature set, by the RRFS algorithm. The proposed methodology is tested on the Princeton Mesh Segmentation project database [47], when considering the 3D steganographic algorithm proposed in [21].

A selection mechanism is first described for deciding which features would be robust enough to be used when addressing the CSM problem. The proposed RRFS defines a criterion for choosing those features that would guarantee the best performance. Most important is that such features are robust at the variation of the cover source, while preserving a relatively strong relevance to the class label as well. Consequently, two criteria are considered during the selection: the relevance of the features to the class label, and the robustness of the selected feature set to the variation of the cover source.

The feature selection algorithm proposed in this chapter belongs to the filter methods [48], considered to be efficient when used for selecting input features for various machine learning algorithms. The filter methods are suitable to be applied in the cover source mismatch situations because they can avoid the overfitting of the training data while being characterized by a better generalization during the testing stage [49]. In the proposed algorithm, the relevance of the features to the class label is estimated by using the Pearson correlation coefficient, calculated between the distribution of each feature and the corresponding objects' classes:

$$\rho(\mathbf{X}_i, \mathbf{Y}) = \frac{\text{COV}(\mathbf{X}_i, \mathbf{Y})}{\sigma_{\mathbf{X}_i} \sigma_{\mathbf{Y}}}, \tag{5.64}$$

where $\mathbf{X}_i$ is the ith feature of a given feature set, $X = \mathbf{X}_i | i = 1, 2, \ldots, N$, where N is the dimensionality of the input feature, $\mathbf{Y}$ is the class label indicating whether the class corresponds to a cover or a stego object, COV represents the covariance, and $\sigma_{\mathbf{X}_i}$ is the standard deviation of $\mathbf{X}_i$. The Pearson correlation coefficient can capture the linear dependencies between features and the label, and it is widely used in science as a measure of the degree of linear dependence between two variables, with $|\rho(\mathbf{X}_i, \mathbf{Y})| = 1$ indicating a high degree of linearity, while $|\rho(\mathbf{X}_i, \mathbf{Y})| = 0$ indicates a scattered dependency. The former value indicates a stronger relevance to the class label. All features are ranked according to their relevance to the class label, calculated using the above equation, in descending order as

$$|\rho(\mathbf{X}_{I_1}, \mathbf{Y})| > |\rho(\mathbf{X}_{I_2}, \mathbf{Y})| > \ldots > |\rho(\mathbf{X}_{I_N}, \mathbf{Y})|, \tag{5.65}$$

where $I = I_1, I_2, \ldots, I_N$ is the feature index.

The robustness of features to the variation of the cover source is related to solving the CSM problem. Ideally, robust features should model the statistical characteristics that distinguish cover and stego objects even after certain distortions are applied on the cover objects. If objects' features do not change much after applying transformations to the cover objects, they would be expected to provide similar steganalysis results to those achieved with the original cover and stego objects. Such features would have a strong robustness in the context of steganalyzers. In the following, two different feature sets are considered for a given set of 3D objects: the first one is extracted from the original objects used as the cover sources for training the steganalyzers, while the other is extracted after applying certain transformations, for instance, mesh simplification and noise addition, to the same objects. Then the Pearson correlation coefficient of two feature sets is calculated as

$$\rho_i(\mathbf{X}_i, \mathbf{X}_{j,i}) = \frac{\mathrm{COV}(\mathbf{X}_i, \mathbf{X}_{j,i})}{\sigma_{\mathbf{X}_i}\sigma_{\mathbf{X}_{j,i}}}, \tag{5.66}$$

where $\mathbf{X}_i$ and $\mathbf{X}_{j,i}$ represent the vector of the feature i extracted from the original set of cover objects, used for training the steganalyzer, and from the objects obtained by applying specific transformations to the same cover source, $j = 1, 2, \ldots, M$, where M represents the number of transformations applied to the original set of cover objects. This formula indicates how well correlated are the initial 3D features with those that are extracted after certain transformations. $|\rho_i(\mathbf{X}_i, \mathbf{X}_{j,i})|$ is normalized to the interval [0, 1]. The robustness is indicated by the average of the absolute values of the Person correlation coefficients, calculated for a specific feature i, for all M transformations:

$$r_i = \frac{1}{M} \sum_{j=1}^{M} |\rho_i(\mathbf{X}_i, \mathbf{X}_{j,i})|, \tag{5.67}$$

where $i = 1, 2, \ldots, N$.

RRFS algorithm starts with a preset number of N features as input. The algorithm aims to find the most N' relevant features that have relatively strong robustness to be used for a steganalyzer that addresses the CSM problem. The N' features are selected by multiple passes through the features ranked according to their relevance. During each pass, a subset of features is selected successively such that:

$$r_i > \theta_p, \qquad (5.68)$$

where θ represents the threshold for the correlation corresponding to the pth percentile of all r_i's, characterizing the robustness of the steganalyzer. Initially, p is set at 90. If the number of selected features $|\mathcal{F}| < N'$, then the threshold is reduced to the value corresponding to the percentile $p - 10$, and consider a new threshold θ_{p-10} instead of θ_p. In this way, with each iteration, additional features added to the set of those selected, the classification capability of the algorithm is still preserved well. The threshold is reduced accordingly, considering lower percentiles p, until the total number of selected features becomes equal to N'. Eventually, N' selected features that are robust enough to the variation of cover source while having at the same time a high relevance to the class label.

Here different feature selection algorithms are compared to evaluate their capabilities, including min-redundancy and max-relevancy (mRMR) [50], double input symmetrical relevance (DISR) [51], and conditional mutual info maximization (CMIM) [53], which have shown very good generalization ability in a wide range of applications [52]. In addition, a simplified version of our algorithm, relevance based feature selection (RFS), which selects the features with higher relevance to the class label, but without considering the robustness to the variation of cover source, is also compared with others. The steganalysis experiments using FLD ensembles are repeated for 10 times, and the median of the resulting errors is considered as the final test results. In summary, this method deals with the cover source mismatch problem of 3D steganalysis and provides several robust features. Its limitation is that the selection of features is restricted to transformations only. A promising improvement would be to experiment on a set of transformed objects originating from completely different cover sources.

5.2 Specific Steganalysis

In this subsection, we discuss two specific steganalysis methods: PCA transform-targeted features and permutation-targeted features.

5.2.1 PCA Transformation Features

The defect of steganography methods based on the PCA transform [20, 21] is noted by Zhou et al. [22]: the preprocessing procedures lead to a location distinction between the cover meshes and the stego meshes, which can be easily attacked by specially designed detectors.

The vertices falling on the two ends of the first principal axis are taken as the end vertices v_i and v_j. Similarly, the vertex falling on the farthest end of the second principal axis is taken as the third end vertex v_k. Then, the cover 3D mesh is transformed to align the unit vectors $\overrightarrow{v_i v_j}$, $\overrightarrow{v_i v_k}$ and $\overrightarrow{v_i v_j} \times \overrightarrow{v_i v_k}$ with the x-axis, y-axis, and z-axis, respectively. Therefore, the transformation matrix $\mathbf{T}$ is defined as

$$\mathbf{T} = [\overrightarrow{v_i v_j}, \overrightarrow{v_i v_k}, \overrightarrow{v_i v_j} \times \overrightarrow{v_i v_k}]. \tag{5.69}$$

Since the first and second principle axes of the stego mesh are near the x-axis and y-axis, respectively, this operation with behavior disorder will cause attackers to be suspicious, and the one-dimensional feature is calculated as the ℓ_1 norm between the above two matrices:

$$\phi_{25} = \|\mathbf{T} - \mathbf{I}\|_1 , \tag{5.70}$$

where $\mathbf{I}$ is the identity matrix. Note that we have also tried cosine distance and ℓ_2 norm between two matrices where the performance does not exceed ℓ_1 norm.

The steganalysis of PCA transform-based steganography algorithms is evaluated empirically using binary classifiers trained on a given cover mesh and its stego version embedded with a fixed relative payload. Five-fold cross validation of support vector machine (SVM) is employed to conduct training and classification. Each test is repeated 10 times, and results are averaged to evaluate the final performance. Soft-margin SVMs with the Gaussian kernel $k(x, y) = \exp(-\gamma_k \|x - y\|_2^2)$, $\gamma_k > 0$ are used. The values of the penalization parameter and the kernel parameter are $C = 5$ and $\gamma_k = 0.5$, respectively. Experiments show that radial basis function (RBF) SVM has competitive results, and LIBSVM [54] is utilized here as the classifier for low computing complexity. In summary, although this method is efficient, it is only effective in detecting PCA transform-based steganographic methods.

5.2.2   Order Permutation Features

Wang et al. [23] proposed the first steganalytic method to break permutation steganography. They found that there are significant differences in the topological distance distribution of consecutive mesh elements between cover and stego meshes. They designed effective steganalytic features by measuring the order of the vertex and triangle lists.

As we all know, for clean meshes, the vertex lists are relatively orderly, while for stego meshes, they have high randomness. Therefore, they utilized the distance term $D(\mathcal{P})$ to measure the order of the vertex list $\mathcal{P}$:

$$D(\mathcal{P}) = \frac{1}{n-1} \sum_{i=1}^{n-1} d(\mathbf{p}_i, \mathbf{p}_{i+1}), \tag{5.71}$$

where $d(\mathbf{p}_i, \mathbf{p}_{i+1})$ is the shortest Euclidean distance between $\mathbf{p}_i$ and $\mathbf{p}_{i+1}$. In most cases, $D(\mathcal{P})$ is very small for cover meshes, where consecutive vertices are close to each other, while for stego meshes, most consecutive vertices are not close to each other, and $D(\mathcal{P})$ may be very large. The order of the face list is similarly designed.

In summary, this method is universal and does not require any prior knowledge, for instance, the concrete steganographic method and embedding payload.

5.3 Cover Source Mismatch Problem

As mentioned before, when a steganalyzer trained on one data source is applied to 3D meshes from a different source, in general, the detection error will increase because of the mismatch between the two different sources, which is recognized as the CSM problem. In fact, CSM hinders the advancement of steganalysis from the laboratory environment to the real world. One possible solution is to use simple measures, such as using several steganalyzers trained on several different sources and testing on a steganalyzer trained on the closest source, or by increasing the diversity of training data.

References

1. M. A. Hearst, S. T. Dumais, E. Osuna, J. Platt, and B. Scholkopf, "Support vector machines," *IEEE Intelligent Systems and their applications*, vol. 13, no. 4, pp. 18–28, 1998.
2. J. Kodovský, J. Fridrich, and V. Holub, "Ensemble classifiers for steganalysis of digital media," *IEEE Transactions on Information Forensics and Security*, vol. 7, no. 2, pp. 432–444, 2012.
3. J. Kodovský, J. Fridrich, and V. Holub, "Ensemble classifiers for steganalysis of digital media," *IEEE Transactions on Information Forensics and Security*, vol. 7, no. 2, pp. 432–444, 2011.
4. Y. Yang and I. Ivrissimtzis, "Mesh discriminative features for 3D steganalysis," *ACM Transactions on Multimedia Computing, Communications, and Applications*, vol. 10, no. 3, p. 27, 2014.
5. Z. Li and A. G. Bors, "3D mesh steganalysis using local shape features," in *IEEE International Conference on Acoustics, Speech and Signal Processing*. IEEE, 2016, pp. 2144–2148.
6. D. Kim, H.-U. Jang, H.-Y. Choi, J. Son, I.-J. Yu, and H.-K. Lee, "Improved 3d mesh steganalysis using homogeneous kernel map," in *International Conference on Information Science and Applications*. Springer, 2017, pp. 358–365.
7. Z. Li, D. Gong, F. Liu, and A. G. Bors, "3D steganalysis using the extended local feature set," in *IEEE International Conference on Image Processing*. IEEE, 2018, pp. 1683–1687.
8. H. Zhou, K. Chen, W. Zhang, C. Qin, and N. Yu, "Feature-preserving tensor voting model for mesh steganalysis," *IEEE Transactions on Visualization and Computer Graphics*, 2019.
9. Z. Li and A. G. Bors, "Steganalysis of meshes based on 3D wavelet multiresolution analysis," *Information Sciences*, 2020.
10. ——, "Selection of robust features for the cover source mismatch problem in 3d steganalysis," in *IEEE International Conference on Pattern Recognition*. IEEE, 2016, pp. 4256–4261.

11. ——, "Selection of robust and relevant features for 3-D steganalysis," *IEEE Transactions on Cybernetics*, 2018.
12. Z. Li, F. Liu, and A. G. Bors, "3d steganalysis using Laplacian smoothing at various levels," in *International Conference on Cloud Computing and Security*. Springer, 2018, pp. 223–232.
13. J. Fridrich, M. Goljan, and D. Hogea, "Steganalysis of JPEG images: Breaking the F5 algorithm," in *International Workshop on Information Hiding*. Springer, 2002, pp. 310–323.
14. J. Kodovský and J. Fridrich, "Calibration revisited," in *ACM Workshop on Multimedia and Security*. ACM, 2009, pp. 63–74.
15. G. Taubin, "A signal processing approach to fair surface design," in *International Conference on Computer Graphics and Interactive Techniques*. ACM, 1995, pp. 351–358.
16. B. Bollobás, *Modern graph theory*. Springer Science & Business Media, 2013, vol. 184.
17. Z. Li and A. G. Bors, "Steganalysis of 3d objects using statistics of local feature sets," *Information Sciences*, vol. 415, pp. 85–99, 2017.
18. M. Lounsbery, T. D. DeRose, and J. Warren, "Multiresolution analysis for surfaces of arbitrary topological type," *ACM Transactions on Graphics*, vol. 16, no. 1, pp. 34–73, 1997.
19. N. Dyn, D. Levine, and J. A. Gregory, "A butterfly subdivision scheme for surface interpolation with tension control," *ACM Transactions on Graphics*, vol. 9, no. 2, pp. 160–169, 1990.
20. C.-M. Wang and P.-C. Wang, "Steganography on point-sampled geometry," *Computers & Graphics*, vol. 30, no. 2, pp. 244–254, 2006.
21. M.-W. Chao, C.-h. Lin, C.-W. Yu, and T.-Y. Lee, "A high capacity 3d steganography algorithm," *IEEE Transactions on Visualization and Computer Graphics*, vol. 15, no. 2, pp. 274–284, 2009.
22. H. Zhou, K. Chen, W. Zhang, Y. Yao, and N. Yu, "Distortion design for secure adaptive 3-D mesh steganography," *IEEE Transactions on Multimedia*, vol. 21, no. 6, pp. 1384–1398, 2018.
23. Y. Wang, L. Kong, Z. Qian, G. Feng, X. Zhang, and J. Zheng, "Breaking permutation-based mesh steganography and security improvement," *IEEE Access*, vol. 7, pp. 183 300–183 310, 2019.
24. Y. Sun, D. L. Page, J. K. Paik, A. Koschan, and M. A. Abidi, "Triangle mesh-based edge detection and its application to surface segmentation and adaptive surface smoothing," in *IEEE International Conference on Image Processing*, vol. 3. IEEE, 2002, pp. 825–828.
25. Kim, H., Choi, H. & Lee, K. Feature detection of triangular meshes based on tensor voting theory. *Computer-Aided Design*. **41**, 47–58 (2009)
26. Medioni, G., Tang, C. & Lee, M. Tensor voting: Theory and applications. *Proceedings of RFIA*. **2000** (2000)
27. Yadav, S., Reitebuch, U. & Polthier, K. Mesh denoising based on normal voting tensor and binary optimization. *IEEE Transactions on Visualization and Computer Graphics*. **24**, 2366–2379 (2017)
28. Rugis, J. & Klette, R. A scale invariant surface curvature estimator. *Pacific-Rim Symposium on Image and Video Technology*. pp. 138–147 (2006)
29. Rusinkiewicz, S. Estimating curvatures and their derivatives on triangle meshes. *Proceedings. 2nd International Symposium on 3D Data Processing, Visualization and Transmission, 2004. 3DPVT 2004.*. pp. 486–493 (2004)
30. Boroumand, M. & Fridrich, J. Boosting steganalysis with explicit feature maps. *Proceedings of the 4th ACM Workshop on Information Hiding and Multimedia Security*. pp. 149–157 (2016)
31. Perronnin, F., Sánchez, J. & Liu, Y. Large-scale image categorization with explicit data embedding. *2010 IEEE Computer Society Conference on Computer Vision and Pattern Recognition*. pp. 2297–2304 (2010)
32. Cho, J., Prost, R. & Jung, H. An oblivious watermarking for 3-D polygonal meshes using distribution of vertex norms. *IEEE Transactions on Signal Processing*. **55**, 142–155 (2006)
33. Yang, Y., Pintus, R., Rushmeier, H. & Ivrissimtzis, I. A 3D steganalytic algorithm and steganalysis-resistant watermarking. *IEEE Transactions on Visualization and Computer Graphics*. **23**, 1002–1013 (2016)
34. Wang, K., Lavoué, G., Denis, F. & Baskurt, A. Hierarchical watermarking of semiregular meshes based on wavelet transform. *IEEE Transactions on Information Forensics and Security*. **3**, 620–634 (2008)

35. Uccheddu, F., Corsini, M. & Barni, M. Wavelet-based blind watermarking of 3D models. *Proceedings of the 2004 Workshop on Multimedia and Security*. pp. 143–154 (2004)
36. Ker, A., Bas, P., Böhme, R., Cogranne, R., Craver, S., Filler, T., Fridrich, J. & Pevnỳ, T. Moving steganography and steganalysis from the laboratory into the real world. *Proceedings of the First ACM Workshop on Information Hiding and Multimedia Security*. pp. 45–58 (2013)
37. Bas, P., Filler, T. & Pevnỳ, T. "Break our steganographic system": the ins and outs of organizing BOSS. *International Workshop on Information Hiding*. pp. 59–70 (2011)
38. Fridrich, J., Kodovskỳ, J., Holub, V. & Goljan, M. Breaking HUGO–the process discovery. *International Workshop on Information Hiding*. pp. 85–101 (2011)
39. Gul, G. & Kurugollu, F. A new methodology in steganalysis: breaking highly undetectable steganograpy (HUGO). *International Workshop on Information Hiding*. pp. 71–84 (2011)
40. Kodovskỳ, J., Sedighi, V. & Fridrich, J. Study of cover source mismatch in steganalysis and ways to mitigate its impact. *Media Watermarking, Security, and Forensics 2014*. **9028** pp. 204–215 (2014)
41. Xu, X., Dong, J., Wang, W. & Tan, T. Robust steganalysis based on training set construction and ensemble classifiers weighting. *2015 IEEE International Conference on Image Processing (ICIP)*. pp. 1498–1502 (2015)
42. Pasquet, J., Bringay, S. & Chaumont, M. Steganalysis with cover-source mismatch and a small learning database. *2014 22nd European Signal Processing Conference (EUSIPCO)*. pp. 2425–2429 (2014)
43. Chaumont, M. & Kouider, S. Steganalysis by ensemble classifiers with boosting by regression, and post-selection of features. *2012 19th IEEE International Conference on Image Processing*. pp. 1133–1136 (2012)
44. Pevnỳ, T. & Ker, A. The challenges of rich features in universal steganalysis. *Media Watermarking, Security, and Forensics 2013*. **8665** pp. 203–217 (2013)
45. Ker, A. & Pevnỳ, T. A mishmash of methods for mitigating the model mismatch mess. *Media Watermarking, Security, and Forensics 2014*. **9028** pp. 189–203 (2014)
46. Lubenko, I. & Ker, A. Steganalysis with mismatched covers: Do simple classifiers help?. *Proceedings of the on Multimedia and Security*. pp. 11–18 (2012)
47. Chen, X., Golovinskiy, A. & Funkhouser, T. A benchmark for 3D mesh segmentation. *ACM Transactions on Graphics (TOG)*. **28**, 1–12 (2009)
48. Chandrashekar, G. & Sahin, F. A survey on feature selection methods. *Computers & Electrical Engineering*. **40**, 16–28 (2014)
49. Guyon, I. & Elisseeff, A. An introduction to variable and feature selection. *Journal of Machine Learning Research*. **3**, 1157–1182 (2003)
50. Peng, H., Long, F. & Ding, C. Feature selection based on mutual information criteria of max-dependency, max-relevance, and min-redundancy. *IEEE Transactions on Pattern Analysis and Machine Intelligence*. **27**, 1226–1238 (2005)
51. Meyer, P. & Bontempi, G. On the use of variable complementarity for feature selection in cancer classification. *Workshops on Applications of Evolutionary Computation*. pp. 91–102 (2006)
52. Brown, G., Pocock, A., Zhao, M. & Luj'an, M. Conditional likelihood maximisation: a unifying framework for information theoretic feature selection. *The Journal of Machine Learning Research*. **13** pp. 27–66 (2012)
53. Fleuret, F. Fast binary feature selection with conditional mutual information. *Journal of Machine Learning Research*. **5** (2004)
54. R.-E. Fan, K.-W. Chang, C.-J. Hsieh, X.-R. Wang, and C.-J. Lin, "LIBLINEAR: A library for large linear classification," *Journal of Machine Learning Research*, vol. 9, no. Aug, pp. 1871–1874, 2008.

Chapter 6
Future Work and Conclusion

Abstract In the previous chapters, we summarized some steganography, steganalysis, watermarking, and 3D printing watermarking methods for 3D meshes. In this chapter, we give several challenges and trends and present some potential solutions.

6.1 Open Problems for 3D Mesh Watermarking

For a wider range of applications, 3D mesh watermarking usually pursues greater robustness for resisting various distortions. Below are two distortion problems that still trouble 3D mesh watermarking. Additionally, we also discuss an interesting potential application of 3D printing watermarking.

6.1.1 Robustness to Causality Problem

For blind 3D mesh watermarking, one critical issue is the causality problem, which means the posteriorly inserted watermark bits would disturb the correctness and the synchronization of the previously inserted ones. The causality problem could be solved by some compensation post-process [1]. Besides, Wang [2] proposes eliminating the causality problem by forbidding most vertices to be adjacent, thus controlling the watermark intensity. In conclusion, proposing new solutions to the causality problem is still worth investigating, as it can improve the blind 3D mesh watermarking robustness to a new level.

6.1.2 Robustness to Representation Conversion

3D object representation conversion, for example, from 3D mesh to voxels, means the mesh model itself no longer exists under such conversion. Only the basic shape of the model could be preserved. Thus, this conversion would invalidate the vast majority of existing 3D mesh watermarks. A possible solution is to leverage the preserved shape information to generate the corresponding features, such as geometric moments, and then use moments to design a watermarking scheme robust to the 3D object representation conversion.

6.1.3 3D Printing-Shooting Resilient Watermark on Curve Surface

Reviewing the existing 3D printing watermarking solutions, we find that their water-mark extraction process requires relatively expansive equipment or cannot embed watermarks on 3D printed objects with complex shapes. Specifically, the scheme proposed by Hou et al. [3] although achieves embedding invisible watermarks on complex objects, its extraction process requires high-precision 3D scanners, which makes it difficult to achieve fast copyright authentication. For LayerCode [4], it can be extracted by camera shot, but its embedding pattern is visible to the human eye. Methods proposed by Delmotte et al. [5] and Dogan et al. [6] could embed watermarks on 3D printed objects with small modifications and the watermark could be extracted by camera shots. However, their embedding positions are restricted to the 3D printed plane and hard to extend to curve surfaces. Therefore, we consider a more convenient way of copyright verification, i.e., 3D printing-shooting resilient watermark on a curve surface. We believe this would be a meaningful direction, and similar work is currently available for watermarking in 3D rendering scenario [7].

6.2 Open Problems for 3D Mesh Steganography

Achieving higher steganographic security is the ultimate goal of 3D mesh steganog-raphy. Below are some ideas toward stronger security.

6.2.1 Combining Permutation and LSB Domain

One way to achieve stronger security is to combine the permutation domain and LSB domain by distributing message bits over the two domains. When the number of vertices of a mesh is 5000, the maximum embedding rate of permutation steganography reaches 11 bit per vertex, which can be considered a large embedding rate. The embedding capacity increases, yet it is inevitable to consider the universal steganalysis and permutation-targeted steganalysis together. The key point lies in devising an optimal message allocation scheme that achieves the optimal steganog-raphic security under the same embedding rate.

6.2.2 Designing Spatial Steganographic Models

Recent developments of adaptive steganography have verified that by designing nonadditive distortion functions, the steganographic security can be improved further by taking advantage of the mutual impact of modifications among local cover pixels [9, 10]. In the work of Zhou et al. [30], they allocate message bits evenly on the xyz-axes without considering the embedding effects on each other. It is suggested to design a joint distortion for a triple unit (a vertex consisting of three components), to utilize the DeJoin [8] scheme to allocate message bits and to implement STCs [32] to embed data.

Additionally, inspired by the success of adversarial attacks in computer vision, adversarial steganography [26–28] has been proposed based on generative adversarial networks (GANs) to deceive CNN-based image steganalyzers. It is vital to design adversarial steganography based on deep generative models to deceive mesh steganalyzers.

6.2.3 Designing Anti-steganalysis Permutation Steganographic Models

Wang et al. [31] proposed a neighborhood embedding scheme that utilizes the next $\lfloor \log_2 i \rfloor$ bits in messages to select from the i unpicked vertices of the 1-ring neighbor of the current vertex. It has been verified that $1 \leq i \leq 11$ and, in most cases, $i = 6$ [33], and the average embedding rate is nearly 2 bit per vertex, which is too small for steganography. Moreover, rigorous experiments on steganalytic security are missing from the work of Wang et al. [31], and it is expected to design a multiple-ring-neighbor-based permutation steganography to boost the embedding rate.

6.2.4 Designing Mesh Batch Steganography Models

Batch steganography and pooled steganalysis [21] have generalized the problems of data embedding and steganalysis to more than one object. It is speculated that, given images with uniform embedding capacity and a steganalytic scheme satisfying certain assumptions, "secure" steganographic capacity is proportional to the square root of the input image number [22]. It is therefore an interesting and challenging problem for researchers to explore the relationship between capacity and the number of vertices of 3D meshes and to design a strategy to allocate messages among cover meshes.

6.2.5 Designing 3D Printing Steganography Models

Since DNA storage offers substantial information density and exceptional half-life, Koch et al. [29] proposed a "DNA-of-things" (DoT) storage architecture to produce materials with immutable memory. They applied the DoT to 3D print a Stanford bunny that contained a 45 kB digital DNA blueprint for its synthesis. Specifically, they stored a 1.4 MB video in its DNA in the plexiglass spectacle lenses and retrieved it by excising a tiny piece of the plexiglass and sequencing the embedded DNA. The DoT could be applied to store electronic health records in medical implants, to hide data in everyday objects and to manufacture objects containing their own blueprint, which can be regarded as robust steganography since they can withstand physical-world attacks such as physical damage. However, the extraction side is expensive and time-consuming. Therefore, how to design an efficient decoder is a future research direction.

6.3 Open Problems for 3D Mesh Steganalysis

6.3.1 Designing Rich Steganalytic Features

Since the steganalysis performance is poor under the low embedding rate of two-state domain and LSB domain steganography, there is much room for improvement in steganalysis. Inspired by the SRM of Fridrich and Kodovský [11], who designed 34,671-D quantized noise residual features acquired by multiple linear and nonlinear high-pass filters, it is possible to take advantage of more than one mesh smoothing technique, including denoising and fairing [12], to extract steganographic residuals. Advanced surface smoothing methods include anisotropic diffusion flow [13], bilateral filtering [14], nonlinear smoothing [15, 16], and neural-network-based filtering [17].

In addition, it may be effective to design more features to boost steganalysis. For example, tensors are helpful feature extractors for a set of locally independent vectors. For instance, tensors based on the vertex normal, edge normal, and edge vector can also reflect the local smoothness, as shown in Fig. 6.1. Another option

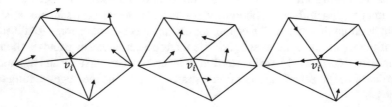

Fig. 6.1 Diagram of local feature set for building tensors: (left) vertex norm, (middle) edge norm and (right) edge vector

is to consider the n-ring-neighborhood-based features ($n > 1$) to scale up areas for feature extraction.

Furthermore, the currently used statistical moments for dimensionality reduction may excessively discard informative features. We find that the dimension of features is equal to the number of vertices, edges, or faces; thus, we believe that training discriminative models for each of the three and reasonably ensembling them may improve the steganalysis performance.

It is worth mentioning that, in addition to the above points, the runtime of the feature extraction of 3D meshes is much greater than that of images. Engineering development of 3D mesh steganalysis should also be considered, such as the use of parallel processing or advanced techniques to resolve the large time consumption of adjacent vertex searching.

6.3.2 Designing Neural Steganalysis Models

The existing methods are all handcrafted features. Note that the designs of these features are cumbersome, and it has been recognized that deep learning has superior performance on classification tasks. These deep neural networks (DNNs), such as convolutional neural networks (CNNs) [19], graph convolutional networks (GCNs) [20], and MeshNet [18], are able to classify testing samples with high accuracy. In addition, CNN based image steganalyzers such as XuNet [24], YeNet [25] and SRNet [23] that use deep models to classify cover images from stego images are maturing fast. The intrinsic topological property of 3D meshes conforms to GCNs and MeshNet; thus, one possible solution is to design an end-to-end modified MeshNet with steganalytic network structures and train it with a back-propagation algorithm to improve the 3D mesh steganalytic performance.

6.3.3 Designing Distance Metric Learning for Permutation Steganalysis

Aiming at the detection of permutation steganography, Wang et al. [31] proposed a theoretical analysis based on the correlation between consecutive mesh elements, but the research is preliminary and quantitative results were not given; thus, there is room for further research. We believe that the distance between two adjacent vertices from the vertex list $\mathcal{P}$ is inadequate for steganalysis and can be improved by calculating the Euclidean distance of adjacent vertices in the permuted order.

6.3.4   Cover Source Mismatch Problem

As mentioned before, when a steganalyzer trained on one data source is applied to 3D meshes from a different source, in general, the detection error will increase because of the mismatch between the two different sources, which is recognized as the CSM problem. In fact, CSM hinders the advancement of steganalysis from the laboratory environment to the real world. One possible solution is to use simple measures, such as by using several steganalyzers trained on several different sources and testing on a steganalyzer trained on the closest source or by increasing the training data diversity.

6.4   Conclusions

Triangle mesh watermarking and steganography are interesting and promising research area, with potential practical applications such as covert communications, copyright protection, integrity authentication, and leak traceability. With the rapid development of vision and graphics, as well as AI and VR technology, 3D models, especially 3D meshes, are widely used in 3D games, virtual reality, film, television animation, and industrial production. The popularity of 3D mesh makes it a suitable carrier for covert communication on the one hand, and the object of intellectual property protection on the other hand. In this book, we gave an overview of 3D mesh watermarking, steganography, and steganalysis. We expect that readers can more or less benefit from this book and be inspired.

References

1. Bors, A. Watermarking mesh-based representations of 3-D objects using local moments. *IEEE Transactions On Image Processing*. **15**, 687–701 (2006)
2. Wang, W., Zheng, G., Yong, J. & Gu, H. A Numerically Stable Fragile Watermarking Scheme for Authenticating 3D Models. *Comput. Aided Des.*. **40**, 634–645 (2008,5), https://doi.org/10.1016/j.cad.2008.03.001
3. Hou, J., Kim, D. & Lee, H. Blind 3D Mesh Watermarking for 3D Printed Model by Analyzing Layering Artifact. *IEEE Transactions On Information Forensics And Security*. **12**, 2712–2725 (2017)
4. Maia, H., Li, D., Yang, Y. & Zheng, C. LayerCode: Optical Barcodes for 3D Printed Shapes. *ACM Trans. Graph.*. **38** (2019,7), https://doi.org/10.1145/3306346.3322960
5. Delmotte, A., Tanaka, K., Kubo, H., Funatomi, T. & Mukaigawa, Y. Blind Watermarking for 3-D Printed Objects by Locally Modifying Layer Thickness. *IEEE Transactions On Multimedia*. **22**, 2780–2791 (2020)
6. Dogan, M., Faruqi, F., Churchill, A., Friedman, K., Cheng, L., Subramanian, S. & Mueller, S. G-ID: Identifying 3D Prints Using Slicing Parameters. *Proceedings Of The* 2020 CHI Conference On Human Factors In Computing Systems. pp. 1–13 (2020), https://doi.org/10.1145/3313831.3376202

7. Yoo, I., Chang, H., Luo, X., Stava, O., Liu, C., Milanfar, P. & Yang, F. Deep 3D-to-2D Watermarking: Embedding Messages in 3D Meshes and Extracting Them from 2D Renderings. *Proceedings Of The IEEE/CVF Conference On Computer Vision And Pattern Recognition*. pp. 10031–10040 (2022)

8. Zhang, W., Zhang, Z., Zhang, L., Li, H. & Yu, N. Decomposing joint distortion for adaptive steganography. *IEEE Transactions On Circuits And Systems For Video Technology*. **27**, 2274–2280 (2016)

9. Li, B., Wang, M., Li, X., Tan, S. & Huang, J. A strategy of clustering modification directions in spatial image steganography. *IEEE Transactions On Information Forensics And Security*. **10**, 1905–1917 (2015)

10. Denemark, T. & Fridrich, J. Improving steganographic security by synchronizing the selection channel. *Proceedings Of The ACM Workshop On Information Hiding And Multimedia Security*. pp. 5–14 (2015)

11. Fridrich, J. & Kodovský, J. Rich models for steganalysis of digital images. *IEEE Transactions On Information Forensics And Security*. **7**, 868–882 (2012)

12. Botsch, M., Kobbelt, L., Pauly, M., Alliez, P. & Lévy, B. Polygon mesh processing. (CRC press,2010)

13. Bajaj, C. & Xu, G. Anisotropic diffusion of surfaces and functions on surfaces. *ACM Transactions On Graphics*. **22**, 4–32 (2003)

14. Fleishman, S., Drori, I. & Cohen-Or, D. Bilateral mesh denoising. *ACM SIGGRAPH*. pp. 950–953 (2003)

15. Schneider, R. & Kobbelt, L. Geometric fairing of irregular meshes for free-form surface design. *Computer Aided Geometric Design*. **18**, 359–379 (2001)

16. Eigensatz, M., Sumner, R. & Pauly, M. Curvature-domain shape processing. *Computer Graphics Forum*. **27**, 241–250 (2008)

17. Zhao, W., Liu, X., Zhao, Y., Fan, X. & Zhao, D. Normalnet: Learning based guided normal filtering for mesh denoising. *ArXiv Preprint ArXiv:*1903.04015. (2019)

18. Feng, Y., Feng, Y., You, H., Zhao, X. & Gao, Y. MeshNet: mesh neural network for 3D shape representation. *Proceedings Of The AAAI Conference On Artificial Intelligence*. **33** pp. 8279–8286 (2019)

19. Krizhevsky, A., Sutskever, I. & Hinton, G. ImageNet classification with deep convolutional neural networks. *Advances In Neural Information Processing Systems*. pp. 1097–1105 (2012)

20. Hamilton, W., Ying, Z. & Leskovec, J. Inductive representation learning on large graphs. *Advances In Neural Information Processing Systems*. pp. 1024–1034 (2017)

21. Ker, A. Batch steganography and pooled steganalysis. *International Workshop On Information Hiding*. pp. 265–281 (2006)

22. Ker, A. A capacity result for batch steganography. *IEEE Signal Processing Letters*. **14**, 525–528 (2007)

23. Boroumand, M., Chen, M. & Fridrich, J. Deep Residual Network for Steganalysis of Digit al Images. *IEEE Transactions On Information Forensics And Security*. **14**, 1181–1193 (2019)

24. Xu, G., Wu, H. & Shi, Y. Structural design of convolutional neural networks for steganalysis. *IEEE Signal Processing Letters*. **23**, 708–712 (2016)

25. Ye, J., Ni, J. & Yi, Y. Deep learning hierarchical representations for image steganalysis. *IEEE Transactions On Information Forensics And Security*. **12**, 2545–2557 (2017)

26. Zhang, Y., Zhang, W., Chen, K., Liu, J., Liu, Y. & Yu, N. Adversarial examples against deep neural network based steganalysis. *Proceedings Of The 6th ACM Workshop On Information Hiding And Multimedia Security*. pp. 67–72 (2018)

27. Tang, W., Li, B., Tan, S., Barni, M. & Huang, J. CNN-based adversarial embedding for image steganography. *IEEE Transactions On Information Forensics And Security*. **14**, 2074–2087 (2019)

28. Bernard, S., Pevný, T., Bas, P. & Klein, J. Exploiting adversarial embeddings for better steganography. *Proceedings Of The ACM Workshop On Information Hiding And Multimedia Security*. pp. 216–221 (2019)

29. Koch, J., Gantenbein, S., Masania, K., Stark, W., Erlich, Y. & Grass, R. A DNA-of-things storage architecture to create materials with embedded memory. *Nature Biotechnology*. **38**, 39–43 (2020)
30. Zhou, H., Chen, K., Zhang, W., Yao, Y. & Yu, N. Distortion design for secure adaptive 3-D mesh steganography. *IEEE Transactions On Multimedia*. **21**, 1384–1398 (2018)
31. Wang, Y., Kong, L., Qian, Z., Feng, G., Zhang, X. & Zheng, J. Breaking permutation-based mesh steganography and security improvement. *IEEE Access*. **7** pp. 183300–183310 (2019)
32. Filler, T., Judas, J. & Fridrich, J. Minimizing additive distortion in steganography using syndrome-trellis codes. *IEEE Transactions On Information Forensics And Security*. **6**, 920–935 (2011)
33. Jiang, R., Zhou, H., Zhang, W. & Yu, N. Reversible data hiding in encrypted three-dimensional mesh models. *IEEE Transactions On Multimedia*. **20**, 55–67 (2017)